1492

Also by Felipe Fernández-Armesto:

Millennium: A History of the Last Thousand Years

Truth: A History and a Guide for the Perplexed

Civilizations: Culture, Ambition, and the Transformation of Nature

Near a Thousand Tables: A History of Food

The Americas: A Hemispheric History

Ideas That Changed the World

So You Think You're Human?

Pathfinders: A Global History of Exploration

The World: A History

Amerigo: The Man Who Gave His Name to America

1492

The Year Our World Began

Felipe Fernández-Armesto

B L O O M S B U R Y

LONDON · BERLIN · NEW YORK

First published in Great Britain 2010

Copyright © 2009 by Felipe Fernández-Armesto

The moral right of the author has been asserted

First published in the United States in 2009 by HarperCollins Publishers,
10 East 53rd Street, New York, NY 10022

Bloomsbury Publishing Plc
36 Soho Square
London W1D 3QY

www.bloomsbury.com

Bloomsbury Publishing, London, New York and Berlin

A CIP catalogue record for this book is available from the British Library

Hardback ISBN 978 1 4088 0070 6
Trade Paperback ISBN 978 1 4088 0498 8

10 9 8 7 6 5 4 3 2 1

Printed in Great Britain by Clays Limited, St Ives plc

Mixed Sources
Product group from well-managed
forests and other controlled sources
www.fsc.org Cert no. SGS-COC-2061
© 1996 Forest Stewardship Council
FSC

Contents

Chapter 1

"This World Is Small"

Prophecy and Reality in 1492

17 June: Martin Behaim is at work making a globe of the world in Nuremberg.

In 1491, a prophet appeared in Rome in rags, flourishing, as his greatest possession, a wooden cross. People thronged large squares to hear him announce that tears and tribulations would be their lot throughout the coming year. An "Angelic Pope" would then emerge and save the Church by abandoning worldly power for the power of prayer.[1]

The prediction could not have been more wrong. There was a papal election in 1492, but it produced one of the most corrupt popes ever to have disgraced his see. Worldly power continued to mock spiritual priorities – though a ferocious conflict between the two began in the same year. The Church did not enter a new age but continued to invite and disappoint hopes of reform. The events the prophet failed to foresee were, in any case, far more momentous than those he predicted. The year 1492 did not just transform Christendom, but also refashioned the world.

Late-fifteenth-century humanists thought Nuremberg as "significant as Athens or Rome". Illustrators of the "world-overview", published there in 1493 "at rich citizens' expense", concurred.

Until then, the world was divided among sundered cultures and divergent ecosystems. Divergence began perhaps about 150 million years ago, with the fracture of Pangaea – the planet's single great landmass that poked above the surface of the oceans. The continents formed, and continental drift began. Continents and islands got ever farther apart. In each place, evolution followed a distinctive course. Every continent had its peculiar repertoire of plants and animals. Life-forms grew apart, even more spectacularly than the differences that grew between peoples, whose cultural variety multiplied, and whose appearance and behaviour diverged so much that when they began to re-establish contact they at first had difficulty recognising each other as belonging to one human family or sharing the same moral community.

With extraordinary suddenness, in 1492 this long-standing pattern went into reverse. The aeons-old history of divergence virtually came to an end, and a new, convergent era of the history of the planet began.

The world stumbled over the brink of an ecological revolution, and ever since, ecological exchanges have wiped out the most marked effects of 150 million years of evolutionary divergence. Today, the same life-forms occur, the same crops grow, the same species thrive, the same creatures collaborate and compete, and the same micro-organisms live off them in similar climatic zones all over the planet.

Meanwhile, between formerly sundered peoples, renewed contacts have threaded the world together to the point where almost everyone on earth fits into a single web of contact, communication, contagion, and cultural exchange. Transoceanic migrations have swapped and swivelled human populations across the globe, while ecological exchange has transplanted other life-forms. Our own mutual divergence lasted for most of the previous one hundred thousand years, when our ancestors began to leave their East African homeland. As they adapted to new environments in newly colonised parts of the planet, they lost touch with each other, and lost even the capacity to recognise each other as fellow members of a single species, linked by common humanity. The cultures they created grew more and more unlike each other. Languages, religions, customs, and lifestyles proliferated, and although a long period of overlapping divergence and contact preceded 1492, only then did a renewal of worldwide links become possible.

For seaborne routes of contact depend on the winds and currents, and until Columbus exposed the wind system of the Atlantic, the winds of the world were like a code that no one could crack. The north-east trades, which Columbus used to cross the Atlantic, lead almost to where the Brazil Current sweeps shipping southward into the path of the westerlies of the South Atlantic and on around the entire globe. Once navigators had detected the pattern, the exploration of the oceans was an irreversible process – though of course slow and long and interrupted by many frustrations. The process is now almost over. "Uncontacted" people – refugees, perhaps, from cultural convergence – still turn up from time to time in the depths of Amazonia, but now the process of reconvergence seems almost complete. We live in "one world".

1492

We acknowledge all peoples as part of a single, worldwide moral community. The Dominican friar, Bartolomé de Las Casas (1484–1566), who was, in effect, Columbus's literary executor, perceived the unity of humankind as a result of his experiences with indigenous people in a Caribbean island that Columbus colonised. "All the peoples of the world," Las Casas wrote, in what has become one of the world's most celebrated tautologies, "are human", with common rights and freedoms.[2]

Because so much of the world we inhabit began then, 1492 seems an obvious – and amazingly neglected – choice, for a historian, of a single year of global history. Its commonest associations are with Columbus's discovery of a route to America – a world-changing event if ever there was one. It put the Old World in touch with the New and united formerly sundered civilisations by turning the Atlantic into a highway instead of a barrier. It made genuinely global history – a real "world system" – possible, in which events everywhere resonate together in an interconnected world, and in which the effects of thoughts and transactions cross oceans like the stirrings aroused by the flap of a butterfly's wings. It initiated European long-range imperialism, which went on to recarve the world. It brought the Americas into the world of the West, multiplying the resources of Western civilisation and making possible the eventual eclipse of long-hegemonic empires and economies in Asia.

By opening the Americas to Christian evangelisation and European migration, the events of 1492 radically redrafted the map of world religions and shifted the distribution and balance of world civilisations. Christendom, formerly dwarfed by Islam, began to climb to rough parity, with periods of numerical and territorial superiority. Until 1492, it seemed unthinkable that the West – a few lands at the poor end of Eurasia – could rival China or India. Columbus's anxiety to find ways to reach those places was a tribute to their magnetism and the sense of the inferiority Europeans felt when they imagined them or read about them. But when Westerners got privileged access to an underexploited New World, the prospects altered. Initiative – the power of some groups of people to change others – had formerly been concentrated in Asia. Now it was accessible to interlopers from elsewhere. In the same year, un-related events on the eastern edge of Christendom, where prophecy was even more heated about the imminent end of the world, elevated a new power, Russia, to the status of a great empire and a potential hegemon.

Columbus has so dominated books about 1492 – they have either been about him or focused on him – that the world around Columbus, which makes the effects of his voyage intelligible, has remained invisible to readers. The worlds Columbus connected; the civilisations he sought and failed to find; the places he never thought about, in recesses of Af-rica and Russia; the cultures in the Americas that he was unable even to imagine – all these were areas of dynamic change in 1492. Some of the changes were effective; that is, they launched transformations that have continued ever since, and have helped shape the world we inhabit today. Others were representative of longer-term changes of which our world is the result.

This book is an attempt to bring them all together by surveying them in a single conspectus, rather as a world traveller might have done on a grand tour of the world, if such a thing were possible, in 1492 – zigzagging around the densely populated band of productive civilisa-tions that stretched around the globe, from the eastern edges of Asia across the Indian Ocean to East Africa and what we now think of as the Middle East, and across the Eurasian landmass to Russia and the Medi-terranean world. From there, by way of the Atlantic, the civilisations of Meso-America and the Andean region were about to become accessible. Only an imaginary traveller could have girdled the whole world at the time. But real travellers pieced world-encompassing routes together, and as far as possible, readers will accompany them, starting in the next chapter, in Granada in January 1492. We shall cross the Sahara from Granada to Gao in West Africa with a Muslim adventurer, and visit the kingdom of Kongo with Portuguese explorers, before returning to ex-plore the Mediterranean with Jewish refugees from expulsion in Spain, pausing in Rome and Florence to witness the Renaissance with pil-grims, preachers, and itinerant scholars. We shall traverse the Atlantic

1492

with Columbus, and the Indian Ocean with another Italian merchant. Further stops on our selective tour of the world embrace the eastern frontier of Christendom and the worlds Columbus sought in China and almost grasped in America.

The motive I have in mind, as I make the journey in my imagination, is to see the world before it ends. In 1492, and as the year approached, expectations of destruction and renewal gripped prophets and pundits in Europe. The seer of Rome, whose name went unrecorded, was one of many who plied their trade in Europe at the time, ministering to sensation-hungry congregations. The world is always full of pessimists, woe-struck by a sense of decline, and optimists grasping for a golden future. There were plenty of both in the late fifteenth century. But in 1492, at least in western Europe, optimists dominated. Two kinds of optimism were rife: one – broadly speaking – religious in inspiration, the other secular.

In the West, religious optimism had accumulated since the twelfth century in circles influenced by the prophecies of the mystical Sicilian abbot Joachim of Fiore. He had devised a new method of divination based on a fanciful interpretation of the Bible. He pressed passages from all over scripture into service, but two texts were especially powerful and appealing: the prophecy that the writers of the Gospels put into Christ's mouth, among his last messages to his disciples, and the vision of the end of the world with which the Bible closes. There was strong, scary stuff here. Christ foresaw wars and rumours of wars, earthquakes, famines, "the beginning of sorrows. . . . The brother shall betray the brother to death, and the father the son; and children shall rise up against their parents, and shall cause them to be put to death. . . . Ye shall see the abomination of desolation. . . . For in those days shall be affliction, such as was not from the beginning of the creation which God created unto this time, neither shall be." The consolation was that after the sun and moon are quenched, and the stars fall, "then shall they see the Son of man coming in the clouds with great power and glory".[3] The visionary of the book of Revelation added more terrors: hail and

Dürer's engravings of the Apocalypse were outstanding examples of a common theme of the art of the 1490s: the end of the world.

fire mingled with blood, the seas turned to blood or wormwood, plagues of giant locusts, scorpions as big as horses, and the earth covered with fire and darkness from "vials full of the wrath of God".[4] Prophets who contemplated these disasters could do so, however, with a certain grim cheerfulness. Schadenfreude was part of it: the tribulations would be permanent only for evildoers. Part of it was relish for disasters as "signs" and portents of the purging of the world.

Anyone who has ever argued with a fundamentalist in our own times will know that you can read any message you like into scripture, but people are so eager for guidance from holy writ that their critical faculties often seem to go into suspension when they read it or receive other people's readings of it. In the texts he selected, Joachim of Fiore detected a providential scheme for the past and future of the cosmos, in three ages. After the Age of the Father, in which God was only partially

1492

The relish with which illustrators of the Nuremberg Chronicle adapted Dürer's drawings of the Dance of Death evokes apocalyptic expectations.

revealed, the incarnation had launched the Age of the Son. A cosmic battle between Christ and Antichrist, good and evil, would inaugurate the Age of the Spirit, which would precede the end of the world, the fusion of earth and heaven, the reimmersion of time in eternity. Readers of Joachim scrutinised the world for the signs he predicted. The "Angelic Pope" would purify the Church and restore the blessings of the time of the apostles. A "Last Emperor" would conquer Jerusalem, unite the world, and champion Christ against the forces of evil. A burst of evangelisation would spread Christianity to parts of the world previous efforts could not reach.

Joachim's message impassioned readers and hearers in every walk of life, but none more than some members of the new order of friars that Francis of Assisi founded in the thirteenth century. Francis seemed to

embody some of Joachim's prophecies. He and his followers exemplified
the life that Christ and the apostles supposedly led. They owned nothing, shared everything, and lived from alms. They were inspired propagandists, evangelising the poor, confronting pagans, even – in Francis's
own case – preaching to ravens when no one else would listen. The
Franciscans radiated a spirit of renewal of the world. When Francis
submitted to what he took to be God's call, he tore off his clothes in the
public square of his home town, to signify his renunciation of wealth
and his utter dependence on God – but it was also the sign of someone
making a new start. His standards of poverty and piety were hard for
his followers to sustain after his death, but a tendency among the friars
insisted on fidelity to his spirit. These "Spiritual" Franciscans, who
grew ever more apart from the rest of the order in the fourteenth and
fifteenth centuries, were aware of the parallels between Francis's life and
Joachim's prophecies, and they became increasingly focused on efforts
to ignite the Age of the Spirit.

Meanwhile, Joachimites scoured the world for a potential "Last Emperor". In the thirteenth century, Joachim's native Sicily became part of
the dominions of the rulers of Catalonia and adjoining regions in eastern Spain, known collectively as the Crown of Aragon. Perhaps for that
reason, candidates for the role of the Last Emperor regularly emerged
from Aragon. To some of his courtiers, Ferdinand of Aragon, who came
to the throne in 1479, seemed a promising choice, especially as he was
already, by marriage, king of Castile, the neighbouring kingdom to the
west, and bore the traditional title "King of Jerusalem". His programme
of conquests in the 1480s, against infidels in the kingdom of Granada
and pagans in the Canary Islands, seemed to invoke implicitly the image
of an all-evangelising, all-unifying monarch.

In part, millenarian fervour in Christendom was a reaction to the
recent and current expansion of Islam and the successes of the Turks.
The horns of the crescent protruded ominously from Constantinople
into central Europe and from Granada into Spain. Aragonese counsellors,
bred in fear of the Turks, hoped that the junction of the Aragonese and

Castilian crowns would provide the strength they needed for the struggle. Castilians agreed. "With this conjuncture of two royal scepters," declared a Castilian chronicler, "Our Lord Jesus Christ took vengeance on his enemies and destroyed him who slays and curses."⁵ Columbus promised the king that the profits of his proposed transatlantic enterprise would meet the costs of conquering Jerusalem from the Muslim rulers of the Holy Land, fulfilling the prophecies and speeding the end of the world.

Ferdinand was not the only ruler to conjure up messianic language and anticipations of an imminent climax of history. Manuel the Fortunate of Portugal was equally susceptible to flatterers who assured him that he was chosen to reconquer Jerusalem and inaugurate the last phase of the world. Charles VIII of France, as we shall see, had a similar notion about himself, and used it to justify the invasion of Italy he launched in 1494. People nowadays generally think of Henry VII, who captured the throne of England in an uprising at the end of a long series of dynastic squabbles in 1485, as an almost boringly businesslike, hardheaded king. But he, too, was a child of prophecy, vaunting his "British" ancestry as evidence that he was destined to return the kingdom to the line of its ancient founders, fulfilling prophecies ascribed to Merlin, or to an "angelic voice" in the ear of an ancient Welsh prophet. In Russia, 1492 was, according to the consensus of the orthodox, to be the last year of the world.

Even secular thinkers, untouched by religious enthusiasms, were susceptible to prophecy. Admiration for ancient Rome and classical Greece was one of the strongest strands in the common culture of the Western elite, and the ancients were enthralled by oracles and auguries, omens and portents. Just as Joachimites sought prophecies in scripture, humanists scoured classical texts. Virgil's prediction of a golden age supplied a kind of secular alternative to the Age of the Spirit. In Virgil's own mind this was not really a prophecy, but flattery addressed to his own patron, Augustus, the first Roman emperor, and calculated to sanctify the emperor's reputation by association with the gods. The golden age, Virgil's readers hoped, was imminent. According to Marsiglio Ficino, presiding genius of Florence's Platonists, it would start in 1492. He was thinking – as a good classicist should – of an ancient Roman prophecy: that in the fullness of time the "Age of Gold" would be renewed – the era that preceded Jupiter's supremacy among the gods, when Saturn ruled the heavens in harmony and peace prevailed on earth. Astrology, in which Ficino and many members of his circle were expert, helped. In 1484 a conjunction of the planets named after Saturn and Jupiter excited expectations of some great mutation in the world. Astrologers in Germany predicted twenty years of tumult, followed by a great reform of church and state.

Naturally, competing prophetic techniques spawned competing prophecies. In the 1480s, some expectations focused on the Last World Emperor, others on the dawn of the Age of Gold, others on cataclysm or reform. Almost no one who made a prediction of the future anywhere in Christendom expected the world to continue as it was.

Though they were wrong about most of the details, the prophets who expected change were right. Events in 1492 would make a decisive contribution towards transforming the planet – not just the human sphere but the entire environment in which human life is embedded – more profoundly and more enduringly than those of any previous single year. Because the story of how it happened is a global story, it has many starting points. But if we start in the southern German city of Nuremberg, we can get a privileged vantage point, from which the whole world becomes visible at a glance.

In Nuremberg, in the course of 1492, the most surprising object to survive from that year was taking shape: the oldest surviving globe of the world. The lacquered wooden sphere, mounted on a metal frame so as to be free to spin at a touch, gleams with continents and islands

1492

painted in tawny browns. Seas shimmer in what at the time would have been expensive dark blue pigment – except for the Red Sea, which is a vivid, and also expensive, carmine. Little, scroll-like insets speckle the surface, full of tiny texts in which the cartographer explained his methods and pretended to esoteric knowledge. It was not the first globe ever made. Nor, even for its time, was it a particularly good attempt at realistic mapping: the length of Africa was distorted; the cartographer wildly misplaced capes along the coast, which explorers had measured with some accuracy; he made up names, otherwise unrecorded, for many places; he inserted evidently false claims to have seen much of coastal Africa for himself.

Despite the errors and rank falsehoods, the globe is a precious record of one vision of what the world was like at the time and a key to what made the year special – why 1492 is the best year from which to date the beginnings of the world we are in now and the era we call modernity. The globe made the world seem small: a nephew of St Francis Borgia's, writing a thank-you letter to his uncle for a gift of a globe in 1566, said that he had never realised how small the world was until he held it in his hands. Martin Behaim, like Columbus – who based his theory of a navigably narrow Atlantic on the conviction that, as he said, "[t]his world is small"[6] – underestimated the size of the planet. But he was a prophet of one of the effects of the processes that started in 1492: the world became smaller in a metaphorical sense, because the whole of it became imaginable and mutually accessible.

Behaim's globe was, at least, an attempt to innovate – an ambition curiously absent in the work of Muslim mapmakers at the time. Perhaps because they were heirs to a rich medieval legacy, scholars in the Islamic world seem to have been satiated with cartography and uninterested in mapping the world afresh until Western advances forced them to try to catch up. One of the classical texts that Europeans hailed as a novelty in the fifteenth century – the *Geography* of the second-century Alexandrian scholar Claudius Ptolemy, had been well known in the Islamic world for many centuries; but until an Italian map based on Ptolemy's informa-

tion arrived in Constantinople in 1469, no Muslim cartographer seems
to have thought of making use of it to enlarge the representation of the
world. In 1513, an Ottoman cartographer produced a world map in
Western style, copied from Western prototypes and using data, apparently captured at sea by Turkish warships, on Columbus's voyages. After
a long period of dominance in all the sciences, the Islamic world seems
to have fallen suddenly behind in that of mapping.

Muslim cartographers largely contented themselves with recycling
Old World images, derived from great pioneers of mapmaking in the
tenth and eleventh centuries. The only innovation in the interim was
the attempt to superimpose a grid of lines of longitude and latitude – a
technique Ptolemy had first proposed – on out-of-date information.
Broadly speaking, Muslims in the 1490s had two types of map at their
disposal: one formal and rigid, with no attempt at realism; the other,
free-flowing and conceived – at least – to be realistic. The first form
was familiar to many readers from the work of Ibn al Wardi, who died
in 1457, and whose compendium of geographical titbits, *The Unbored
Pearl of Wonders and the Precious Gem of Marvels*, was much copied. In
his version of the world, Arabia is tiny but perfectly central, gripped
between the Indian Ocean and the Red Sea like a nail head in a vice.
Africa extends eastward almost to the limits of the Ecumene. Deep in
East Africa, the legendary Mountains of the Moon – twin triangles of
gold – seem to pour the Nile across the continent. Opposite the great
river's mouth, the Bosporus flows to the northern edge of the world,
dividing Europe from Asia. The more informal maps that appeared
frequently in fifteenth-century works derived from the work of one of
the finest mapmakers of the Middle Ages – the twelfth-century Sicilian
master al-Idrisi. Typically, they also placed Arabia in the centre of the
composition, but they gave it a reliable shape, and showed the Nile
flowing from the Mountains of the Moon, located a little way beyond
the equator.

If Muslim cartography made it hard to picture the world of 1492,
surviving Chinese sources are even less helpful. Chinese attempts to

map the world existed in the thirteenth and fourteenth centuries. None
has survived, however, beyond purely schematic representations of the
cosmos – a circle representing heaven, a rectangle representing the earth
– designed to evoke the old Chinese saying that the heavens are round
but the earth has sharp corners. For an idea of how Chinese cartography
made the world look, the best map to turn to is Korean. The *Kangnido*
was made in 1402 and much copied, not only in Korea but also in Japan
and the Ryukyu Islands. A copy dated 1470 survives. In a passage of
promotional writing accompanying the map, the principal patron, the
Confucian scholar Kwon Kun, describes "looking on in satisfaction" as
the map took shape and describes its purpose – to inform and enhance
government – as well as the process by which the cartographer, Yi Hoe,
who is also known for maps of Korea and celestial maps, made it. "The
world is very wide," the text observes. "We do not know how many tens
of millions of li [a unit of distance equal to less than half a kilometre]
there are from China in the centre to the four seas at the outer limits."
The writer condemns most maps as "too diffuse or too abbreviated" but
says that Yi Hoe compiled his work from reliable Chinese predecessors of
the fourteenth century with corrections and additions, "making it a new
map entirely, nicely organized and well worth admiration. One can indeed know the world without going out of his door!"[7]

The map shows Eurasia and Africa in a great sweep from a huge and
detailed Korea to a vaguely delineated Europe, sketchy in outline but
emblazoned with about one hundred place-names. China is copiously
detailed, India less so – though recognisable in shape, with Sri Lanka
like a round ball at its toe. Indochina and the Malay Peninsula are a
tiny, insignificant stump. Japan is displaced well to the south of its real
position, and none of the islands of Indonesia or even of the China Sea,
except the Ryukyus, are identifiable. Africa and Arabia are etiolated and
squashed towards the western edge of the world. A huge inland sea occupies most of the African interior. The map exudes pride and ambition
– an effort at a global vision; a belief, at least, that such a vision was pos-

sible. The excitement the globe of 1492 aroused in Nuremberg seems closely paralleled in Korea.

Martin Behaim made the Nuremberg globe in his native city. A merchant by vocation, he had travelled around western Europe making deals and knew parts of the Low Countries and Portugal well. One of his trips abroad, in 1483, probably had an ulterior motive: to postpone or avoid a sentence of three weeks' imprisonment for dancing during Lent at a Jewish friend's wedding. He was in Lisbon in 1484 and seems to have caught the geography bug in that city of Atlantic explorers, where coastal surveying voyages down the west of Africa were under way, mapping the regions Martin would get so badly wrong on his globe. His claim to have accompanied those expeditions is unsupported by any other evidence, and seems incompatible with his errors. His ambitions exceeded his knowledge.

When he got back to Nuremberg in 1490, his tales excited expectations he could not honestly or perfectly fulfil. Still, although he had little or no practical experience in navigating or surveying, he was a representative armchair geographer of his day, who conscientiously compiled information of varying degrees of reliability from other people's maps and from sailing directions recorded by real explorers. The data he brought to Germany from Portugal was bound to arouse the enthusiasm owing to shards of insight from the cutting edge of the exploration of the earth.

The most conspicuous feature Martin incorporated from the latest Portuguese discoveries was his depiction of the Indian Ocean as accessible from the west, around the southern tip of Africa. He shows the African coast trailing a long way eastward – a relic of an old mapmaking tradition that represented the Indian Ocean as landlocked and effectively barricaded to the south by a great arc of land, stretching all the way from southern Africa to easternmost Asia. Not until the 1490s, or the very end of the 1480s at the earliest, did Portuguese geographers feel certain that the sea lay open beyond what by then they began to call the Cape of Good Hope. Speculative cartography had broached the possibility for nearly a century and a half, but the first map to reflect explicitly the observations of Portuguese navigators was made in Florence in 1489. Even then, the trend of the African coast beyond the Cape of Good Hope remained in doubt, and before commissioning more voyages, the Portuguese court waited – as we shall see – for reports from agents sent overland into the Indian Ocean to assess the ocean's accessibility from the south.

Behaim's effort was amateurish. On his globe, the old information was familiar and most of what was new was false. But his representation of the world is more important for some of the ways in which it is wrong than for the few things he got right. For many of his errors and assumptions fitted the agenda of an increasingly influential group of geographers in Nuremberg, Florence, Portugal, and Spain, who corresponded with one another and propagated their own, revolutionary way of imagining geography.

In Nuremberg, the person who did most to promote and organise the globe-making project was the merchant and city councillor Georg Holzschuher, who had made a pilgrimage to Jerusalem and became disinterestedly curious about the geography of the world beyond his reach. The Jerusalem pilgrimage had long been a focal theme of mapmakers in southern Germany, and Holzschuher – whom, exceeding the evidence, I imagine as awestruck by the wonders of creation – appreciated the possibilities of integrating all the available data in a single map. Part of a pious beholder's wonder at the diversity of the world was delight in the myths and marvels of traditional travel literature and chivalric romance. Behaim's globe included many of the imaginary isles and prodigies that speckled other medieval maps. He featured the island where, in hagiographical literature, St Brendan the Navigator found paradise, along with Antilia, the mythical Atlantic land where escapees from the Moors supposedly founded seven cities. The island home of the Amazons appears, with another inhabited exclusively by men with whom the Amazons supposedly got together from time to time in order to breed.

Alongside religious inspiration, traditional sensationalism, and scientific curiosity, hard-headed commercial interest motivated Nuremberg's merchant-patricians. Johannes Müller Regiomantanus, the leading cosmographer in the city's lively scholarly community until his death in 1476, was in no doubt that the city's advantages for "very great ease of all sorts of communication with learned men everywhere" derived from the fact that "this place is regarded as the centre of Europe because the routes of the merchants lead through it".[8] The town council voted to finance Behaim's work, and he loaded his globe with information directed at these patrons. He focused on the sources of spices – the most valuable products of Asia. In practice, pepper dominated the spice trade. Most of it came from south-western India. It accounted for more than 70 per cent of the global market by volume. High-value, low-bulk products, however, were disproportionately important: cinnamon from Sri Lanka, and cloves, mace, and nutmeg from specialised producers in the Banda Islands and the Moluccas. Europeans speculated rhapsodically about the provenance of the spices. St Louis' biographer imagined fishermen of the Nile filling their nets with ginger, rhubarb, and cinnamon dropped from the trees of the earthly paradise and floated downstream from Eden.

The idea that the demand for spices was the result of the need to disguise tainted meat and fish is one of the great myths of the history of food. Fresh foods in medieval Europe were fresher than they are today, because they were produced locally. Preserved foods were just as well preserved by salting, pickling, drying, or conserving in fat and sugar as by canning, refrigeration, freeze-drying, and vacuum-packing today. In any case, as we shall see, taste and culture determined the role of spices in cooking. Spice-rich cuisine was desirable because it was expensive, flavouring the status of the rich and the ambitions of the aspirant. Moreover, the preponderant fashion in cuisine in late-medieval Europe imitated Arab recipes that called for sweet flavours and scented ingredients: milk of almonds, extracts of perfumed flowers, sugar, and all the delicacies of the East.

1492

A menu from Richard II's England featured small birds boiled in almond paste with cinnamon and cloves, served with rose-scented rice boiled soft in almond milk, mixed with chicken's brawn, scented with sandalwood and flavoured with more cinnamon and cloves together with mace. European cookbooks advised adding spices to dishes at the last possible moment so as to lose none of the precious flavour to the heat. A fourteenth-century merchant's guidebook lists 288 distinct spices. In a fifteenth-century cookbook written for the king of Naples, there are about 200 recipes, 154 of which call for sugar; 125 require cinnamon, and 76 need ginger. Spices for the wedding banquet of George "the Rich", Duke of Bavaria, and Jadwiga of Poland in 1475 included 386 pounds of pepper, 286 pounds of ginger, 257 pounds of saffron, 205 pounds of cinnamon, 105 pounds of cloves, and 85 pounds of nutmeg. Medicine, as much as cuisine, demanded spices, almost all of which were part of the Eurasian pharmacopoeia, as needful in the apothecary's shop as in the kitchen. Medieval recipes involve the combination of medical and culinary lore in order to balance the bodily properties – respectively, cold, wet, hot, and dry – that were believed to cause disease when their equilibrium was disturbed. Most spices were hot and dry. In sauces, they could correct the moist and wet properties physicians ascribed to meat and fish. Pharmacists' records feature pepper, cinnamon, and ginger in prescriptions for almost every ailment from pimples to plague.[9]

European markets had always been at a disadvantage in securing spice supplies. China absorbed most of the production. The residue available to Europeans had to travel long distances, through the hands of many middlemen. Europe, which was still a poor and backward corner of Eurasia compared with the rich economies and civilisations of maritime Asia, produced nothing that Asian markets wanted in exchange. Only cash would do. In the first century BC, Rome's greatest natural historian complained that a taste for spice-rich food enriched India and impoverished Europe. Europeans "arrive with gold and depart with spice", as a Tamil poet put it.[10] A fourteenth-century guidebook for Italian merchants in the East explained that there was no point in taking anything to China except silver, and reassured readers that they would be able to rely on the slips of paper – a kind of money still unfamiliar in Europe – that Chinese customs officers gave them at the border.[11]

Profit beckoned anyone ingenious or determined enough to buy spices at or near their source. Medieval merchants made heroic efforts to penetrate the Indian Ocean. The routes all involved hazardous encounters with potentially hostile Muslim middlemen. You might try to cross Turkey or Syria to the Persian Gulf or, more usually, attempt to get a passport from authorities in Egypt and ascend the Nile, transferring, via desert caravan, to the Red Sea at a port controlled by Ethiopians. Not surprisingly, many attempts failed. When they succeeded, they remained dependent on native shipping to get the goods across the Indian Ocean and on local middlemen for transport to the shores of the Mediterranean. European merchants who overcame the difficulties became part of the existing trading networks of maritime Asia. Before the 1490s, no one had opened direct routes of access from the European market to the Eastern sources of supply.

Behaim designed his globe to address that problem directly. He was "well fitted to disclose the east to the west".[12] That was the opinion of his friend and a fellow merchant of Nuremberg, Hieronymus Münzer, who also travelled extensively on the Iberian Peninsula and took part in the network of correspondence that united Portuguese and Nuremberg geographers with counterparts in Florence. The letters of recommendation Münzer wrote on Behaim's behalf show the values they all shared. They advocated belief in "experience and trustworthy accounts" over book learning and reliance on ancient geographers.[13] To that extent, they shared the worldview of modern science, but it would be rash to see them as precursors of the scientific revolution. For wishful thinking, rather than reason or evidence, made them reject classical wisdom.

In particular, they rejected classical traditions about the size of the world. But the ancients had probably got it roughly right. Eratosthenes, the librarian of Alexandria, had calculated the girth of the globe around the turn of the third and second centuries BC. He measured the elevation of the sun at two points on the same meridian and the distance between the same points on the surface of the earth. The angular difference was a little over seven degrees, or about a fiftieth of a circle. The distance – in miles of value roughly corresponding to those most of Eratosthenes' interpreters used at the time – was about five hundred miles. So the size of the world would work out, correctly, to about twenty-five thousand miles.

For Behaim and his collaborators, that seemed far too much. They felt either that the calculations were wrong or that miles of smaller value should be used. The evidence they cited was consistent with their prejudice in favour of observation over tradition. Whatever the ancient books said, Münzer insisted, the fact was that there were elephants in Africa and Asia, so those continents must be close to one another. "The habitable east," he concluded, "is very near the habitable west." China "can be reached in a few days" westward from the Azores.[14] Other evidence pointed the same way: driftwood washed ashore on Europe's ocean edge; reports of castaways of allegedly oriental appearance on the same shores. A map described in Florence in 1474 illustrated the theory: it put Japan only about twenty-five hundred miles west of mythical Antilia, which probably appeared in the vicinity of the Azores, and located China a little over five thousand miles west of Lisbon. The details of what might lie in the unexplored ocean between Europe and Asia were in dispute, but one shared conclusion stood out. As Christopher Columbus put it, as he contemplated the theories that came out of Nuremberg, Florence, and Lisbon, "This world is small." A viewer of Martin Behaim's globe could sense the smallness, cupping the image of the world between his hands, seeing the whole of it with a single spin. The gaps in Behaim's mapping symbolise the mutual ignorance of people in non-communicating regions.

Events that began to unfold in 1492 would dispel that ignorance, reunite the world's sundered civilisations, redistribute power and wealth among them, reverse formerly divergent evolution, and reforge the world. Of course, a single year can hardly have wrought so much work on its own. Strictly speaking, it was not until 1493 that Columbus was able to explore exploitable two-way routes across the ocean. The route he used to reach the Caribbean in 1492 was, as we shall see, not viable in the long run and had to be abandoned. The linking of the hemispheres was clearly a huge step towards the making of what we think of as "modernity" – the globalising, Western-dominated world we inhabit today – but it was hardly complete even in 1493. All Columbus really did was open possibilities that took his successors centuries to follow up. And even the potential was hardly the product of a couple of years. Only in the following few years could the possibilities of remaking the world, with a new, previously unimaginable balance of wealth and power, really be glimpsed. Other explorers developed more routes back and forth across the North and South Atlantic, to open connections with other parts of the Americas, and created a new seaborne link, or reconnoitred new land routes, from Europe to southern and central Asia.

To most people, anyway, it was not 1492. Even to people in Christendom, it was not yet necessarily 1492 when, by our reckoning, the year began on 1 January. Many communities reckoned the year as beginning on 25 March, the presumed anniversary of Christ's conception. A spring beginning had logic and observation on its side. In Japan, television still broadcasts the opening of the first cherry blossom every year. Each culture has its own way of counting time.

The Muslim world, which dwarfed Christendom at the time, counted – and still counts – the years from Muhammad's exile from Mecca, and divided them into lunar months. In India, outside Muslim areas, the numbering of years was an indifferent matter when viewed against the longevity of the gods, whose world was renewed every 4.32 million years in an eternal cycle. Their current age had begun in what we count as 3012 BC. For everyday purposes, in northern India, people generally counted the years from a date corresponding to 57 BC in our calendar. In the south of the subcontinent, the year AD 78 was the

1492

preferred starting point. For much of their past, the Maya of Meso-America recorded all important dates in three ways: first, in terms of a long count of days, starting from an arbitrary point over five thousand years ago; second, according to the number of years of just over 365 days each of the current monarch's reign; and third, in terms of a divinatory calendar of 260 days, arrayed in twenty units of 13 days each. By the late fifteenth century, only the last system was regularly used. The Incas recorded dates for only 328 days of the solar year. The remaining 37 days were left out of account while farming ceased, after which a new year commenced.

In China and Japan, there was no fixed date on which a new year started; each emperor designated a new date. Meanwhile, people celebrated New Year's Day on different dates, according to local custom or family tradition. Years were named after one of twelve animals, as they still are: rat, ox, tiger, rabbit, dragon, snake, horse, sheep, monkey, bird, dog, and pig. The cycle of twelve interlocked with another cycle of ten, so that no year name was repeated until sixty years had elapsed. In a parallel system, years were also numbered in order from the start of an emperor's reign. The 1st January 1492 was the day named Jia Chen, the second day of the twelfth month of the year Xin Hai, or the fourth year of the Hongxi reign. Xin Hai had begun on 9 February 1491 and would end on 28 January 1492. The year Ren Zi then began and lasted until 17 January 1493. The 31st December 1492 was the thirteenth day, named Ji You, of the twelfth month of Ren Zi, the fifth year of the Hongxi reign.

So a book about a year is fundamentally ahistorical if it treats the events that occurred between 1 January and 31 December, by Western reckoning, of a given year as a coherent entity. Most people would not have thought of those days as constituting a year, any more than any other combination of days amounting to about 365 in all – or 260 days, or 330, or whatever other number happened to be conventional in their culture. In any case, no sequence of days encloses events so discrete that they can be understood except in a longer context. So in this book the rules shall be flexible about dates, ranging back and forth from what we now think of as 1492 into adjoining years, decades, and ages.

A book like this, moreover, is necessarily about more than the past. Because we are imposing a modern notion of a year on people unaware of it at the time, this book, like other histories of particular years, is self-condemned to be retrospective. It is as much about us – how we see the world and time – as about people in the past. Historians' job is not to explain the present but to understand the past – to recapture a sense of what it felt like to live in it. But, for present purposes, I want to depart from my usual historian's chores. What I expect readers of this book to want to know about 1492 is not only or even primarily what it felt like to experience it, because most people had no sense of experiencing anything of the sort, but what its events contributed to the world we inhabit now.

Still, a year really did mean something, in a way no longer easily accessible to us in urban, industrial or post-industrial environments. The succession of seasons is hardly noticeable, except superficially – as hemlines rise and fall with the mercury in the thermometer, and as the density of clothing matches cloud cover. Heating and insulation indemnify us against summer and winter. US homes are now typically hotter in winter than summer, thanks to the ferocity of the boilers and the frigidity of the air-conditioning. Global trade brings out-of-season food even to relatively poor people in relatively rich countries. Most modern Westerners have lost the lore of knowing when to eat what.

In 1492, almost the entire world lived by farming or herding, and the whole of the rest by hunting. So the cycle of the seasons really did determine almost everything that mattered in life: the rhythms at which crops grew or animals migrated determined what one ate, where one lived, what clothes one wore, how much time one spent at work, and what sort of work one did. Reminders of the passage of time, carved on church doors for worshippers to see as they entered, commonly included scenes, arrayed month by month, of the activities the cycles of weather regulated: typically, tilling in February, pruning in March, hawking in April, mowing in June, grape treading in October, ploughing in November. Japanese poems conventionally began with invocations of the season. Chinese writers associated each season with its appropriate food, clothes, and decor. The whole world lived at a pace and rhythm adjusted to the seasons.

Everywhere people watched the stars. In Mediterranean Europe, the motions of Orion and Sirius, as they climbed to mid-sky, signalled the wine harvest. The rising of the Pleiades announced harvest time for grain, their setting the time to plant. The Maya watched the motion of Venus anxiously, because the planet governed days propitious respectively for warmongering and peacemaking. Muhammad had taught Muslims that new moons are "signs to mark fixed periods for men and for the pilgrimage".[15] In China, astronomers were vital policy consultants, because the prosperity of the empire depended on the accurate timing of imperial rites according to the motions of the stars, and part of the emperor's duty was to monitor the skies for signs of celestial "disharmony". For this was a world without escape from the elements, or relief from the demons that filled the darkness, the storms, the heat and cold and hostile wastes and waters. Witchcraft persecution was not a medieval vice but an early modern one, which started as a large-scale enterprise in much of Europe in the late fifteenth century. In Rome in 1484, the pope heard reports of many men and women who "deny with perverse lips, the faith in which they were baptised" in order to "fornicate with demons and harm men and beasts with their spells, curses, and other diabolical arts". Regulations for persecuting witches followed.[16]

Nature seemed capricious, gods inscrutable. Plague in Cairo in 1492 reputedly killed twelve thousand inhabitants in a single day. A flood wiped out most of the army of the ruler of Delhi a year later. Many Jews expelled from Spain in 1492 perished in North African famines. The infections Columbus's men took to the New World wrought near-destruction on the unaccustomed, unimmunised inhabitants. There were over one hundred thousand people on the island of Hispaniola, by a conservative estimate, in 1492. Only sixteen thousand survived a generation later.

Yet, although they were at the mercy of nature, people could change the world by reimagining it, striving to realise their ideas, and spreading them along the new, world-girdling routes explorers found. The changes wrought in 1492, and their world-shaping consequences, are proof of that. Most of the transforming initiatives that helped to produce modernity came, ultimately, from China. Paper and printing – the key technologies in speeding and spreading communications – were Chinese inventions. So was gunpowder, without which the world could never have experienced the "military revolution" that based modern warfare on the massed firepower of huge armies; nor could the traditional balance of power, which kept sedentary civilisations at the mercy of horse-borne enemies, ever have been reversed. The "gunpowder empires" that outclassed ill-equipped enemies around the early modern world, and the modern nation-state, which arose from the military revolution, would simply never have come about.

Industrialisation would have been impossible without the blast furnace and the exploitation of coal for energy, both of which originated in China. Modern capitalism would have been impossible without paper money – another idea Westerners got from China. The conquest of the world's oceans depended on Western adaptations of Chinese direction-finding and shipbuilding technologies. Scientific empiricism – the great idea on which Westerners usually congratulate themselves for its impact on the world – had a much longer history in China than in the West. So in science, finance, commerce, communications, and war, the most pervasive of the great revolutions that made the modern world depended on Chinese technologies and ideas. The rise of Western powers to global hegemony was a long-delayed effect of the appropriation of Chinese inventions.

Nevertheless, the effective applications came from Europe, and it was in Europe that the scientific, commercial, military, and industrial revolutions began. To recapitulate: this perplexing shift of initiative – the upset in the normal state of the world – started in 1492, when the resources of the Americas began to be accessible to Westerners while remaining beyond the reach of other rival or potentially rival civilisations. In the same year, events in Europe and Africa drew new frontiers between Christendom and Islam in ways that favoured the former. These events were surprising, and this book is, in part, an attempt to explain them. For Europe – formerly and still – was a backwater, despised or ignored in India, Islam, China, and the rest of East Asia, and outclassed in wealth, artistry, and inventiveness. The ascent of the West, first to challenge the East and ultimately to dominate the world, began in earnest only in 1492. People in every generation have their own modernity, which grows out of the whole of the past. No single year ever inaugurated anyone's modernity on its own. But for us, 1492 was special. Key features of the world we inhabit – of the way power and wealth, cultures and faiths, life-forms and ecosystems are distributed around the planet – became discernible in the historical record for the first time. We are still adjusting to the consequences.

Chapter 2

"To Constitute Spain
to the Service of God"

The Extinction of Islam in Western Europe

2 January: Granada falls to Christian conquerors.

"The king of Granada rose early . . . and made his person ready in the way that Moors do when faced with danger of death." His mother clung to him despairingly.

"Leave me, my lady," he said. "My knights await me."

As he rode to confront the enemy camped outside the walls of his capital, after eight months of siege, throngs of starving citizens assailed him, with weeping mothers and howling babies, "to shout out that . . . they could no longer bear the hunger; for this reason they would abandon the city and go over to the enemy camp, allowing the city to be captured, and all of them to be taken prisoner and killed". So he relented of his determination to fight to the death, and decided to try to negotiate an honourable surrender.[1]

1492

Working in the
year Granada
fell, illustrators
of Diego de
San Pedro's
Cárcel de amor
unmistakably
depicted the
siege, under a
commander with
King Ferdinand's
features.

Presumably, the chronicler who told this impressive but improbable tale – with its chivalric touches and heart-tweaking sentiments – was romanticising. For most of the previous ten years of warfare in Granada, Abū 'Abd Allāh Muhammad – Muhammad XI, or "Boabdil," as Christians called him – had not behaved with exemplary valour but had relied on conspiracy, compromise, and a series of tactical alliances to stave off what seemed like inevitable defeat for his realm at the hands of the hugely bigger neighbouring kingdoms of Castile and Aragon.

Granada already seemed an anachronism – the last Muslim-ruled state on the northern shore of the western Mediterranean. Muslims lost Sicily three centuries earlier, and by the mid-thirteenth century, Christian conquerors from the north had swept up all the remaining kingdoms of the Moors – as they called Muslims – in what are now

Spain and Portugal. Ferdinand and Isabella, joint monarchs of Aragon and Castile, or, as they preferred to say, "of Spain", justified the war with religious rhetoric in a letter to the pope:

> We neither are nor have been persuaded to undertake this war by desire to acquire greater rents nor the wish to lay up treasure. For had we wished to increase our lordships and augment our income with far less peril, travail, and expense, we should have been able to do so. But our desire to serve God and our zeal for the holy Catholic faith have induced us to set aside our own interests and ignore the continual hardships and dangers to which this cause commits us. And thus we may hope both that the holy Catholic faith may be spread and Christendom quit of so unremitting a menace as abides here at our gates, until these infidels of the kingdom of Granada are uprooted and expelled from Spain.[2]

In a sense what they said was true, for they could have saved the costs of the war and exacted handsome tribute from the Moors. But other considerations impelled them, of a nature more material than they admitted to the pope. Granada was a rich country. It was not particularly populous. Despite wildly excessive guesses in the traditional literature, it is hard to make the total population add up to much more than three hundred thousand. But it could feed many more with its prodigious harvests of millet, which Christians would not eat. The products of Granada's industries – silk, leather wares, arms, ceramics, jewel work, dried fruits and nuts, almonds and olives – were bountiful, and increasing demand for silk in Europe boosted the economy. About a tenth of the population lived in the capital, served by the 130 water mills that ground the daily millet.

The kingdom of Granada represented a source not only of revenue but also of patronage. Many of the nobles who fought for Ferdinand and Isabella in the civil war that inaugurated their reign remained inadequately rewarded and potentially restive. The royal patrimony had shrunk, and the monarchs did not wish to relinquish more of it to already overmighty subjects. The towns of the kingdoms had resolutely opposed attempts to appropriate their lands. Acquisition of Granada would solve the monarchs' problems. According to the laws, rulers were not allowed to alienate their inherited patrimony but could do what they liked with conquered lands. By the end of the conquest of Granada, more than half the surface area of the kingdom would be distributed among nobles.

Thanks to Granada's economic boom, the Moors' strength to defy and attack their Christian neighbours was greater in the late fifteenth century than for a long time previously. The lords of neighbouring lands responded with mingled fear and aggression. But the war was not only a matter of frontier security or territorial aggression. It has to be considered in the context of the struggle against the rising power of the Turks of the Ottoman Empire, whom the Spanish monarchs perceived as their most formidable enemies in the long run. The pressure of Islam on the frontiers of Christendom had mounted since mid-century, when the Turks seized Constantinople. The loss of Constantinople ratcheted up the religious content of Christian rhetoric. The Ottoman Empire, meanwhile, launched a huge naval offensive, invaded Italy, and developed relations with Muslim powers in North Africa and with Granada itself. Ferdinand was not just the ruler of most of Christian Spain. He was also heir to wider Mediterranean responsibilities as king of Sicily, protector of Catalan commerce in the eastern Mediterranean and North Africa, and hereditary stakeholder in the legacy of the crusader kingdom of Jerusalem. He was apprehensive of the Ottoman advance and eager to clear what seemed like a Muslim bridgehead from Spain.

Meanwhile, each side in the potential conflict over Granada was succouring the other's enemies. In the 1470s, rebel refugees from Ferdinand's and Isabella's vengeance took shelter at the court of the ruler of Granada, Mulay Hassan, while Ferdinand encouraged and negotiated in secret with dissidents in Granada. For Mulay Hassan's crown, too, was disputed. Doubts of the propriety of his accession (for the rules of succession in Granada were never clearly defined) disturbed the scruples of members of his dynasty. Court intrigue and seraglio conspiracies bedevilled the throne, and rebellions were common.

Finally, among the causes of the conflict, Ferdinand and Isabella hoped that war would distract their nobles from their own squabbles and bring internal peace to Castile. Although, in the opinion of at least one chronicler, Christians who made allies of the Moors "deserved to die for it", and although the law expressly forbade it, the practice was common, and the private wars of the aristocracy in regions bordering Granada thrived on the exotic diet of infidel support. As a device for getting Spanish nobles to co-operate against a common enemy, the war worked. Once the fighting began, such inveterate foes as the Marquess of Cadiz and the Duke of Medina Sidonia – "my enemy incarnate", as Cadiz called him – joined forces and exerted themselves in each other's support. Isabella's secretary reminded her that Tullius Hostilius, one of the legendary kings of ancient Rome, had made unprovoked war merely in order to keep his soldiers busy. The enterprise against the Moors would "exercise the chivalry of the realm".[3]

The war fed on religious hatreds and generated religious rhetoric. But more than a clash of civilisations, a crusade, or a jihad, the war resembled a chivalresque encounter between enemies who shared the same, secular culture. Throughout the fighting, as always in medieval wars between Spanish kingdoms, there were warriors who crossed the religious divide.

Fighting began as an extension of business by other means. For most of the fifteenth century, Granada's internal struggles weakened the kingdom and invited conquest, but Castilian kings reckoned that it was easier and more profitable to collect tribute. Traditionally, Granada bought peace by paying tribute to Castile every three years. The sources are imperfect, but contemporaries – presumably exaggerating – reckoned the value of the tribute at 20 to 25 per cent of the revenue of the king of Granada. Even at more modest cost, the system was inherently unstable, because in order to sell truces, the Castilians had to keep up raids, and Granadines exploited breaches of the peace to launch counter-raids of their own. Renewals of the truce were therefore always tense. Both sides appointed arbitrators to settle disputes arising from breaches of the peace, but the machinery seems to have been ineffective. Instances were repeatedly referred to the Spanish monarchs, who could respond only by making overtures to the king of Granada; and he, on the Moorish side, was one of the worst offenders in the matter of truce breaking. The Moors, the chronicler Alonso de Palencia thought, were "more astute in taking advantage of the truce" – by which he meant that the balance of profit from raiding accrued to their side.

Mulay Hassan committed his greatest outrage in 1478, when he sacked the Murcian town of Cieza, putting eighty inhabitants to the sword and carrying off the rest. The helplessness of Ferdinand and Isabella in the face of such action was disturbing. They could not obtain the hostages' release by diplomacy and could not afford ransom. Instead, to those families too poor to pay the price they gave permission to beg alms for the ransoms, and relieved them of the need to pay dues, tolls, and taxes on money sent to Granada to obtain the Ciezans' release.

By the end of the 1470s, however, Ferdinand and Isabella no longer needed peace on the Moorish front. War with Portugal and Castile's own war of succession subsided. Unemployed warriors turned to the Moorish frontier, where Castilian noblemen were waging private war for profit. Mulay Hassan tried to quell them by seizing frontier strongholds. On a moonless and unsettled December night in 1481 they lunged forward against Záhara and other fortified places. The Christians were unprepared for an attack that was no longer a mere raid but an attempt to occupy permanently the assailants' targets. At Záhara the attackers

> scaled the castle and took and killed all the Christians whom they found within, save the commander, whom they imprisoned. And when it was day they sallied forth . . . made captive one hundred and fifty Christian men, women, and children, and sent them bound to Ronda.[4]

Perhaps Mulay Hassan thought he could get away with it because the lord of the place was one of Isabella's opponents. The Spanish monarchs, however, reacted with anger

> both because of the loss of this town and fortress and, even more, on account of the Christians who died there. . . . And if we can say we find any cause for pleasure in what has happened, it is only because it gives us an opportunity to put into immediate effect a plan which we have had in mind and which would one day surely come to fruition. In view of what has happened, we have resolved to authorize war against the Moors on every side and in such a manner that we hope in God that very soon not only will we recover the town that has been lost, but also conquer others, wherein Our Lord may be served, His holy faith may be increased, and we ourselves shall be well served.[5]

The king of Granada is supposed to have explained to his courtiers how the Christians would beat them bit by bit, like rolling up a carpet from the corners. The story is a literary commonplace – the Ottoman sultan Mehmet II is said to have used the same image to explain his own strategy for conquering Europe a few years earlier. But it does describe what happened: a slow war of attrition, in which the invaders devoured the kingdom inwards from the edges, slowly, exploiting internal conflicts among the defenders to make up for the deficiencies in their own strength.

For although the Christian kingdoms were much bigger than Granada, with opportunities for mobilising far more men and ships, the aggressors could never make the disparity in resources work to their advantage as they should. At the height of the war, the aggressors numbered ten thousand horse and fifty thousand foot.

Armies on this scale were hard to gather and keep in the field, and harder still to keep supplied. The struggle for money, horses, men, siege equipment, arms, and grain dominates the surviving documents. Diego de Valera, a chronicler who was the monarchs' household steward, advised King Ferdinand to "eat off earthenware, if necessary, and melt down your tableware, sell your jewels, and appropriate the silver of the monasteries and churches, and even sell off your land".[6] The monarchs were entitled to interest-free loans from their subjects, and sometimes delayed repayment. As security for a sum raised from the city authorities of Valencia in 1489 – a particularly tough year for the war budget – Isabella deposited a crown of gold and diamonds and a jewelled necklace. The Church was a willing source of subsidies for so holy an enterprise. Papal bulls from November 1479 authorised the monarchs to use some of the proceeds from the sale of indulgences for the expenses of the war. Early Christian victories convinced the pope to renew the grant until the end of the war. The Jews, who were exempt from military service, paid a special levy.

To some extent, medieval wars could help to pay for themselves. Booty was an important source of finance. A fifth of it belonged to the crown by law, while the captains responsible divided the rest between them. The capture of Alhama, the first Christian sortie of the war, yielded

infinite riches in gold and silver and pearls and silks and clothes of silk and striped silk and taffeta and many kinds of gem and horses and mules and infinite grain and fodder and oil and honey and almonds and many bolts of cloth and furnishings for horses.[7]

Prisoners could be ransomed for cash. The size of the booty determined the scale of a victory, and it was no praise for Alonso de Palencia to say of the Marquess of Cadiz that he gained "more glory than booty". Only the nobility and their retainers served for booty. Most soldiers received wages, some paid by the localities where they served as militia, others directly out of royal coffers.

The money available was never enough, and Ferdinand and Isabella fell back on a cheap strategy: divide and conquer. In effect, for

much of the war, the Spanish monarchs seemed less focused on conquering Granada than on installing their own nominee on the throne.
The Granadines fought each other to exhaustion. The invaders
mopped up. The most important event of the early phase of the war
was the capture in 1483 of Boabdil, who was then merely a rebellious
Moorish prince. He was the plaything of seraglio politics. His mother,
estranged from the king, fomented his opposition. His support came
at first from factions at court but spread with the strain and failures of
the war. A conflict that Mulay Hassan hoped would strengthen his
authority ended by undermining it. A combined palace putsch and
popular uprising drove Mulay Hassan to Málaga and installed Boabdil
in his place in Granada. But the upstart's triumph was short-lived.
The internecine conflict weakened the Moors. Boabdil proved inept as
a general and fell into Christian hands after a disastrous action at
Lucena.

The Christians called Boabdil "the young king" from his nineteen
years and "Boabdil the small" for his diminutive stature. His ingenu-
ousness matched his youth and size. He had little bargaining power in
negotiating for his release, and the terms to which he agreed amounted
to a disaster for Granada. He recovered his personal liberty and obtained Ferdinand's help in his bid to recover his throne. In return he
swore vassalage. In itself, this might have been no great calamity, as
Granada had always been a tributary kingdom. But Boabdil seems to
have made the mistake of disbelieving Ferdinand's rhetoric. Except as a
temporary expedient, Ferdinand was unwilling to tolerate Granada's
continuing existence on any terms. Boabdil's release was merely a strategy for intensifying Granada's civil war and sapping the kingdom's
strength. The Spanish king had tempted Boabdil into unwilling collaboration in what Ferdinand himself called "the division and perdition of
that kingdom of Granada".

Boabdil's father resisted. So did his uncle, Abū 'Abd Allāh Muhammad, known as el Zagal, in whose favour Hassan abdicated, while the

Christians continued to make advances under cover of the Moorish civil war. Boabdil fell into Ferdinand's hands a second time, and agreed to even harsher terms, promising to cede Granada to Castile and retain only the town of Guadix and its environs as a nominally independent kingdom. The Granadine royal family seems to have retreated into a bunker mentality, squabbling over an inheritance no longer worth defending. It is hard to believe that Boabdil can ever have intended to keep the agreement, or that Ferdinand can have proposed it for any reason other than to prolong Granada's civil war.

For the invaders, the most important success of the succeeding campaigns was the capture of Málaga in 1487. The effort was costly. As Andrés de Bernáldez, priest and chronicler, lamented, "[T]he tax-gatherers squeezed the villagers because of the expenses of that siege." The rewards were considerable. Castile's armies in the war zone could be supplied by sea. The loss of the port impeded the Granadines' communications with their co-religionists across the sea. The whole western portion of the kingdom had now fallen to the invaders.

Even in the face of Ferdinand's advance, the Moors could not end their internal differences. But Boabdil's partial defeat of el Zagal and return to Granada, with Christian help, had the paradoxical effect of strengthening Moorish resistance, although Boabdil's was the weaker character and weaker party. Once Granada was in his power, he found it impossible to honour his treaty with Ferdinand and surrender the city into Christian hands. Nor was it in his interests to do so once el Zagal was out of the running.

By 1490 nothing but the city of Granada was left, occupying a reputedly impregnable position, but highly vulnerable to exhaustion by siege. Yet at every stage the war seemed to take longer than the monarchs expected. In January 1491 they set a deadline of the end of March for their final triumphant entry into Granada, but the siege began in earnest only in April. At the end of the year they were still in their makeshift camp nearby. Meanwhile the defenders had made many successful sorties, seizing livestock and grain-laden wagons,

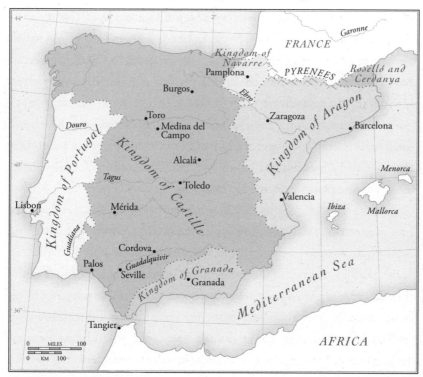

The Kingdom of the Iberian Peninsula, 1492.

and the besiegers had suffered many misadventures. Hundreds of tents in their camp burned in a conflagration in July, when a candle flame in the queen's tent caught a flapping curtain. The monarchs had to evacuate their luxurious pavilion.

The militant mood of the city's inhabitants limited Boabdil's freedom. The ferocity with which they opposed the Christians determined his policy. His efforts, formerly exerted in the Spaniards' favour, were now bent on the defence of Granada. There was no way of supplying the city with food, and by the last stage of the war refugees crammed it to bursting. Yet even in the last months of 1491, when the besiegers closed around the walls of Granada, and Boabdil decided to capitulate, still the indomitable mood of the defenders delayed surrender. The last outlying redoubt fell on 22 December. The Spanish troops entered the citadel by night on the eve of the capitulation in order to avoid "much scandal" – that is, the needless bloodshed a desperate last resistance might otherwise have caused. Did Boabdil really say to Ferdinand, as he handed over the keys of the Alhambra on 2 January 1492, "God must love you well, for these are the keys to his paradise"?[8]

"It is the extinction of Spain's calamities," exclaimed Peter Martyr of Anghiera, whom Ferdinand and Isabella kept at their court to write their history. "Will there ever be an age so thankless," echoed Alonso Ortíz, the native humanist, "as will not hold you in eternal gratitude?" An eyewitness of the fall of the city called it "the most distinguished and blessed day there has ever dawned in Spain". The victory, according to a chronicler in the Basque country, "redeemed Spain, indeed all Europe".[9] In Rome, bonfires burned all over the city, nourished into life in spite of the rain. By order of the pope, the citizens swept Rome's streets clean. When dawn broke, the bell at the summit of the Capitoline Hill in Rome began ringing with double strokes – a noise never otherwise heard except on the anniversary of a papal coronation, or to announce the feast of the Assumption of the Virgin in August. But it was a cold, wet morning in early February 1492 when the news of the fall of Granada was made public. Equally unseasonally, celebratory bullfights aroused such enthusiasm that day that numerous citizens were gored and killed before the bulls were dispatched. Races were held – separately for "old and young men, boys, Jews, asses and buffaloes". An imitation castle was erected, to be symbolically stormed by mock assailants – only the ceremony had to be deferred because of the rain. Pope Innocent VIII, already so old and infirm that his entourage were in permanent fear for his life, chose to celebrate mass in the hospital of the Church of St. James the Great, the patron saint of Spain. A procession of clergy joined him there from St Peter's, in a throng so irrepressibly tumultuous that he had to postpone his sermon because of the noise they made.[10] The pope called the royal conquerors "athletes of Christ" and conferred on them the new title, which rulers of Spain bore ever after, of "Catholic Monarchs". The joy evoked in Rome echoed through Christendom.

Yet every stage of the conquest brought new problems for Ferdinand and Isabella: the fate of the conquered population; the disposal, settlement, and exploitation of the land; the government and taxation of the towns; the security of the coasts; the assimilation and administration of the conflicting systems of law; and the difficulties arising from religious differences. The problems all came to a head in the negotiations for the surrender of the city of Granada. The Granadine negotiators proposed that the inhabitants would be "secure and protected in their persons and possessions", except for Christian slaves. They would retain their homes and estates, and the king and queen would "honour them and regard them as their subjects and vassals". Muslims would enjoy the right to continue practising Islam, even if they had once been Christians, and to keep their mosques with their schools and endowments. Mothers who converted to Christianity would have to renounce gifts received from their parents or husbands, and lose custody of their children. The native merchants of Granada would have free access to markets anywhere in Castile. Citizens who wished to migrate to Muslim lands could keep their belongings or dispose of them at a fair price and remove the proceeds from the realm. All clauses were to apply to Jews as well as Muslims.

Astonishingly, the monarchs accepted all these terms – on the face of it, an extraordinary departure from the tradition established by earlier Castilian conquests. Except in the kingdom of Murcia, to the east of Granada, Castilian conquerors had always expelled Muslims from land they conquered. In effect, this meant scrapping the entire existing economic system and introducing a new pattern of exploitation, generally based on ranching and other activities practicable with small populations of new colonists. Initially, the deal struck with Granada more resembled the traditions established in the Crown of Aragon, in Valencia, and in the Balearic Islands, where the conquerors did all they could to ensure economic continuity, precisely because they lacked the manpower to replace the existing population. Muslims were too numerous and too useful. In the kingdom of Valencia, the running of agricultural estates depended on the labour of Muslim peasants, who continued to be the bedrock of the regional economy for well over a hundred years. Granada, however, was not like Valencia. It could prosper even without the Muslim population, whose fate, despite the favourable terms of surrender, remained insecure.

By Granada's terms of surrender, the Moors, as subjects and vassals of the monarchs, not only could remain to keep the economy going, but also incurred obligations of military service. Ferdinand and Isabella even attempted to organise them to provide coastal watches against invasion, but that part of their policy was outrageously overoptimistic. If Maghrebis or Turks invaded, most Christians were in no doubt of whose side the defeated Moors would favour. As Cardinal Cisneros wrote during his stay in Granada, "Since there are Moors on the coast, which is so near to Africa, and because they are so numerous, they could be a great source of harm were times to change."

At first, the conquerors seemed anxious to act in good faith. Ferdinand, despite his reluctance to have more Muslim subjects, acted as if he realised that the ambition of an all-Christian Spain, "constituted to the service of God", was impractical. The governor and archbishop of Granada shared power with Muslim "companions", and for a while their collaboration kept the peace. The companions ranged from respected imams, such as Ali Sarmiento, who was reputedly a hundred years old and immensely rich, to shady capitalists, such as al-Fisteli, the money lender who served the new regime as a tax collector. In 1497, Spain offered refuge to Moors expelled from Portugal. So expulsion was not yet imminent.

Yet if the monarchs had kept to the terms of the bargain they made when the city fell, it would have been honorable, but it would also have been incredible. Ferdinand, as we have seen, declared in correspondence with the pope their intention of expelling the Muslims. In 1481 he wrote in similar terms to the monarchs' representative in the north-west of Spain: "[W]ith great earnestness we now intend to put ourselves in readiness to toil with all our strength for the time when we shall conquer that kingdom of Granada and expel from all Spain the enemies of the Catholic faith and dedicate Spain to the service of God."[11] Most of the conquered population did not trust the monarchs. Many took immediate advantage of a clause in the terms of surrender that guaranteed emigrants right of passage and provided free shipping. Granada leached refugees. Boabdil, whose continued presence in Spain the monarchs clearly resented, left with a retinue of 1,130 in October 1493.

Indeed, the policy of conciliating the conquered Moors, while it lasted, was secondary to the monarchs' main aim of encouraging them to migrate. This had the complementary advantages of reducing their potentially hostile concentration of numbers and of freeing land for resettlement by Christians. The populations of fortified towns were not protected by the terms negotiated for the city of Granada. They had to leave. Their lands were confiscated. Many fled to Africa.

Eventually, Ferdinand and Isabella abandoned the policy of emigration in favour of expulsion. In 1498, the city authorities divided the city into two zones, one Christian, one Muslim – a sure sign of rising tensions. Between 1499 and 1501, the monarchs' minds changed as turbulence and rebellion mounted among the Moors and most of them evinced unmistakable indifference to the chance to convert to Christianity. The fate of former Christians provoked violence when the Inquisition claimed the right to judge them. There were only three hundred of them, but they were disproportionately important: "renegades" to the Christians, symbols of religious freedom to the Moors. Muslim converts to Christianity were exempt from the Inquisition's ministrations for forty years. The new archbishop of Granada, Hernando de Talavera, procured that concession for them, partly because he disliked and mistrusted the Inquisition, and partly because he realised that converts needed time to adjust to their new faith. Apostates, however, were in a special category. It was hard to fend the Inquisition off. In 1499, Ferdinand and Isabella sent the primate of Spain, Cardinal Cisneros, to sort the problem out.

Cisneros might have been expected to take a sympathetic line. He was an admirer and probably a practitioner of mysticism. He was a great patron of humanist scholarship. His reputation for learning, piety, reasonableness, and diplomatic skill was unexcelled. However, whereas Talavera and the governor of Granada, the Conde de Tendilla, tried to attract former Christians back to the fold, Cisneros sought to bribe or pressure them into conversion. He suspended teaching in Arabic. He also took advantage of a loophole in the terms of Granada's surrender that allowed Christians to interrogate Muslims' formerly Christian wives and their children to see whether they wanted to return to their former faith. He did not, he declared, want to force them: that was against canon law. Their response to pressure was in their own hands. But the line between coercion and force was blurred, and Cisneros's methods seemed to the Muslims generally to be forcible in effect and therefore in breach of the terms of the surrender of Granada. A report drawn up for the monarchs explained what happened. "Since this was a case in which the Inquisition could take an interest," Cisneros, the report said,

> thought he could find some way to get them to admit their fault and bring them back to our faith, so that perhaps some of the Moors would be converted . . . and our Lord was pleased to grant that, thanks to the archbishop's preaching, and his gifts, some of the Moors did convert. . . . Because slight pressure was being applied to the renegades to make them admit their errors and convert to our faith, as is legally permissible, and also because the archbishop's men were converting the renegades' sons and daughters at a tender age, as is legally permissible, the Moors . . . , concluding that the same thing would happen to them all, rioted and killed an officer of justice who went to arrest one of them, so they rose up, barricaded the streets, brought out their hidden arms, made new ones for themselves, and set up a resistance.[12]

The first riot broke out when a woman, seized by interrogators, called for help. The rioters desisted, in obedience to Archbishop Talavera, but Cisneros imposed a new condition: they had to submit to baptism or leave the city. This was man-on-the-spotism: an extemporised decision that forced policy makers' hands. Fifty or sixty thousand people, if we can believe the claims of Cisneros's propagandists, were received into the Church.

Coming after the erosion of their culture by the large-scale emigration and conversions that followed the conquest, the new turn of events scared some of the Muslims into rebellion. Berber raiding parties took part. Outside the city of Granada the scale of the uprising was enormous. Chroniclers estimated at up to ninety-five thousand the number of troops needed to quell it. The king himself took command. Atrocities multiplied. When rebel villages refused to submit to terms that now always included the demand to accept Christianity, they were bombarded into submission and the defenders were enslaved. At Andarax the Christians put three thousand rebel prisoners to death and blew up a mosque to which hundreds of women and children had fled for refuge. The rebels dealt harshly, in their turn, with anyone in their communities who would not join them. One petitioner who survived complained to the monarchs of how the rebels burned his home and granary and carried off his wife, daughter, and livestock.

The monarchs, still fearful of collusion with the Turks, grew alarmed when the rebels appealed to the Ottomans to help them. In 1502, after a series of measures restricted Muslims' freedom of movement, those who refused baptism were expelled from Castile, including Granada. In acknowledgement of the fact that the economy in Valencia depended on Muslim labour, they were allowed to remain in the Crown of Aragon. The rebels' terms of surrender show what conversion meant in real terms. Though the monarchs promised that former Muslims would have clergy to instruct them in Christianity, doctrine hardly featured: rather, the victors demanded a modified form of cultural conversion in which the vanquished submitted to what nowadays would be called "integration". Their former crimes were pardoned. They could keep their traditional dress "until it wore out". They could have their own butchers, but meat had to be slaughtered in the Castilian fashion. They could record legal transactions in Arabic, but only the law of Castile would apply in the courts. They could keep their baths. They would pay only Christian taxes, but at a special – effectively punitive – rate three times higher than that of "old Christians". Their charitable endowments were to continue, though no longer for maintaining mosques and Islamic schools: road maintenance, poor relief, and the ransoming of captives would be the only permitted objectives. The past would be confined to oblivion, and to call someone "Moor" or "renegade" became an offense.[13]

The conquest of Granada and its aftermath changed the profile of Europe for a half a millennium. Outside the range of Ottoman conquests, no Muslim-ruled state ever re-emerged in Europe. Until the creation of sovereign Albania in 1925, there was no state with a Muslim majority. It became possible – though perhaps not convincing – to claim that the culture of Europe, if such a thing exists, is Christian. The habit of identifying Europe with Christendom went almost unchallenged until the late twentieth century. Only then, with large-scale Muslim migrations and the emergence, in Bosnia, of another European state with a Muslim majority, did Europeans have to recraft their self-image to take the Muslim contribution to the making of Europe into account.

The events of 1492 did not, however, contribute much to the making of modern political institutions. Spain did not become a modern state in any of the ways usually alleged: not unified, not centralised, not subject to absolute rule, certainly not bureaucratic or "bourgeois". Only in one respect did Ferdinand and Isabella practise a new technique of government: they used printing to distribute their commands faster and more efficiently around their realms. In other respects, they ruled a typically chaotic, heterogeneous medieval state, in which the monarchs shared power with the "estates" of Church, nobility, and towns.

Monarchs were "natural lords" over their people. Their leadership was as the head's over the limbs of the human body – and everyone knew that the human body was a microcosm of the universe. Nature was a hierarchy: even the most cursory examination of different creatures and natural phenomena made that obvious. Church windows depicted the ranks of creation, from the heavens to the plants and creatures beneath Adam's feet, with a place for everything and everything in its place. Sacred writings and the traditions of mystical theology portrayed a similar establishment among God and the various orders of angels. The same state naturally characterised human affairs.

Although Aragon and Castile remained separate states, the monarchy of Ferdinand and Isabella derived a new and exalted dignity from the union of the monarchs. "You shall hold the monarchy of all the Spains," Diego de Valera assured the king, "and shall renew the imperial seat of the Goths, from whence you come."[14] The Goths whom Valera had in mind were the last rulers of a state that covered the whole – or almost the whole – of the Iberian Peninsula back in the sixth and seventh centuries. But Ferdinand and Isabella could not re-create a peninsula-wide state and probably never even thought of trying to do so. Even their personal union was an emergency measure – a political solution improvised to meet temporary problems.

The fact that Isabella was a woman created some of the problems. Until the mid-sixteenth century, when Falloppio sliced women's bodies open and saw how they really work, medical science classed women as defective men – nature's botched jobs. Isabella needed Ferdinand at her side in a calculated display of essential equipment. Earlier queens in Castilian history, moreover, had been condemned as disastrous. The image of Eve – seducible, fickle, wilful, and selectively subrational – dogged women and made them seem unfit for rule. Works intended for young Isabella's edification included Juan de Mena's *Laberinto de Fortuna*, first printed in 1481, which stressed the importance of female self-discipline for a well-ordered household and kingdom, and Martín de Córdoba's *Jardín de nobles doncellas*, which paraded exemplars of feminine virtues. As well as of sexual coquetterie, Isabella was the target of misogynistic pornography. A work from probably a few years after her death, the *Carajicomedia*, frankly aligns her with whores and sluts.[15]

The monarchs' conflicting pretensions made matters worse. The rivalry is apparent between the lines of the address Isabella delivered at the conference in 1475 that settled their differences over how they would share power: "My lord, . . . where there exists that conformity that by God's grace ought to exist between you and me, there can be no dispute." By implication, the conformity was lacking and the dispute obvious. In exchange for parity of power with Isabella in her lifetime, Ferdinand had to renounce his own claim to the throne in favour of his offspring by his wife. Isabella made him her "proctor" in Castile, with power to act on her behalf. He made her "co-regent, governor, and general administrator in the kingdoms of the Crown of Aragon . . . in our presence and absence alike".[16]

The image of unity papered over the cracks in the monarchs' alliance. Almost all the documents of the reign were issued in the monarchs' joint names, even when only one of them was present. They were said to be "each other's favourite", "two bodies ruled by one spirit", "sharing a single mind". Theirs was the equality of Tweedledum and Tweedledee. To mask their differences, their propaganda made a display of mutual love. Love knots and yoke-and-arrows were their most favoured decorative motifs. The conjugal yoke bound the weapons of Cupid. Pictures of the monarchs exchanging rather formal kisses illuminated presentation copies of royal decrees.[17]

Were the king and queen in love? Their biographers seem unable to abjure this silly question. The coquetterie in which she encouraged court poets was part of Isabella's armoury. Ferdinand's dislike of her favourites is well attested, and Isabella responded by removing her husband's mistresses from the court. "She loved after such a fashion," said one of the court humanists, "so solicitous and vigilant in jealousy, that if she felt that he looked on any lady of the court with a look that evinced desire, she would very discreetly find ways and means to dismiss that person from the household."[18] Her object in persecuting her husband's floozies was, however, according to the same source, her own "honour and advantage" rather than amorous satisfaction. A document often cited as evidence of her affection for her husband is the letter she wrote to her confessor describing Ferdinand's escape from an assassination attempt in Barcelona in December 1492, but the incident reveals feelings deeper, in Isabella, than love. A knife-wielding maniac, "long crazy and out of his mind", as an eyewitness observed, took advantage of one of the regular Friday audiences, at which petitioners were allowed to confront the monarch in person. On the face of it, the sentiments the queen declared at the time seemed admirably, lovingly selfless. "The wound was so big," she bleated,

> so Dr Guadalupe says, for I hadn't the heart to behold it – so wide and so deep that four fingers' lengths would not equal its depth and its width was a thing of which my heart trembles to tell. . . . and it was one of the griefs I felt to see the king suffer what I deserved, without deserving the sacrifice he made, it seemed, for me – it quite destroyed me.

Yet for all her expressions of tenderness for her spouse, it was evidently for herself that Isabella most grieved and feared. She made her sorrow seem worse than her husband's affliction. A professional court flatterer, Alonso Ortiz, told her that her suffering "seemed greater than the king's". She congratulated herself on persuading the would-be assassin to confess, thereby saving his soul. And she took up most of her letter to her confessor with reflections on her own unpreparedness for death. Ferdinand's plight convinced her "that monarchs may die from any sudden disaster, the same as other men, and it is reason enough to be ready always to die well". She went on to ask her confessor to prepare a handy list of all her sins, including especially the vows she had broken in the pursuit of power.[19]

The monarchs' affection for each other may have become a fact, but it began as an affectation. The language of love the king and queen exchanged in public had little to do with real sentiments and much to do with the courtly ethos that made the monarchs' style of government seem far removed from modernity: the cult of chivalry, which was probably the nearest they got to an ideology. Isabella's mental image of heaven is suggestive. She saw it as a sort of royal court, staffed by paragons of knightly virtue. Chivalry could not, perhaps, make men good, as it was supposed to do. It could, however, win wars. Granada fell, said the Venetian ambassador, in "a beautiful war. . . . There was not a lord present who was not enamored of some lady", who "often handed warriors their weapons . . . with a request that they show their love by their deeds". The queen of Castile died uttering prayers to the archangel Michael as "prince of the chivalry of angels".[20]

To see how important chivalry was, the best measure is the frequency and intensity of jousting. (The joust was chivalry's great rite – a sport of unsurpassed nobility, which afforded many opportunities for political jobbery.) In April 1475, in the midst of war with Portugal, the monarchs held a tourney at Valladolid that the local chronicle acclaimed as "the most magnificent that had ever been seen, men said, for fifty years and more". The host and master of the joust, the Duke of Alba, exhibited the value of valour. He "fell from his horse on his way to risk himself at the tilt and was rendered dumb, unable to speak, and he hurt his head, and they bled him. Yet he still came out armed and jousted twice." The king displayed a tribute on his shield that read, "I suffer without making sound / For as long as I am bound." The king's secretary, however, confided the underlying purpose of assembling the monarchs' most powerful supporters: they had to know who was with them and who against them. The magnates had their own agenda, according to Alonso de Palencia: they intended to exploit the occasion to distract Ferdinand from matters of state and lure him into expenditure and concessions.

Not all the nobility upheld the standards of chivalrous behaviour. One of the most barbarous cases on record concerned Don Fernando de Velasco, brother of the highest courtier in the kingdom, who burned to death some yokels who, in their drunkenness, had mistaken him for a Jewish rent collector and abused him accordingly. The king replied to subsequent complaints that he regretted the wretches' deaths, without benefit of prior confession, but that Velasco had acted nobly in exacting satisfaction for the outrage they had committed against him.

Noble scions began to throng Castile's many universities. Education, as well as arms, conferred nobility. "My lineage is for me enough, / Content to live without expensive stuff" was Alonso Manrique's motto, but he was an accomplished poet. With the expansion of taste came an increased interest in the accumulation of wealth. The Admiral of Castile (whose title was a hereditary dignity, not a naval office) obtained a dyestuffs monopoly from the crown, though he employed an agent to run it for him: a wealthy Genoese merchant in Seville – Francisco da Rivarolo, who was one of Columbus's financial backers. The dukes of Medina Celi, who were in the vanguard against Granada, had their own merchant fleet and tuna fishery and processing plant. Their neighbours and rivals, the dukes of Medina Sidonia, invested heavily in another growth industry of the time – sugar production. All noblemen had to be good estate managers in order to keep pace with inflation, which was beginning to be a normal feature of economic life. The Medina Celi dexterously increased their income from food rents and seigneurial taxes, and the record books of monastic and clerical lordships show how they increased incomes to match rising costs.

Some writers questioned the true nature of nobility, pointing out, under the influence of Aristotle and his commentators, whose works were easily accessible in every serious library, that gentility lay in the cultivation of virtue. "God made men, not lineages" was a theme of Gómez Manrique, knight, poet, warrior against the Moors, and close courtier of the king and queen. This did not mean that all men were social equals, but that humble men could rise to power if they possessed the requisite merit. The king could ennoble those who deserved it. The merits that earned ennoblement could be intellectual. "I know," declared Diego de Valera, "how to serve my Prince not only with the strengths of my body but also with those of my mind and intellect." Alonso de Palencia's *Treatise on Knightly Perfection* personifies Chivalric Practice as a Spanish nobleman in search of Lady Discretion. He finally encounters her in Italy, the homeland of humanism.

These modifications of noble behaviour and language should not be mistaken for a "bourgeois revolution". Although they spread their wings economically and culturally, nobles remained true to the traditions of their class, whose virtue was prowess and whose pursuit was power. As Isabella's secretary wrote to a magnate wounded in battle with the Moors, "The profession you make in the order of chivalry obliges you to undergo more perils than common men, just as you merit more honour than they, because if you had no more spirit than the rest in the face of such affrights, then we should all be equals."[21]

Because of the court's obligation to impress, ostentation and pageantry were an important part of court daily life. The monarchs learned from Burgundy, and from the northern artists they employed at court, the importance of rich and impressive display in affairs of state and the usefulness of pageant that emphasised symbolically the pre-eminence of the king. Large numbers of observers detailed the apparel the monarchs wore on every occasion, because every gold stitch was significant. Isabella felt guilty about the opulence of her garb and liked to stress its relative simplicity. "I wore only a simple dress of silk with three gold hem bands," she protested on one occasion in a letter to her confessor. Her affectations of austerity deceived no one.

Her biggest expenditure was on clothing and furnishings. Prodigious quantities of black velvet were used for mourning clothes, for death was a frequent visitor to the family and the court. Jewels, especially those of a sacred nature, figure largely. From 1488 Isabella's chapel must have been a veritable thesaurus of jewelled golden crosses, encrusted as they were with diamonds and rubies. Political expenditure thrust its way into these intimate ledgers. When Granada was conquered, Isabella contributed to the campaign for forcible acculturation of the Moors by providing cash for them to be reclothed in Castilian fashion. When the son of the king of Granada was a prisoner in 1488, she equipped him with the right clothes. She gave fat tips – bribes, in effect – to foreign ambassadors. She paid to rebuild the walls of the town of Antequera. And seven of those bolts of black velvet went to the messenger who brought news that Ferdinand had captured the Moorish town of Loja in 1486.

Alongside this sort of expenditure one finds the record of purchases of sweets for the children, wages for the masters who taught them Latin, and the upkeep of a painter to do their portraits. The monarchs liked to keep Christmas as a family occasion. They would stock up with quince jam well in advance and buy presents to exchange at the end of the holiday. In 1492 they gave their daughters painted dolls with changeable blouses and skirts. Prince John, who as a man child and heir to the throne was meant to be above such things, got an embroidered purse and four dozen bolts of finely spun silk. For the family generally, the king supplemented the Christmas sweetmeats with plenty of lemon preserves.

As far as government was concerned, the most important feature of court life was mobility. The monarchs ruled not as later Spanish kings did, from a fixed central capital, but led a peripatetic existence as they crossed the country from town to town, taking the court with them like a menagerie on a lead. They were Spain's most-travelled rulers, penetrating parts of the kingdom that had not seen the sovereign for decades. Some areas were better frequented than others, according to their importance. They spent most time in the heartlands of old Castile between the central mountain ranges and the River Duero, but they often visited New Castile and Andalusia. They would go to Extremadura when Portuguese affairs were prominent, and made excursions into Aragon and Catalonia. In this way not only was the monarchs' contact with their subjects and personal role in government maintained, but the monarchs also spread the burdensome cost of entertaining the court, which fell on the localities where the court resided or the lords who acted as hosts. However, they had to meet the cost of transporting their own cumbrous and colourful caravan. The baggage that Isabella took with her wherever she went filled sixty-two carts.

Ferdinand and his wife were distinctly unmodern monarchs. They helped usher in the modern world by accident, as they adjusted to emergencies and reverted to traditions. Their conquests and "cleansings" – as we now say – of hated minorities were too cruel to be called Christian, but they were religious. The monarchs used credal differences to identify enemies, religious rhetoric to justify their campaigns. They reigned in a time of aggressive religious fervour, induced by the alarming territorial gains Islam had made in the previous years. It was natural that Ferdinand's Aragonese counsellors, heirs to the Aragonese tradition of enmity for the Turks, would want to appropriate Castilian resources for war on the Eastern frontier of Mediterranean Christendom, while Castilians in their turn expected Aragonese help to be valuable in the continuing war against the Moors. Mingled with these expectations was millennial fever. Nothing Ferdinand and Isabella did can make perfect sense except against the background of renewal of the long-persistent belief that a Last World Emperor would appear who would defeat Islam and face the Antichrist. They were consciously preparing for the end of the world. Instead, they helped bring into being a new order, in which credal boundaries coincided with the frontiers of civilisations.

For a moment, in the aftermath of the fall of Granada, it looked as if a "concert of Christendom" and a crusade against the Turks were about to take shape. Islam and Christendom clawed at one another across the sea, at times exchanging rhetoric, at times overtly waging war, at times merely struggling to win the outlying and uncommitted peoples of the world to their cause. A local victory seemed to have acquired global importance. And while Ferdinand and Isabella struggled to cope with the consequences of their success, events – to which we must now turn – across the Straits of Gibraltar combined to settle the future limits of Christendom and Islam in Africa.

Chapter 3

"I Can See the Horsemen"

The Strivings of Islam in Africa

20 December: Sonni Ali the Great of Songhay dies.

He can have been only five or six years old when his family joined the flood of refugees from Granada, but al-Hasan ibn Muhammad ibn Ahmad al-Wazzan always called himself "the Granadine". His exile was the beginning of a life of travel, first as a fugitive, then as a merchant, later as an ambassador, and later still as the captive of Christian pirates. He claimed unconvincingly to have been as far as Armenia, Persia, and the Eurasian steppes. He certainly knew much of the Mediterranean and of West and North Africa at first hand. His spiritual journeys were equally far-reaching. As a prisoner in Rome, he became a Christian, a papal favourite, and under the name of Giovanni Leone – or "Leo Africanus", as most title pages say – was the author of the most authoritative writings on Africa in his day. When invaders sacked Rome in 1527, Leo fled back to Africa and to Islam.

His most spectacular itineraries were across the Sahara to what he and his contemporaries called the Land of the Blacks. He could never quite

1492

The north-west Africa of Leo Africanus.

make up his mind about black people, for he felt torn between conflicting literary traditions that clouded his perceptions. Prejudices about black people were routine in Morocco and other regions of North Africa where black slaves arrived as common items of trade. Leo inherited those prejudices from Ibn-Khaldūn, the greatest historian of the Middle Ages, whose works he plundered. "The inhabitants of the Land of Blacks," he wrote, ". . . lack reason . . . and are without wits and practical sense. . . . They live like animals, without rule or law." Leo found, however, "the exception . . . in the great cities, where there is a little more rationality and human sentiment". Blacks generally, he concluded, were:

people of integrity and good faith. They treat strangers with great kindness, and they please themselves all the time with merry dancing and feasting. They are without any malice, and they do great honour to all learned men and all religious men.[1]

This disposition was the key to the slow but sure success of Islam in the region, seeping gradually south of the Sahara, into the Niger Valley and the Sahel, the great savanna.

By his own account, Leo went twice to the Sahel – once as a boy, and later as an envoy of the ruler of Fez, where he spent part of his childhood and adolescence. He had to cross the Atlas Mountains, narrowly escaping robbers – on his first journey – by excusing himself in order to pee and then disappearing into a snowstorm. He must have seen the white peaks of the Sierra Nevada from his home in Granada, but after shivering nearly to death in the Atlas he hated snow for the rest of his life. He crossed a ravine over the River Sebou in a basket strung on pulleys. In retrospect, it made him sick with terror. He reached Taghaza, the fly-blown mining town that produced the salt Sahelian palates craved. Here, where even the houses were hewn from blocks of salt, Leo joined a salt caravan, waiting three days while the gleaming slabs were roped to the camels.

The object of the journey was to exchange salt for gold, literally ounce for ounce. You can live without gold, but not without salt. Salt not only flavours food but also preserves it. Dietary salt replaces the vital minerals the body loses in perspiration. Dwellers in the Niger Valley and in the forests to the south, where there were no salt mines and no access to sea salt, lacked a basic means of life. The Mediterranean world, meanwhile, had adequate supplies of salt but needed precious metals. From the northern shores of the Mediterranean, the source of the gold could be glimpsed only with difficulty across the glare of the Sahara. Even the Maghrebi merchants who handled the trade were unsure of the location of the mines, secreted deep in the West African interior, in the region of Bure between the headwaters of the rivers Niger, Gambia, and Senegal, and, farther west, around the middle Volta.

The gold came north along routes secret to the traders who handled it along the way. "Dumb trade" procured it, according to all the accounts Europeans had at their disposal, written perhaps from convention rather than conviction. Merchants supposedly left goods – sometimes textiles, always salt – exposed for collection at traditionally appointed places. They then withdrew, and returned to collect the gold that their silent, invisible customers left in exchange. Bizarre theories circulated. The gold grew like carrots. Ants brought it up in the form of nuggets. It was mined by naked men who lived in holes. It probably really came from mines in the region of Bure, around the upper Gambia and Senegal, and perhaps from the middle Volta.

In the mid-fourteenth century, Ibn Battuta, the most-travelled pilgrim in the Islamic world, joined a southbound trading caravan at Sijilmassa, where the gold road began, and headed south in search of the place of origin of the trade. His motive, he claimed, was curiosity to see the Land of the Blacks. He left an unsurpassed description of the terrible journey across the desert, between "mountains of sand. . . . You see them in one place. Then you look again, and they have shifted to a new position." Blind men, it was said, made the best guides, because in the desert visions were deceptive, and devils amused themselves by misleading journeyers.

It took twenty-five days to reach Taghaza. The water here, though salty, was a precious commodity that the caravanners paid dearly for. The next stage of the journey usually involved ten days with no possibility of replenishing water supplies – unless perhaps occasionally by extracting it from the stomachs of dead animals. The last oasis lay nearly three hundred kilometres from the caravan's destination, in a land "haunted by demons", where "no road is visible, . . . only the drifting, wind-blown sand".[2]

Despite the torments of the road, Ibn Battuta found the desert "luminous, radiant", and inspiring – until his caravan reached an even hotter region, near the frontier of the Sahel. Here they had to travel in the cool of the night, before at last, after a journey of two months, they reached Walata, where black customs officials were waiting and vendors offered sour milk laced with honey.

Here, at the southern end of the Golden Road, lay the empire of Mali, renowned as the remotest place to which gold could reliably be traced. Mali dominated the middle Niger, controlling, for a while in the fourteenth century, an empire that included all three great riverside emporia – Jenne, Timbuktu, and Gao. The power of the Mande, the West African elite who ran the empire's affairs, extended over great stretches of the Sahel and southward into the edges of the forest. They were a commercial and imperial people, strong in war and wares. The merchant caste, known as Wangara, thrust colonies beyond the reach of the empire's direct authority, founding, for instance, a settlement inside the forest country, where they bought gold cheaply from the local chiefs. It was frustrating to be so close to the source of such wealth while having to rely on middlemen to supply it.

But they never succeeded in controlling production of the gold, for the mines remained outside their domains. Whenever they attempted to exert political authority in the mining lands, the inhabitants resorted to a form of passive resistance or "industrial action" – downing tools and refusing to work the mines. Mali, however, did control the routes of access to the north and the points of exchange of gold for salt, which tripled or quadrupled in value as it crossed Malian territory. The rulers took the gold nuggets for tribute, leaving the dust to the traders.

The Mansa, as the ruler of Mali was known, attained legendary renown because of the fame of Mansa Musa, who reigned from about 1312 to 1337. In 1324 he undertook a spectacular pilgrimage to Mecca, which spread his reputation far and wide. He was one of three Mansas to make the hajj. This alone shows how stable and substantial the Malian state was, for the journey took over a year, and few rulers in the world could risk such a long absence from their bases of power. Musa made his trip in lavish style, with conspicuous effect. People in Egypt remembered it

1492

for centuries, for the Mansa stayed there for over three months and distributed so much gold that he caused inflation. By various accounts, the value of gold in Egypt fell by between 10 and 25 per cent. Musa gave fifty thousand dinars to the sultan of Egypt and thousands of ingots of raw gold to the shrines he visited and the officials who entertained him. Though he travelled with eighty camels, each laden with three hundred pounds of gold, his munificence outstripped his supplies. He had to borrow funds on his homeward journey. Reputedly, on his return to Mali he repaid his loans at the rate of seven hundred dinars for every three hundred he had borrowed.

The ritual magnificence of Mali's court impressed visitors almost as much as the ruler's wealth. Ibn Battuta thought the Mansa commanded more devotion from his subjects than any other prince in the world. Arab and Latin authors were not always appreciative of blacks' political sophistication. This makes the goggle-eyed awe of the sources in this case all the more impressive. Everything about the Mansa exuded majesty: his stately gait; his hundreds of attendants, bearing gilded staves; the way subjects communicated with him only through an intermediary; the acts of humiliation – prostration and heaping one's head with dust – to which his interlocutors submitted; the reverberant hum of bowstrings and murmured approval with which auditors greeted his words; the capricious taboos that enjoined death for those who wore sandals in his presence or sneezed in his hearing. The range of tributaries impressed Ibn Battuta, especially the cannibal envoys, to whom the Mansa presented a slave girl. They returned to thank him, daubed with the blood of the gift they had just consumed. Fortunately, reported Ibn Battuta, "they say that eating a white man is harmful, because he is unripe".[3]

This exotic theatre of power had a suitably dignified stage and numerous company. The Mansa's audience chamber was a domed pavilion in which Andalusian poets sang. His bushland capital had a brick-built mosque. The strength of his army was cavalry. Images of Mali's mounted soldiery survive in terracotta. Heavy-lidded aristocrats with lips curled in command and haughtily uptilted heads come crowned with crested helmets, riding rigidly on elaborately bridled horses. Some have cuirasses or shields on their backs, or strips of leather armour worn apron-fashion. Their mounts wear halters of garlands and have decorations incised into their flanks. The riders control them with short reins and taut arms, like practitioners of dressage. For most of the fourteenth century they were invincible, driving invaders from desert or forest out of the Sahel.

Around the Mediterranean, Maghrebi traders and travellers scattered stories about the fabled realm, like grains of sand dusted from expansive hands. The image of the Mansa's splendor reached Europe. In Majorcan maps from the 1320s, and most lavishly in the Catalan Atlas of the early 1380s, the ruler of Mali appears like a Latin monarch, save only for his black face, bearded, crowned, and throned – a sovereign equal in standing to any Christian prince. "So abundant is the gold that is found in his country," reads the text placed alongside his picture, "that this lord is the richest and noblest king in all the land."[4] The image might have been transferred, with little modification, to a painting of the Three Kings of Christ's epiphany – which was the context in which European artists regularly painted imaginary black kings at the time. And the black king's gift to the divine infant would be the mighty gold nugget the Mansa brandished in the map.

Europeans strove to cut out the middlemen and find routes of access to the gold sources for themselves. Some of them tried to follow the caravans over the desert. In 1413 the trader Ansleme d'Isaguier returned to his native Toulouse with a harem of negresses and three black eunuchs, whom he claimed to have acquired in Gao, one of the great emporia of the middle Niger. No one knows how he can have got so far. In 1447, the Genoese Antonio Malfante reached Tuat, garnering only rumours about the gold. In 1470, in Florence, Benedetto Dei claimed to have been to Timbuktu and observed a lively trade there in European textiles. Between 1450 and 1490, Portuguese merchants strove to open a route towards the Niger across country from their newly founded

1492

trading station at Arguim on the Saharan coast, and succeeded in diverting some gold-bearing caravans to trade there.

Like every El Dorado, however, Mali and its people could be disappointing to those who actually got that far. "I repented of having come to their country," Ibn Battuta complained, "because of their deficient manners and contempt for white men."[5] By the middle of the fifteenth century, as Mali declined, impressions were generally unfavourable. The empire was in retreat, ground between the Tuareg of the desert and the Mossi of the forest. Usurpers eroded the edges, while factions subverted Mali at the centre. The emperors lost control over great marketplaces along the Niger. Cut-price successors to the famed poets and scholars of earlier generations cheapened arts and learning at the court. When European explorers at last penetrated the empire in the 1450s, they were disillusioned. Where they had expected to find a great, bearded, nugget-wielding monarch, such as the Catalan Atlas depicted, they found only a poor, harassed, timorous ruler. New maps of the region cut out the image of the sumptuously arrayed Mansa and substituted crude drawings of a "stage nigger", dangling simian sexual organs. It was a dramatic moment in the history of racism. Until then, white Westerners saw only positive images of blacks in paintings of the magi who acknowledged the baby Jesus. Or else they knew Africans as expensive domestic slaves who shared intimacies with their owners and displayed estimable talents, especially as musicians. Familiarity had not yet bred contempt.

Disdain for blacks as inherently inferior to other people and the pretence that reason and humanity are proportional to the pink pigment in Western flesh were new prejudices. Disgust with Mali fed them. Attitudes remained equivocal, but the balance of white assumptions tilted against blacks. If white respect for black societies had survived the encounter with Mali, how different might the subsequent history of the world have been? Mass enslavement of blacks would not have been averted, for Islam and the Mediterranean world already relied heavily on the African slave trade. But the subordination of the black world would surely have been contested early and with more authority – and there-fore, perhaps, with more success.

While Europeans beheld Mali's travails with disappointment, the empire's neighbours contemplated the same developments with glee. For the pagan, forest-dwelling Mossi, advancing from the south, Mali was like a beast felled for scavenging: bits could be picked off. For the Tuareg, raiding from the desert to the north, the stricken emperors were potential vassals to be manipulated or milked. In the last third of the fifteenth century, rulers of the people known as Songhay, whose lands bordered Mali to the east, began to conceive a grander ambition: they would supplant Mali altogether.

Historians called the ruling family of Songhay the Sonni, though that seems to have been the most commonly used of their titles rather than a family name. They were a long-lived dynasty, founded, so the legend said, by a dragon slayer who invented the harpoon and used it to liberate the peoples of the Niger from a sorcerer-serpent. Since then, by 1492, eighteen of his heirs had reigned successively, according to most tradi-tional counts. We can recognise the legend as a typical story of a stranger-king who brings the glamour and objectivity of an outsider to power struggles he can transcend and ends up as ruler.

The historical record of the Sonni began in the early fourteenth cen-tury, when they were governors of Gao, as restless subordinates of Mali. Gao was an impressive city, unwalled and, said Leo Africanus, full of "ex-ceeding rich merchants". Hundreds of straight, long, interlocking streets with identical houses surrounded a great marketplace specialising in slaves. You could buy seven slave girls for a fine horse and, of course, swap salt for gold or sell Maghrebi and European textiles. There were whole-some wells, and corn, melons, lemons, and rice as abundant as flesh. The governor's palace was filled with concubines and slaves. "It is a wonder to see what plentie of Merchandize is dayly brought hither," wrote Leo Afri-canus in the version of his work produced by a sixteenth-century English translator, "and how costly and sumptuous all things be." Horses cost four or five times as much as in Europe. Fine scarlet cloth from Venice or Turkey commanded thirty times its Mediterranean price. "But of all other commodities salt is the most extremelie deere."[6]

The city's governors had plenty of opportunities for self-enrichment, and plenty of temptations to declare independence. To ensure good behaviour, the Mansa Musa took the ruler's children as hostages when he passed through Gao in 1325. But such measures could have only temporary effects. The Sonni were free of Malian supremacy by early in the fifteenth century. Probably around 1425, Sonni Muhammad Dao felt secure enough to lead a raid against Mali, reaching Jenne, seizing Mande captives, and generating legends.

The Sonni bestowed on their children such names as Ali, Muhammad, and Umar, suggesting a commitment to Islam or at least familiarity with it. For centuries, Islam had overspilled the Sahara, lapping the kings and courts of the western African bulge. As early as the ninth century, Arab visitors to Soninke chiefdoms and kingdoms noted that some people followed "the king's religion" – some form of pre-Islamic paganism – while others were Muslims. Although Islam made little documented progress in West Africa before the eleventh century, immigration and acculturation along the Saharan trade routes prepared the way for Islamisation. The main reasons for Muslims to go to the Land of the Blacks were commercial, although they also went south to make war, find patronage if they were scholars or artists, and make converts to Islam. On this frontier, therefore, Islam lacked professional missionaries, but occasionally a Muslim merchant might interest a trading partner or even a pagan ruler in Islam.

A late-eleventh-century Arab compiler of information about West Africa tells such a story, from Malal, south of the Senegal. At a time of terrible drought, a Muslim guest advised the king of the consequences if he accepted Islam: "You would bring Allah's mercy on the people of your country, and your enemies would envy you." Rain duly fell after prayers and Quranic recitations. "Then the king ordered that the idols be broken and the sorcerers expelled. The king, together with his descendants and the nobility, became sincerely attached to Islam, but the common people remained pagans."[7]

As well as peaceful missionising, war spread Islam. The region's first well-documented case of Islamisation by jihad occurred in the Soninke kingdom of Ghana in the eleventh and twelfth centuries. This kingdom anticipated Mali and Songhay, thriving on the taxation of trans-Saharan trade and occupying a similar environment around the upper Niger, somewhat to the east of Mali's future heartland. In the mid-eleventh century the Almoravids – as Westerners call the al-Murabitun, a movement of warrior-ascetics – burst out of the desert, conquering an empire from Spain to the Sahel. They targeted Ghana as the home of "sorcerers", where, according to collected reports, the people buried their dead with gifts, "made offerings of alcohol", and kept a sacred snake in a cave. Muslims – presumably traders – had their own large quarter in or near the Ghanaian capital, Kumbi Saleh, but apart from the royal quarter of the town. The Soninke fought off Almoravid armies with some success until 1076. In that year, Kumbi fell, and its defenders were massacred. The northerners' political hold south of the Sahara did not last, but the struggle of Islam against paganism continued.

Spanish and Sicilian travellers' reports give us later snapshots of the history of Ghana. The most extensive account is full of sensational and salacious tales praising the slave women, excellent at cooking "sugared nuts and honeyed donuts", and with good figures, firm breasts, slim waists, fat buttocks, wide shoulders, and sexual organs "so narrow that one of them may be enjoyed as though she were a virgin indefinitely".[8] But a vivid picture emerges of a kingdom with three or four prosperous, populous towns, productive in copper work, cured hides, dyed robes, and Atlantic ambergris as well as gold. The authors also make clear the means by which Islam spread in the region, partly by settlement of Maghrebi merchants in the towns, and partly by the efforts of individual holy men or pious merchants establishing relationships of confidence

1492

with kings. Interpreters and officials were already typically Muslims, and every town had several mosques, but even rulers sympathetic to Islam maintained their traditional court establishments, and what Muslims called "idols" and "sorcerers".

By the mid-twelfth century, Islam was clearly in the ascendant. Arab writers regarded Ghana as a model Islamic state, whose king revered the true caliph in Baghdad and dispensed justice with exemplary openness. They admired his well-built palace, with its objects of art and windows of glass; the huge natural ingot of gold that was the symbol of his authority; the gold ring by which he tethered his horse; his silk clothes; his elephants and giraffes. "In former times," reported a scholar based in Spain, "the people of the country professed paganism. . . . Today there are Muslims and they have scholars, lawyers, and Koran readers and have become pre-eminent in these fields. Some of their chief leaders . . . have travelled to Mecca and made the pilgrimage and visited the Prophet's tomb."9

Archaeology confirms this picture. Excavations at Kumbi reveal a town of nearly one and a half square miles, founded in the tenth century, housing perhaps fifteen to twenty thousand, with a regular plan and evidence of large, multi-storey buildings, including what excavators have designated as nine-roomed "mansions" and a great mosque. Artefacts include glass weights for weighing gold, many finely wrought metal tools, and evidence of a local form of money.10 This magnificence did not last. After a long period of stagnation or decline, pagan invaders overran the Soninke state and destroyed Kumbi. But Islam had spread so widely by then among the warriors and traders of the Sahel that it retained a foothold south of the Sahara for the rest of the Middle Ages.

The big questions, for the history of the world, were: how tenacious would that hold prove? How far would it extend? How deep would Islam penetrate? And how would it change the way people lived and thought? For the future of Islam in West Africa, the attitude of Songhay's rulers was critical.

For in Songhay, Islam remained superficial. The kings relied on the Muslim intelligentsia of Gao for scribes, bureaucrats, encomiasts, and diplomats at literate courts. But they also had to wield the traditional magic of their people. To rule Songhay, a leader had to combine uneasily compatible roles as a good Muslim and a good magus, both at the same time. He had to be what his people called a *dali* – both king and shaman, endowed with powers of prophecy, capable of contacting the spirits as well as praying to God.

Sonni Ali Ber – "Ber" means "Great" – who succeeded to the throne in the 1460s, had been raised in his mother's land, around Sokoto. Here Islam had barely arrived and was hardly practised, even in the royal court. Sonni Ali drank *djitti*, the magic potion that protected against witchcraft, literally with his mother's milk. He knew something of Islam. He learned bits of the Quran in childhood. His parents submitted him to be circumcised. But he always seemed to prefer paganism: at least, that is how the sources – all written by clerics or their cronies – represent him. Some of his objectively verifiable behaviour seems to match his anticlerical reputation. Rather than residing in Gao, for instance, which was cosmopolitan, and therefore Muslim, Sonni Ali preferred the second city of his kingdom, Koukya, a palace town where caravans did not come.

The way the kingdom worked bound Sonni Ali to an ancient, pagan past. Songhay was a tributary state. At Sonni Ali's birth, tribute of millet and rice converged from around the kingdom. Forty head each of oxen, heifers, goats, and chickens were decapitated and the meat distributed to the poor. It was an ancient rite of agrarian kingship, for the king's role was to garner food and control its warehousing, ensuring equitable shares for all and stocks against times of famine. Iron tribute arrived, forged in fires lit by the bellows of the fire god. Each smith paid a hundred lances and a hundred arrows a year for the king's army. Of twenty-four subject peoples who supplied the palace slaves, each paid special tribute: fodder for the king's horses, dried fish, cloth.

Dominion of the river was vital to making the system work, for the Niger was the great highway that linked the forest to the desert. But to possess the river, control over the Sahel was indispensable. Sonni Ali knew that and acted accordingly. His reputation for cruelty owed much to embellishment by his clerical foes, but something, too, to his own strategy. To conquer, he had to inspire fear. He drove back the Tuareg and Mossi – the previously unconquerable warrior bands around the upper Volta – and ruled by razzia, descending periodically on his tributaries' lands to enforce their compliance. He built three palace garrisons around his kingdom to facilitate control.

He established a monopoly or near-monopoly of violence and cowed the kingdom into peace. Sonni Ali's peace favoured trade and especially, therefore, the elites of the Niger Valley towns. At the time, Timbuktu was the greatest of them – "exquisite, pure, delicious, illustrious, blessed, lively, rich". Leo Africanus described the notable buildings: the houses of Timbuktu of clay-covered wattles with thatched roofs, the great mosque of stone and mortar, the governor's palace, the "very numerous" shops of the artisans, the merchants, and especially weavers of cotton cloth. Like every vibrant urban space, the city was "very much endangered by fire". Leo saw half of it burn "in the space of five hours" as a violent wind fanned the flames and the inhabitants of the other half of the city shunted their belongings to safety.[11]

"The inhabitants," he reported, "are very rich", especially the immigrant Maghrebi elite of merchants and scholars, who generated so much demand for books imported from the Maghreb that – so Leo claimed – "there is more profit made from this commerce than from all other merchandise". The people, Leo declared, "are of a peaceful nature. They have a custom of almost continuously walking about the city in the evening (except for those that sell gold), between ten and one o'clock, playing musical instruments and dancing. . . . The citizens have at their service many slaves, both men and women. The women of the city maintain the custom of veiling their faces, except for the slaves who sell all the foodstuffs."[12]

Gold nuggets and cowrie shells were exchanged for salt, which was "in very short supply", slaves, European textiles, and horses. "Only small, poor horses," according to Leo, "are born in this country. The merchants use them for their voyages and the courtiers to move about the city. But the good horses come from Barbary. They arrive in a caravan and, ten or twelve days later, they are led to the ruler, who takes as many as he likes and pays appropriately for them."[13]

By Sonni Ali's time, Malian sovereignty over Timbuktu was nominal. The city was poised between two potential masters: the Tuareg herdsmen of the desert, against whom the Malians could no longer offer protection, and the Sonni. Preserving effective independence required a careful balancing act, playing off the rivals against one another. In the early years of Ali's reign, Muhammad Nad, the wily old governor of Timbuktu, treated the Sonni with circumspection – appeasing him with tribute and deterring him with the threat of Tuareg intervention. The magnificence of Muhammad Nad's court was fit for a king. Leo describes him riding a camel, hearing pleas from prostrate subjects, and garnering a treasure of coins, ingots, and immense gold nuggets. This wealth paid for an army of "about three thousand horsemen and infinity of foot soldiers". War was waged for tribute and captives: "[W]hen he has gained a victory, he has all of them – even the children – sold in the market at Timbuktu." Still, Muhammad Nad knew how to defer when it mattered. He joined Sonni Ali in his first campaigns of conquest against the forest dwellers to the south: participation in campaigns was a rite of submission, part of the normal relationship of tributaries to their lords.

Muhammad Nad's son and successor, Ammar, was less diplomatic. Resentful of admitting to being Songhay's dependant, he sent a letter of defiance: "My father quit this life possessing nothing but a linen shroud. The force of arms at my disposal surpasses belief. Let him who doubts it come and count." But it soon became obvious that he could not do without Songhayan help. When the Tuareg descended on the town and intimidated him into releasing part of the governor's traditional income from tolls on the trade of the river, Ammar cut a deal with the Sonni.

He was entertaining Akil, the Tuareg chief, in January 1468, when a cloud of dust appeared on the horizon.

"A sandstorm," ventured the host.

"You have wasted your eyes on books," replied Akil. "My eyes are old, but I can see the armed horsemen approaching."[14]

The Tuareg abandoned Timbuktu to Sonni Ali, who – so tradition asserted – likened the city to a woman "rolling her eyes in terror and sashaying her body to seduce us".[15] The mullahs, however, did not join in the seductive performance or the submissive posture of the governor and merchant elite. They supported the Tuareg. It is hard to separate cause and effect: were the clergy repelled by Sonni Ali's paganism? Or was his identification with the old gods part of his response to clerical hostility? In any event, his overtly contemptuous and vindictive treatment of them became obvious for the remaining years of his reign.

It seems more convincing to see his attitude as part of the power play that balanced factions in Timbuktu than to suppose that he practised anticlericalism out of pagan devotion or principled detestation of the mullahs. Anticlericalism and piety are not incompatible, and Ali's religious views and sentiments seem to have been much more deeply imbued with reverence for Islam than clerical propaganda made out. Sonni Ali performed the holiday prayers of Ramadan year by year during his campaigns. "Despite his ill treatment of scholars," reported a late but generally fair chronicler, "he acknowledged their worth and often said, 'Without the clergy the world would no longer be sweet and good.'"[16] Muhammad Nad's sons and grandsons, by contrast, were lax in performing Muslim rites. Yet they incurred much less clerical obloquy.

On the other hand, evidence of Sonni Ali's hostility towards the city patriciate of Timbuktu is ample, especially in an intense period of mutual distrust from 1468 to 1473. Muhammad Nad had been a great friend to the city's elite, as Leo Africanus observed. "There are in Timbuktu numerous judges, teachers and priests, all properly appointed" by Muhammad Nad, who "greatly honours learning".[17] Ali abjured this attitude, treated the city with disdain, and rarely paused there on his progresses around the kingdom.

His conquest provoked a massive exodus of the elite. A caravan of one thousand camels took the exiles to Walata, where they could rely on Tuareg protection, while Ali killed, enslaved, or imprisoned the children of one of the chief judges of the city, And-agh-Muhammad al-Kabir. He humiliated – the chroniclers are not explicit about the details – the family of the other, al-qadi al-Hajj, and massacred a party of them who tried to flee to Walata. His policy was not solely to do with vengeance, but was also designed to contain potential opposition within Songhay, for al-Hajj was close to the family of Sonni Ali's lieutenant and most successful general, Askia Muhammad – the only possible rival to the Sonni's supremacy. Rebellion, massacre, and a further exodus followed in 1470 or 1471. The feud between Ali and Timbuktu was beginning to damage the kingdom. The new refugees sowed martyrdom stories among exiles and initiated the implacably hostile scholarly tradition against Ali. Worse for the Sonni's revenues, the decline of the city disrupted trade.

By now, however, Sonni Ali was beginning to feel secure. In 1471 (or perhaps a little later – the chronology of the sources is confused), he conquered Jenne, despite the fire ships the defenders launched against the Songhayan fleet. Jenne was the last and largest of the great river ports of the Niger, where the call from the great minaret, so it was said, echoed in seven thousand places. Ali had now constructed an empire comparable in extent to Mali at its height. Consolidation rather than conquest became his main aim. From about 1477, for eight or nine years, he tried to rebuild his relationship with Timbuktu's patricians and scholars, and reinvigorate the kingdom's trade. He projected a canal from Niger to Walata, though he never got around to building it. To the office of chief judge of Timbuktu, he appointed a descendant of a sage whom Mansa Musa had brought to the Sahel: it was an emphatic gesture of deference to tradition. He sent women captured on campaigns against the Fulani as a present to the scholars of Timbuktu – though some of the recipients treated the gift as an insult. If Ali's intentions were good, they were too little too late. Renewed war with the Mossi interrupted his plans for reconstruction and provoked him into a new bout of repression.

In 1485 he dismissed Muhammad Nad's son from the governorship of Timbuktu and installed a nominee of his own. Probably in 1488, he ordered what the chroniclers call the "evacuation" of Timbuktu.[18] Other evidence does not support clerical sources' picture of a devastated and depopulated city; so this was probably just the expulsion of suspect families. The clergy intensified their counter-campaign of propaganda. Sonni Ali became a bogeyman for the godly. In Egypt his rise was reported as a calamity for Islam, comparable to the loss of al-Andalus to Christian conquerors. In 1487, mullahs in Mecca raised imprecations against him. A Maghrebi jurist later denied that Ali was a Muslim at all.[19] Meanwhile, back in the Sahel, Ali's priority for war continued to shift power from the mullahs and merchants to warrior chiefs.

Askia Muhammad Touray was the greatest of them. As one of Ali's closest companions, commanders, and counsellors, he evinced total loyalty, but the Sonni's opponents naturally cast him as their potential champion, or at least as an intermediary whose favour they needed. Askia Muhammad's popularity and success were vexing to Sonni Baro, the heir to the throne. Baro tried to arouse in his father suspicions against Muhammad by alleging that the general's Muslim piety implied alliance with traitorous clergy.

The charges had some credibility. Muhammad had tried to save massacre victims in Timbuktu and had used his influence to moderate Sonni Ali's anticlerical excesses. In consequence he had a powerful constituency of admirers and partisans, especially in the city that regarded him as its protector. Sonni Baro, by contrast, was a hateful figure, identified with all his father's most obnoxious traits – his adherence to pagan forms, his humbling of the clerics, his oppression of Timbuktu. By December 1492, when news arrived that Sonni Ali had died, many of the mullahs and merchants were ready to incite rebellion. Askia

Muhammad was in Timbuktu when news of the king's death broke there on 1 January 1493.

One of the elite messengers, trained to spend up to ten days in the saddle and cross the entire kingdom, arrived with a breathless message:

Ali the Great, your master and mine, king of Songhay, star of the world, shining sun of our hearts, terror of our enemies, died ten days ago. . . . He was on his way back to Gao from an expedition. . . . As he was crossing a small tributary of the Niger, a sudden swell arose and carried off our lord, his horse, his baggage, and his train in the surging waves. The army watched powerless from the shore. I was there. We could do nothing. It all happened so fast.[20]

The citizens of the town came out of their dwellings and raised the cry: "The tyrant is dead! Long live King Muhammad!" But their hero cut short a preacher who denounced the memory of "the impious and terrible tyrant, the worst oppressor ever known, the destroyer of cities, of hard and cruel heart, who killed so many men whose names are known to God alone and who treated the learned and godly with humiliation and contempt".[21] Muhammad's display of loyalty to his dead master only increased his devout reputation and the clamour for him to be king. Chroniclers gilded his iron ambition with the gleam of piety.

He was reluctant – so it was said – to accept the throne. The people besought him; the army acclaimed him. Messengers from the old king's deathbed assured him that Ali had wanted him to save the kingdom from Sonni Baro's impiety or incompetence. The truth is that Muhammad dared not defer to Sonni Baro. For too long, they had been rivals in the old king's esteem, and contenders for influence over him. Muhammad marched against Baro, claiming to demand from him accession to the true faith. It was an old and enduring pretext for violence: jihad against an alleged apostate.

The surviving chronicles, which are uniformly favourable to Askia Muhammad, portray Sonni Baro preparing for battle in drugged ecstasy, communing with his idols, especially Za Beri Wandu, the god who be-got the River Niger. A sorcerer conjured for Baro a vision of his father's spirit. Baro saw the ghost's lips move but heard nothing. The medium gave him the message: "[T]he king rejoices in your valour and urges you to combat Islam courageously." Sonni Baro, meanwhile, treated Muhammad's emissary, an old sheikh who brought the insulting de-mand for repentance and conversion, to a display of magic. A fakir dis-gorged a chain of pure gold. Another made a tree shake in a windless landscape. When the sheikh tried to escape the scene of devilry, Sonni Baro himself rose and beat him almost to death. "I reign by right of birth," he cried, "and the protection of the gods."[22]

To the chroniclers who recorded or constructed this scene, it was a double blasphemy, for only Allah conferred kingship. False auguries deceived Baro, even at the height of the battle that followed. The deci-sive element in Muhammad's victory, however, seems not to have been supernatural intervention, but the Tuareg allies who descended from the desert in his support.

It was one of the great decisive battles of the world – though West-ern tradition has forgotten or ignored it. Sonni Baro owed nothing to the mullahs and had every reason to arrest the spread of Islam south of the Sahara. Had he triumphed, Islam might have been stopped at the edge of the Sahel. Askia Muhammad, on the other hand, owed his throne to Muslims and invested heavily in practising and promoting their religion. In 1497, he re-enacted the most ostentatious of the dis-plays of piety of the Mansas of Mali by making a pilgrimage to Mecca with one thousand foot soldiers and five hundred horse, bidding to emu-late the Mansa Musa's dazzling retinue. He legitimised his usurpation of power in Songhay by submitting his claim to the throne to the Sharif of Mecca. On his return to Songhay in 1498, he adopted the title of ca-liph – the most ambitious claim any ruler could make to the legacy of the Prophet.

Muhammad's reason for arrogating the title to himself perhaps owed something to regional power struggles: Ali Ghadj, the redoubtable king of Bornu – the state that straddled the Sahel around Lake Chad – used the same title until his death in 1497. Bornu was a warrior state, exchanging slaves for horses. Ali Ghadj's successor, Idris Katakarmabi, was on the throne when Leo Africanus turned up. He found Bornu rich in rare kinds of grain and with wealthy merchants in the villages, but the highland people were naked or clad in skins. "They embrace no religion at all, . . . living in a brutish manner, and having wives and children in common." Still, Bornu had three thousand horsemen, and huge numbers of infantry, maintained by a tithe of the people's grain and the spoils of war. Though stingy with merchants – so merchants said – "the king seemeth to be marveilous rich; for his spurres, his bridles, platters, dishes, pots, and other vessels . . . are all of pure golde: yea, and the chaines of his dogs and hounds are of golde also".[23] Bornu, in short, was a major regional power against which the parvenu Songhayan state had to measure itself. In any case, the style of caliph fitted Muhammad's Muslim self-projection. When he made war, he called it jihad.

Islam's progress was now irreversible. That does not mean that it was uncontested or unlimited. Paganism, though bloodied and bowed, survived. In the long run it was ineradicable, subsisting as a form of popular religion or "alternative" subculture, and always polluting Islam with syncretic influences. When conspirators deposed the ageing Askia Muhammad in 1529 and confined him to an island in the Niger, his heirs slid back into ambiguous practices reminiscent of those of Sonni Ali.

Moreover, even while Sonni Ali died in the Niger, a newly arrived religion was intruding in sub-Saharan West Africa. As a rival to Islam, Christianity had one big advantage: its adherents carried it by sea. They could outflank Islam and dodge the forests, reaching directly deep into tropical Africa via the coasts.

The first outpost was the fort that Portuguese explorers founded in 1482 at São Jorge da Mina, on the underbelly of the African bulge, near the mouths of the rivers Benya and Pra, about a hundred kilometres from the Volta. For over half a century, the Portuguese had justified their slave raids and trading ventures on the coast of the African Atlantic as part of a crusade to spread Christianity. The ambitious prince Dom Henrique, whom historians call "the Navigator" (rather misleadingly, as he made only two short sea trips), sponsored the voyages until his death in 1460, with support from successive popes, and sent expeditions as far as what is now Sierra Leone; but he never honoured his promises to send missionaries to the region. Spanish friars strove to fill the gap, but the Portuguese detested them as foreign agents, and they made little or no progress. The merchants and private entrepreneurs who ran the Portuguese effort from 1469 to 1475 had no reason to waste hard-nosed investment on spiritual objectives.

In 1475, however, the crown took over the enterprise, perhaps in order to confront Spanish interlopers. West African navigation became the responsibility of the senior prince of the royal house, the infante Dom João. Henceforth, Portugal had an heir and, from his accession in 1481, a king committed to the further exploration and exploitation of Africa. He seems to have conceived of the African Atlantic as a sort of "Portuguese main", fortified by coastal trading establishments. Numerous informal and unfortified Portuguese outposts already dotted the Senegambia region. Freelance expatriates set most of them up, "going native" as they did so. Dom João, however, had a militant and organising mentality, forged in the war he waged against Spanish interlopers on the Guinea coast between 1475 and 1481.

When he sent one hundred masons and carpenters to build the fort of São Jorge, therefore, he was doing something new: inaugurating a policy of permanent footholds, disciplined trading, and royal initiatives. The natives could see and fear the transformation for themselves. A local chief said that he had preferred the "ragged and ill dressed men who had traded there before".[24] Another prong of the new policy was the centralisation of the African trade at Lisbon, in warehouses below the royal palace, where all sailings had to be registered and all cargo stored. An even more important element in João's plan was the cultivation of friendly relations with powerful coastal chieftains: the Wolof chiefs of Senegambia; the rulers – or "obas", as they were called – of the lively port city of Benin; and ultimately – much farther south – the kings of Kongo. Conversion to Christianity was not essential for good relations – but it helped. In Europe, it served to legitimise Portugal's privileged presence in a region where other powers coveted the chance to trade. In Africa, it could create a bond between the Portuguese and their hosts.

Dom João therefore presided over an extraordinary turnover in baptisms and rebaptisms of rapidly apostatising black chiefs. In one remarkable political pantomime in 1488, he entertained an exiled Wolof potentate to a full regal reception, for which the visitor was decked out with European clothes and the table laden with silver plate.[25] Farther east along the coast, Portuguese missionary effort was still feeble, but the fort of São Jorge was Christianity's shop window in the region, contriving an attractive display. Its wealth and dimensions were modest, but mapmakers depicted it as a splendid place, with high fortifications, pennanted turrets, and gleaming spires – a sort of black Camelot. It had no explicit missionary role, but it did have resident chaplains, who became foci of enquiries from local leaders and their rivals, who realised that they could get help in the form of Portuguese technicians and weapons if they expressed an interest in Christianity. The obas of Benin played the game with some skill, never actually committing to the Church but garnering aid like supermarket customers targeting "special offers". Not much came of any of the contacts, in terms of real Christianisation, and in competition in the region neither Christianity nor Islam was very effective at first. But West Africa had become what it has remained ever since: an arena of spiritual enterprise in which Islam and Christianity contended for religious allegiance.

Farther south, where Portuguese ships reached but where Muslim merchants and missionaries were unknown, was the kingdom of Kongo. Here people responded to Christianity with an enthusiasm wholly disproportionate to Portugal's lacklustre attempts at conversion. The kingdom dominated the River Congo's navigable lower reaches, probably from the mid-fourteenth century. The ambitions of its rulers became evident when Portuguese explorers established contact in the 1480s. In 1482, battling against the Benguela Current, Diogo Cão reached the shores of the kingdom. Follow-up voyages brought emissaries from Kongo to Portugal and bore Portuguese missionaries, craftsmen, and mercenaries in the reverse direction.

In Kongo, the rulers sensed at once that the Portuguese could be useful to them. They greeted them with a grand parade, noisy with horns and drums. The king, brandishing his horsetail whisk and wearing his ceremonial cap of woven palm fibre, sat on an ivory throne smothered with the gleaming pelts of lions. He graciously commanded the Portuguese to build a church, and when protesters murmured at the act of sacrilege to the old gods, he offered to put them to death on the spot. The Portuguese piously demurred.

On 3 May 1491, King Nzinga Nkuwu and his son, Nzinga Mbemba, were baptised. Their conversion may have started as a bid for help in internal political conflicts. The laws of succession were ill defined, and Nzinga Mbemba, or Afonso I, as he called himself, had to fight for the succession. He attributed his victory to battlefield apparitions of the Virgin Mary and St James of Compostela – the same celestial warriors that had often appeared on Iberian battlefields in conflicts against the Moors and would appear again on the side of Spain and Portugal in many wars of conquest in the Americas. Kongo enthusiastically adopted the technology of the visitors and embraced them as partners in slave raiding in the interior and warfare against neighbouring realms. Christianity became part of a package of aid from these seemingly gifted foreigners. The royal residence was rebuilt in the Portuguese style. The kings issued documents in Portuguese, and members of the royal family went to Portugal for their education. One prince became an archbishop, and the kings continued to have Portuguese baptismal names for centuries thereafter.

The Portuguese connection made Kongo the best-documented kingdom in West Africa in the sixteenth century. However Afonso I came

to Christianity in the first place, he was sincere in espousing it and zeal-
ous in promoting it. Missionary reports extolled the "angelic" ruler for
knowing

> the prophets and the gospel of Our Lord Jesus Christ and all the
> lives of the saints and everything about our sacred mother the church
> better than we ourselves know them. . . . It seems to me that the
> Holy Spirit always speaks through him, for he does nothing but
> study, and many times he falls asleep over his books, and many
> times he forgets to eat and drink for talking of Our Lord, . . . and
> even when he is going to hold an audience and listen to the people,
> he speaks of nothing but God and His saints.[26]

Thanks in part to Afonso's patronage, Christianity spread beyond
the court. "Throughout the kingdom", the same writer informed the
Portuguese monarch, Afonso

> sent many men, natives of the country, Christians, who have schools
> and teach our saintly faith to the people, and there are also schools
> for girls where one of his sisters teaches, a woman who is easily sixty
> years old, and who knows how to read very well and who is learned
> in her old age. Your Highness would rejoice to see it. There are also
> other women who know how to read and who go to church every
> day. These people pray to Our Lord at mass and Your Highness will
> know in truth that they are making great progress in Christianity
> and virtue, for they are advancing in the knowledge of the truth;
> also, may Your Highness always send them things and rejoice in
> helping them and, for their redemption, as a remedy, send them
> books, for they need them more than any other things for their re-
> demption.[27]

Afonso may have loved books. His own priority, however, was to
ask for what we would now call medical aid – physicians, surgeons,

apothecaries, and drugs – not so much in admiration of Western medicine as in fear of the link between traditional cures and pagan practices,
for, as Afonso explained to the king of Portugal,

> we always have many different diseases, which put us very often in
> such a weakness that we reach almost the last extreme; and the same
> happens to our children, relatives and natives owing to the lack in
> this country of physicians and surgeons who might know how to
> cure properly such diseases. And as we have got neither dispensaries
> nor drugs which might help us in this forlornness, many of those
> who had been already confirmed and instructed in the holy faith of
> Our Lord Jesus Christ perish and die; and the rest of the people in
> their majority cure themselves with herbs and spells and other an-
> cient methods, so that they put all their faith in the said herbs and
> ceremonies if they live, and believe that they are saved if they die;
> and this is not much in the service of God.[28]

Not all Afonso's efforts to convert his people were entirely benign.
The missionaries also commended him for "burning idolaters along
with their idols". How much the combination of preaching, promotion,
education, and repression achieved is hard to gauge. Portugal stinted
the resources needed to Christianise Kongo effectively. And the rapacity of Portuguese slavers hampered missionary efforts. Afonso complained to the king of Portugal about white slavers who infringed the
royal monopoly of European trade goods and seized slaves indiscrimi-
nately. "In order to satisfy their voracious appetite", they

> seize many of our people, freed and exempt men, and very often it
> happens that they kidnap even noblemen and the sons of noblemen,
> and our relatives, and take them to be sold to the white men who are
> in our Kingdoms; and for this purpose they have concealed them;
> and others are brought during the night so that they might not be
> recognised. And as soon as they are taken by the white men they are

immediately shackled and branded with fire. . . . And to avoid such a
great evil we passed a law so that any white man living in our Kingdoms and wanting to purchase goods in any way should first inform
three of our noblemen and officials of our court whom we rely upon
in this matter, . . . who should investigate if the mentioned goods are
captives or free men, and if cleared by them there will be no further
doubt nor embargo for them to be taken and embarked. But if the
white men do not comply with it they will lose the aforementioned
goods. And if we do them this favour and concession it is for the part
Your Highness has in it, since we know that it is in your service too
that these goods are taken from our Kingdom.[29]

Despite the limitations of the evangelisation of Kongo, the dynamism of Christianity south of the Sahara set a pattern for the future.
The region was full of cultures that adapted to new religions with surprising ease. Until the intensive missionary efforts of the nineteenth
century, Christianisation was patchy and superficial, but Christians
never lost their advantage over Muslims in competing for sub-Saharan
souls.

By adhering to Christianity, the Kongolese elite compensated, to
some extent, for the isolation and stagnation of Christian East Africa at
about the same time. Christianity had been the religion of Ethiopia's
rulers since the mid-fourth century, when King Ezana began to substi-
tute invocations of "Father, Son, and Holy Spirit" for praise of his war
god in the inscriptions that celebrated his campaigns of conquest and
enslavement. The empire's next thousand years were chequered with
disaster, but Ethiopia survived – an aberrant outpost of Christendom,
with its own distinctive heresy. For the Ethiopian clergy subscribed to
the doctrine, condemned in the Roman tradition in the mid-fifth century, that Christ's humanity and divinity were fused in a single, wholly
divine nature. In the late fourteenth century, in near-isolation from contact with Europe, the realm again began to reach beyond its mountains
to dominate surrounding regions. Monasteries became schools of

Map redrawn from Fra Mauro's Venetian Mappamundi of the 1450s, showing how well informed Latin Christendom was about Ethiopia.

missionaries, whose task was to consolidate Ethiopian power in the conquered pagan lands of Shoa and Gojam. Rulers, meanwhile, concentrated on reopening their ancient outlet to the Red Sea and thereby the Indian Ocean. By 1403, when King Davit recaptured the Red Sea port of Massaweh, Ethiopian rule stretched into the trade route along the Great Rift Valley, where slaves, ivory, gold, and civet headed northward, generating valuable tolls.

Yet by the time of the death of King Zara Yakub, towards the end of the 1460s, expansion was straining resources, and conquests stopped. Saints' lives are a major source for Ethiopian history in this period. They tell of internal consolidation rather than outward expansion as monks converted wasteland to farmland. The kingdom began to feel beleaguered, and rulers sought outside help, looking as far as Europe for allies. European visitors were already familiar in Ethiopia, for Ethiopia's Massaweh Road was a standard route to the Indian Ocean. Italian merchants anxious to grab some of the wealth of the Indian Ocean for themselves would head up the Nile as far as Keneh, where they joined camel caravans across the eastern Nubian desert for the thirty-five-day journey to the Red Sea. Encouraged by these contacts, Ethiopian rulers sent envoys to European courts and even flirted with the idea of submitting the Ethiopian church to the discipline of Rome. In 1481, the pope provided a church to house visiting Ethiopian monks in the Vatican garden.

The kingdom was still big enough and rich enough to impress European visitors. When Portuguese diplomatic missions began to arrive – the first, in the person of Pedro de Covilhão, in about 1488; a second in 1520 – they found "men and gold and provisions like the sands of the sea and the stars in the sky", while "countless tents" borne by fifty thousand mules transported the court around the kingdom.[30] Crowds of two thousand at a time would line up for royal audiences, marshalled by guards on plumed horses, caparisoned in fine brocade. To the ruler of Ethiopia, Negus Eskendar, Covilhão was immediately recognisable as a precious asset, whom he retained at his court with lavish rewards.

Ethiopia, however, had already overreached its potential as a conquest state. Pagan migrants permeated the southern frontier. Muslim invaders pressed from the east, building up the pressure until within a couple of generations they threatened to conquer the highlands. Ethiopia barely survived. The frontier of Christendom began to shrink.

Meanwhile, beyond Ethiopia, the east coast of Africa was accessible to Muslim influence but cut off from that of Christians. In the sixteenth century the sea route around the Cape of Good Hope brought Portuguese merchants, exiles, and garrisons to the region. Here, however, Christianity never had the manpower or appeal to compete with Islam, while the inland states remained largely beyond the reach of missionaries of either faith.

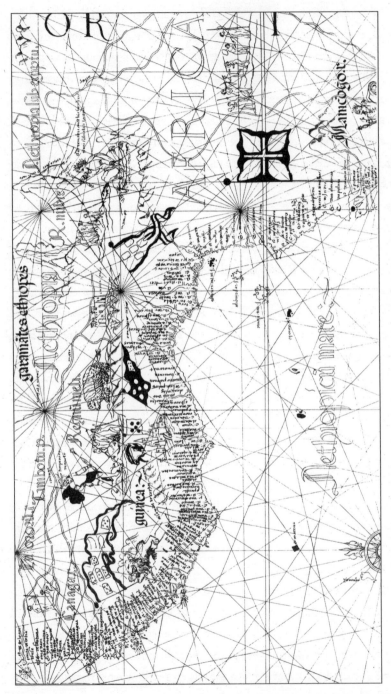

Diogo Homem's map of West Africa (1558) shows São Jorge da Mina (topped with five-dotted flag), indigenous slave-raiding, and the ruler of Songhay, extravagantly behatted.

The greatest of these states were at the far end of the Rift Valley, around the gold-strewn Zambezi. The productive plateau beyond, which stretched to the south as far as the River Limpopo, was rich in salt, gold, and elephants. Like Ethiopia, these areas looked towards the Indian Ocean for long-range trade with the economies of maritime Asia. Unlike Ethiopia, communities in the Zambezi Valley had ready access to the ocean, but they faced a potentially more difficult problem. Their outlets to the sea lay below the reach of the monsoon system and, therefore, beyond the normal routes of trade. Still, adventurous merchants – most of them, probably, from southern Arabia – risked the voyage to bring manufactured goods from Asia in trade for gold and ivory. Some of the most vivid evidence comes from the mosque in Kilwa, in modern Tanzania, where fifteenth-century Chinese porcelain bowls – products Arabian merchants shipped across the whole breadth of the ocean – line the inside of the dome.

Further evidence of the effects of trade lie inland, where fortified, stone-built administrative centres – called "zimbabwes" – had been common for centuries. In the late fourteenth and fifteenth centuries, the zimbabwes entered their greatest age. The most famous, Great Zimbabwe, included a formidable citadel on a hill 350 feet high, but remains of other citadels are scattered over the land. Near stone buildings, the beef-fed elite were buried with gifts: gold, jewellery, jewelled ironwork, large copper ingots, and Chinese porcelain.

In the second quarter of the fifteenth century, the centre of power shifted northward to the Zambezi Valley, with the expansion of a new regional power. Mwene Mutapa, as it was called, arose during the northward migration of bands of warriors from what are now parts of Mozambique and KwaZulu-Natal. When one of their leaders conquered the middle Zambezi Valley, he took the title Mwene Mutapa, or "lord of the tribute payers" – a name that became extended to the state. From about the mid-fifteenth century, the pattern of trade routes altered as Mwene Mutapa's conquests spread eastward towards the coast. But Mwene Mutapa never reached the ocean. Native merchants, who traded at inland fairs, had no interest in a direct outlet to the sea. They did well enough using middlemen on the coast and had no incentive for or experience of ocean trade. The colonists were drawn, not driven, northward, though a decline in the navigability of the River Sabi may have stimulated the move.

The events of 1492 hardly affected the remote interior and south of Africa. But the death of Sonni Ali Ber in the waters of the Niger, the consolidation of Portuguese influence that followed the baptism of Nzinga Nkuwu in Kongo, and the renewal – which was going on at about the same time – of Ethiopia's diplomatic contact with the rest of Christendom were decisive events in carving up the continent between Islam and Christianity. With Askia Muhammad's triumph in Songhay, the accession of Afonso I in Kongo, and the success of Pedro de Covilhão's mission to Ethiopia, the configurations of the religious map of Africa today – where Islam dominates across the Sahara and in the Sahel, as far as the northern forest belt, and along the Indian Ocean coast, with Christianity preponderant elsewhere – became, if not inevitable, highly predictable.

Chapter 4

"No Sight More Pitiable"

The Mediterranean World
and the Redistribution of the Sephardim

*1 May: The royal decree expelling unbaptised Jews
from Spain is published.*

"There was not a Christian who did not feel their pain," reported Andrés de Bernáldez, priest and chronicler, who watched the crowds of Jews making their way into exile from Castile in the summer of 1492. Making music as they went, shaking their tambourines and beating their drums to keep their spirits up, "they went by the roads and fields with great labour and misery, some falling, some struggling again to their feet, others dying or falling sick". When they saw the sea, "they uttered loud screams and wailing, men and women, old and young, begging for God's mercy, for they hoped for some miracle from God and that the sea would part to make a road for them. Having waited many days and seen nothing but trouble, many wished they had never been born." Those who embarked "suffered disasters, robberies, and death on sea and on land, wherever they went, at the hands of Christians and Moors alike". Bernáldez knew "no sight more pitiable".[1]

Despite this avowal of compassion, Bernáldez hated Jews. By contumaciously refusing to recognise their Messiah, they had forfeited to Christians their heritage as God's chosen people. The roles in the book of Exodus were now reversed: the Jews were the "evil, unbelieving idolaters", and Christians were "the new children of Israel". Bernáldez hated Jews for their arrogance in claiming God's special favour. He hated the stink he scented on their breath and in their homes and synagogues, and which he attributed to the use of olive oil in cooking – for, amazing as it seems to anyone familiar with Spanish cooking today, medieval Castilians eschewed olive oil and used lard as their main source of dietary fat. He hated them with hatred born of economic envy, as dwellers "in the best locations in cities and towns and the choicest, richest lands" and as work-shy capitalists who "sought prosperous occupations, so as to get rich with little work, . . . cunning people, who usually lived off the many extortions and usuries they gained from Christians".[2]

He hated them, above all, for their privileges. Jews were exempt from tithes and, if they lived in their own ghettos (which by no means all did), were not obliged to pay municipal taxes. They elected the officials of their own communities. They enjoyed their own jurisdiction, and until 1476 they regulated their own business affairs among themselves according to their own laws. Even after that date, lawsuits between Jews were settled outside the common legal system, by judges specially appointed by the crown. The Inquisition – the tribunal everyone else feared – could not touch them unless they were suspected of suborning Christians or committing blasphemy. Because their own customs allowed higher rates of interest than those chargeable under Christian law, they had an advantage in any form of business that involved handling debt. They farmed taxes and occupied positions of profit in royal and seigneurial bureaucracies – though diminishingly so by the late fifteenth century. They lived – in many cases – as tenants and protégés of church, crown, or aristocracy. Most Jews, of course, were poor artisans, small tradesmen, or labourers, but Bernáldez observed what we would now call a trickle-down effect, with the wealthy members of the community supporting the less fortunate. In that respect, Jews were a typical group in medieval society – an "estate" that transcended class, with fellow feeling and a sense of common interest uniting people at different levels of wealth and education in defence of their shared identity and collective privileges.

"Jew" became a term of abuse. Terms of abuse are rarely used literally. Nowadays "fascist" is an insult hurled undiscriminatingly at people who have no resemblance to fascists. "Liberal" is fast becoming a similarly unspecific term in the United States. Few of the people foul-mouthed as "motherfuckers" in gangland parlance actually practise incest. Of most of the people denounced as Jews in fifteenth-century Spain, there is no independent evidence to connect them with Jewish ancestry, culture, or beliefs. If the term meant anything, it seems to have meant something like "thinking in an allegedly Jewish way" – which meant, in practice, thinking pharisaically: having, for instance, a literal-minded attitude to the law, or being more concerned with material or legalistic values than with spirituality. Of course, these thought patterns were not genuinely Jewish – you can find them in people of all religions and none – but readers of the letters of St Paul would recognise them as the sort of thoughts the apostle regarded as un-Christian.

Anti-Semitism is so perversely irrational that it is hard for any clear-headed person to understand. Christians, especially, ought to be immune to its venom, because their religion originated in Judaism and owes much of its doctrine, ritual, and scripture to the Jewish past. Christ, his mother, and all the apostles were Jews. The good that Jews have done the world by way of science, art, literature, and scholarship has been out of all proportion to their numbers. No community of similar size can rival Jews for the blessings they have brought the rest of us. Yet any conspicuous minority – and Jews have always formed conspicuous minorities – seems to ignite prejudice and attract odium. Privileged minorities stoke hatred even more intensively. And though

Hartmann Schedel, the principal author of the Nuremberg Chronicle, collected Hebrew books, perhaps in the hope of sparing them from the burning he anticipated as a harbinger of the imminent end of the world.

Christianity did not cause anti-Semitism, which was rife in the ancient Greek and Roman worlds before Christ, it provided a new pretext. Mobs regularly plundered Jews when readings in church reminded them that Christ's co-religionists demanded his crucifixion and cried, "His blood be upon us and on our children!"

In a notorious case heard in Ávila in 1491, on evidence recorded by hearsay or extracted by torture, Jews and some former Jews were condemned for crucifying a child, with a lot of mocking mummery of Christ's crucifixion, and eating his heart in a parody of the mass, as well as stealing and blasphemously abusing a consecrated Host for purposes of black magic. The allegedly murdered child – never convincingly named, never produced – probably never existed, but he became the hero of sensationalist literature, the object of a popular cult, and the genius of a shrine that attracts worshippers to Ávila to this day. The supposed perpetrators of the crimes were garrotted, or dismembered with red-hot pincers, and their grisly remains were burned so as not to pollute the earth. The Inquisition gave the case a huge billing. Much of it was heard in the presence of the Grand Inquisitor himself, and the findings – suitably massaged to conceal the implausibility of most of the charges and the contradictions of most of the testimony – were lavishly publicised. Some of the most learned jurists in Spain endorsed the sentence, despite the outrageous deficiencies of the evidence.

The case revealed three troubling aspects of the deteriorating reputation of Jews in the kingdom. First, public credulousness was an index of how far anti-Semitism had penetrated the culture. Second, the imagery of Christ's sacrifice on the cross and in the Eucharist, despite Christians' moral debt to Judaism, could easily be twisted into service against Jews. Finally, the trial seems, in retrospect, obviously contrived to serve political ends. By showing Jews and former Jews colluding in ritual murder and black magic, the inquisitors managed to establish in policy makers' minds a suppositious link between Judaism and Christian apostasy.

For what really worried the partisans of expulsion of the Jews was that, while Jewish communities remained in place, converts from Judaism could not escape the corroding effects of a Jewish environment. In the La Guardia case, the only charge that was proved against one of the alleged conspirators was that

not content with the fact that, for humanity's sake alone, as our holy faith prescribes, he, together with all other Jews, has the right to consort and converse with faithful Catholic Christians, he seduced certain Christians to his damnable law with false and deceitful preachings and suggestions, as a fautor of heresy, saying and expounding to them that the law of Moses was the only true law, in which they must be saved, and that the law of Jesus Christ was a feigned and dissembled law, never imposed or established by God.[3]

It was therefore the policy of the Inquisition to insulate society from Jewish influence. It was also a popular cause. The result of free association between Christians and Jews, according to Bernáldez, who was dim enough to be representative of popular prejudices, was that converts from Judaism and their descendants tended to be either "secret Jews" or "neither Jews nor Christians" – "like Muhammad's beast of burden, neither horse nor mule", as a tract of 1488 said.[4] Rather, they were godless antinomians who withheld their children from baptism, respected no fasts, made no confession, and gave no alms, but lived for gluttony and sexual excess or, in the case of backsliders into Judaism, ate Jewish food and observed Jewish customs.

There was probably some truth in the less sensational of these accusations: in a culturally ambiguous, transgressive setting, people can easily transcend traditions, escape dogma, and create new synergies. Investigations by the Inquisition uncovered many cases of religious indifference or outright scepticism. The late-fifteenth-century convert Alfonso Fernández Semuel asked to be buried with a cross at his feet, a Quran on his breast, and a Torah "high on his head" – as we know from a satire denouncing him for behaving crazily.[5] A sophisticated Jewish convert who became a bishop and a royal inquisitor felt that "because converts from Judaism are learned and intelligent, they cannot and will not believe or engage in the nonsense believed and diffused by Gentile converts to Catholicism".[6] In areas where Jews were relatively numerous, their practices infected culture generally. "You should know," Bernáldez asserted, "that the habits of the common people, as the Inquisition discovered, were no more nor less than those of the Jews, and were steeped in their stench, and this was the result of the continual contact people had with them."

Anti-Semitism was part of the background that makes the expulsion of the Jews intelligible, but it was not its cause. Indeed, Iberia tolerated its Jews for longer than other parts of western Europe. England expelled its Jews in 1291, France in 1343, and many states in western Germany followed suit in the early fifteenth century. The big problem of the expulsion is not why it happened, but why it happened when it did. Money grubbing was not the motive. By refusing a bribe to abrogate the decree of expulsion, the monarchs of Castile and Aragon surprised the Jewish leaders who thought the whole policy was simply a ruse to extort cash. The Jews were reliable fiscal milch-cows. By expelling those who worked as tax gatherers, the monarchs imperilled their own revenues. It took five years for returns to recover their former levels. The Ottoman sultan Suleiman I is said to have marvelled at the expulsion because it was tantamount to "throwing away wealth".[7] "We are astonished," the king wrote in self-vindication to one opponent of the expulsion,

> that you should think we want to take the Jews' possessions for ourselves, for that is very far from our thoughts. . . . While we want to recover for our court, as is reasonable, all that rightfully belongs to us by way of debts the Jews owe in taxes or other dues owed by their community, once their debts to us and other creditors have been paid, what remains should be returned to the Jews, to each his own, so that they may do as they wish with it.[8]

The monarchs seem to have been entirely sincere in their determination not to profit from the expulsion: to them, it was a spiritual purgation. Synagogues were seized for conversion into churches, alms-houses, and other public institutions, and cemeteries were generally turned over to common grazing; but other Jewish communal property was assigned to be held in escrow for settlement of Jews' debts, which, in theory, were recoverable by Christian and Jewish creditors alike. Jews could realise the value of their assets in cash and, by a modification of the original decree of expulsion, take the proceeds abroad with them, together with unlimited moveable wealth in the form of jewels, bonds, and bills of exchange. This was a remarkable concession, as the laws of the realms of Aragon and Castile were strict about absolutely prohibiting the export of money and valuables. Some exceptions were even granted for the removal of bullion: the leading figure among the expulsees, Isaac

Abranavel, was allowed ten thousand ducats in gold and jewels. Probably no more than a dozen individuals in the entire kingdom could lay their hands on that much cash.

In every diocese, the monarchs appointed administrators to look after personal property that Jews left unsold at the expulsion and, when its value could be realised, to pay the proceeds to the expulsees in their new homes abroad, and to recover and remit unpaid debts owed to expelled Jews. Some of these administrators laboured for years at the job, with mixed results, and their records show how evil some of the unintended consequences were. Buyers extorted property from desperate expulsees. Municipalities acted illegally in seizing Jews' assets and used every imaginable form of prevarication to avoid disgorging them. In a buyers' market, it was impossible to get a fair price for Jewish property. Rapacious officials robbed exiles of cash or extorted unlawful bribes or illegal fees. Debtors to Jewish creditors evaded their obligations. Freighters overcharged. Despite honest efforts by administrators the crown appointed, most wrongs were probably never righted. The entire process was ill thought out, and the monarchs had simply not allowed enough time for all the problems to be solved before the Jews were made to leave.

The real motives for the expulsion, the reasons that can explain its timing, must be sought in the immediate circumstances of the event. In part, an exalted mood of religious fervour was responsible, kindled by war and fanned by fear. The war with Granada demanded a united effort from the monarchs' subjects. Legend ascribed to the Jews a supporting role in the first Muslim conquests of Iberian soil nearly eight hundred years before. Scouring the past for material, propagandists reawakened old anxieties about where Jewish loyalties lay. In 1483, the monarchs responded to local petitions by permitting the expulsion of all Jews from Andalusia, as if clearing the frontier zone of suspect aliens. As they conquered territory from Granada, the monarchs shifted Jews out of it, piece by piece, as if afraid of nurturing a potentially traitorous fifth column clandestinely undermining stability from within. And as with the conquest of Granada, the threat or promise of the millennium was like a shadow over the Jews. The conversion of the world, according to traditional Christian eschatology, was one of the signs of its approaching end.

The Inquisition contributed. In 1478, the monarchs persuaded the pope to give them control over appointments and operations of the Inquisition in Spain, turning it effectively from an arm of the Church into a scourge of the state. It was the only institution that operated in the territories of both Aragon and Castile without having to respect the frontiers and the peculiarities of the laws. Previously, the Inquisition had been barely active in the Iberian Peninsula, concentrating strictly on matters of dogma and dealing only with serious heresies. It now became a kind of thought police, a terrifyingly omniscient network of tribunals and informers, prying into people's lives at every social level and extending its jurisdiction from matters of faith to morals and private life. The rather weak theological justification for this was that moral misbehaviour was prima facie evidence of incorrect belief, and that personal lives and customs exhibited practitioners' true religion.

The Inquisition became an organ for policing and enforcing social conformity – a cauldron for brewing a consistent state, into which elements of heterogeneity were flung and boiled to a pulp. Nominally, the organisation's job was to expunge "heretical depravity". The only common deviations from orthodoxy in Spain were the result of ignorance, poor education, and inadequate catechisation by overworked or undertrained clergy. But the widespread conviction that heresy arose mainly from Jewish example, or from the memory of Judaism in the progeny of converts, trumped the truth. The "justice" the Inquisition delivered was attractive to anyone who wanted to denounce a neighbour, a competitor, or an enemy. It was perilous to anyone who was a victim of envy or revenge. And it was cheap. In no other court could you bring charges without incurring costs or risks. Inquisitorial justice was also secretive. In no other court could you bring a charge without disclosing your identity to the accused. Because the courts had the power to sequester the assets of accused people during their trials, the Inquisition had a vested interest in treating denunciations seriously and protracting cases. All of these features made the Inquisition a popular tribunal, to which complainants were keen to recur, and a juggernaut that its own officials could barely manage and no one could control. Rather, as happened in other parts of Europe at the time, where a craze for witchcraft persecution took off, or as we have seen in our own time with the proliferation of cases of alleged child abuse based on supposedly "recovered" memories, the numbers of accusations seemed to corroborate the Inquisitors' fears. On flimsy evidence, Spain seemed suddenly to be awash with apostasy.

Ferdinand and Isabella took the peril seriously. Because Ferdinand was a hero of Machiavelli's, who saw him as ruthlessly calculating, dedicated to success, and unconstrained by moral scruples, a myth has grown up of Ferdinand as a modern-minded, secular politician. On the contrary, he was conventionally pious, susceptible to prophecy, and deeply aware of his responsibilities to God. No monarch of the day could escape exposure to traditional ideas of kingship – in their daily education as princes, in the readings their tutors prescribed, and in sermons and in the confessional when in power. One of the most frequently repeated principles of tradition was the ruler's responsibility for his subjects' salvation.

Bernáldez, perhaps, highlighted the most urgent reason for the expulsion. The numbers of conversos – Jewish converts to Christianity – were multiplying alarmingly. Minorities are easy to tolerate until their numbers reach a critical threshold, which varies from case to case and society to society, but which always exists and which, when crossed, seems trapped with trip wires that set off terrible alarms. Against the background of war, the growth of a potentially subversive minority nourished widespread neurosis. Spain was in the grip of a Great Fear – irremediable because irrational and therefore impervious to facts, like the equally irrational fear of terrorists and poor immigrants and "rising crime" in Western democracies today. Crown and Church should have been pleased with the growing number of converts to Christianity, but fear subverted pleasure. Every convert was a potential apostate or "secret Jew". The large turnover in conversions suggested that converts were superficially instructed and perhaps in many cases opportunistic. In the circumstances it might have made more sense to expel the converts than the Jews, but that was an unthinkable strategy. There were too many of them. Society could not function without their services. Natural law and the law of the Church protected them, whereas Jews were technically at the mercy of the crown – present on sufferance, dependent on revocable royal grace. The Inquisition, moreover, had jurisdiction over converts and could command their beliefs, whereas the tribunal had no right to interrogate the faith of Jews. Inquisitors believed, therefore, that without Jews to seduce them into heresy or apostasy, converts could be redeemed or coerced into salvation.

So inquisitors lobbied the crown to remove what they thought was the cause of the problem. They issued the decree expelling Jews from Andalusia. Exceeding their lawful powers, they attempted – unsuccessfully, because of local resentment of their high-handed tactics – to launch similar initiatives in other parts of the realm. The Grand Inquisitor, Tomás de Torquemada, made the first draft of the decree expelling the Jews from the whole kingdom in March 1492. The document, modified at the royal court, and signed and sealed by the king and queen on the last day of the month, was explicit about the arguments that swayed the monarchs. There is no reason to mistrust its declarations. What the monarchs believed about the Jews may not have been true. But it is true that they believed it. "We were informed," the decree began, "that in our realms there were some bad Christians who Judaised and apostasised from our holy Catholic faith, and much of the cause of this was the communication between Christians and Jews." The decree went on to detail the particular instances – most of them verified at hearings before the Inquisition – of

> the great damage to the Christians . . . from the information, contacts, and communication exchanged with the Jews, who, according to the

1492

evidence, always seek by whatever means they can to subvert and sub-
tract faithful Christians from our holy Catholic faith and part them
from it and attract and pervert them to their accursed faith and opinion, instructing them in the rites and observances of their tradition;
convening assemblies where they read out and teach what they must
believe and observe according to their tradition; seeking to circumcise
them and their sons; giving them books in which to read their prayers
and explaining to them the fasts they have to keep, and joining with
them to read and teach their versions of their history; keeping them
informed in advance of the dates of Passover and advising them of
what acts and observances they must perform at that time; giving
them, and taking from their houses, the unleavened bread and ritually
slaughtered meats; instructing them in what to avoid, both in terms of
foodstuffs and other matters their law requires; and persuading them
as far as they can to hold and keep the law of Moses and giving them
to understand that there is no other law or truth beside it; all of which
appears from many statements and confessions both by Jews themselves and those whom they have perverted and deceived.[9]

The document continued by explaining that the monarchs had
hoped to solve the problem by permitting the expulsion of the Jews from
Andalusia, where most of the harm had been done. The results, however, had been unsatisfactory, and they had decided to resort to a more
radical policy because "the said Jews increase and continue their evil
and accursed purpose wherever they dwell in company" with Christians. A scruple, however, arising from considerations of natural justice
troubled the monarchs: by expelling all the Jews, they were, in effect,
punishing the avowedly innocent along with the allegedly guilty. They
dealt with this by arguing that the Jews together formed a single corpo-
ration, by analogy with a college or university:

because when any grave or detestable crime is committed by certain
members of a college or university, it is right that such college or

university be dissolved and abolished and that the lesser members incur the consequences on account of their superiors and vice versa.

Like most hurriedly formulated policies, the expulsion had the opposite of its intended effect: it enormously increased the numbers of insincere, under-evangelised, and uncommitted converts. The demographics of the expulsion have generated ferocious and inconclusive debate, but two disarming facts are incontrovertible: There were never very many Jews to expel. And many of them – probably most, including most of the rabbis, according to contemporary assertions by a Jewish observer – preferred baptism to expulsion.[10] "Expulsion" seems a misnomer. The event should perhaps rather be called a forcible conversion.

Though no reliable records exist, the consensus of the sources suggests a total Jewish population of at least 150,000 at the time of the expulsion, and perhaps as many as 200,000. There is no warrant in the sources for any significantly higher estimate. Chroniclers' estimates of the number of expulsees are probably, like almost all other chroniclers' estimates, inflated by delusion or design. Christian chroniclers who tried to compute figures put the total at between 100,000 and about 125,000; Jewish chroniclers, who might be pardoned for exaggerating, aired figures of 200,000 or 300,000, which would at least equal and probably exceed all the Jews of the kingdoms. If we allow that large numbers accepted baptism, and others returned to do so after despairing of making a life abroad, it would be rash to assert that the expulsees numbered more than 100,000 and prudent to bear in mind that the real tally may have been much lower. The decree of expulsion created more converts than expulsees.

Most of those who persevered in exile endured harrowing privations or died along the way. The neighbouring kingdoms of Navarre and Portugal admitted refugees – but not for long. Diplomatic pressure from Ferdinand and Isabella, combined with the fear and resentment any foreign influx brings, made the rulers of both countries anxious to usher the Jews along their way. A few families bought the right of residence in Portugal, but it proved a poor bargain, abrogated when expulsions of native Jews followed, in Portugal in 1497, as the price of negotiating a dynastic alliance with Castile, and in Navarre in 1512 when Ferdinand conquered and annexed the portions of the kingdom south of the Pyrenees. Refugees who entered Portugal illegally or broke the terms of their visas were liable to be enslaved. Their children were seized and shipped off to the remotest and deadliest destination in the Portuguese world, the island of São Tomé, in the Gulf of Guinea, amid unravelling Portuguese dreams of starting sugar plantations and trading in such mainland treasure as slaves, copper, ivory, and condiments. Almost all the handful of colonists – who even at the end of the decade numbered only fifty – were exiled criminals. The land, the governor reported, was evil, and the colony so penniless that there was no truck to trade with and no food to spare for the Jewish children. They had to be shipped off to the nearby island of Príncipe, "in order to be able to eat".[11]

Some refugees went to Morocco. The Spanish chronicler who recorded their sufferings may have exaggerated, because he wanted to show "what calamities, dishonours, tribulations, pain, and suffering" ensue from unbelief. He also relished an opportunity to catalogue Muslim barbarities. But he claimed to have heard the stories he told from returnees relieved to have got back home "to a land of reasonable people". The list of atrocities is depressing: along the roads "the Moors came and stripped them to their skins, raped the women, murdered the men, and slit their stomachs open, searching for gold in their bellies, because they knew they had swallowed it".[12]

In Morocco, the courtly city of Fez was one of the destinations the Jews most favoured. Leo Africanus knew Fez well. He was equivocal about the city. He invited readers to marvel at "how large, how populous, how well-fortified and walled this citie is".[13] He made a list of its amenities: the sewers that carried all the filth into the river through 150 conduits; the houses finely built and curiously painted, and gaily tiled and roofed with "gold, azure, and other excellent colours", and the summer houses of the nobility outside the town, each with its "christall-fountain environed with roses and other odoriferous flowers and herbes". There were more than one hundred baths, and two hundred inns fairer than any buildings in Christendom save the Spanish College in Bologna. There were two hundred schools, seven hundred mosques, and more than two thousand flour mills. The nine hundred lamps in the main mosque were forged from bells captured from Christian churches. But the hospitals were decayed and the colleges impoverished – "and this," Leo opined, "may be one reason why the government is so base." The city's elite was equally degenerate: "If you compare them with the noblemen and gentlemen of Europe, they may seem to be miserable and base fellowes; not for any want or scarcitie of victuals, but for want of good manners and cleanliness." They sat on the ground to eat and used "neither knives or spoones but only their ten talons. . . . To tell you the very truth, in all Italie there is no gentleman so meane, which for fine diet and stately furniture excelleth not the greatest potentates and lords of all Africa."[14]

Those who got there suffered "all the curses of the Torah and more" – as one of them, who was ten years old at the time of the expulsion – later recalled.[15] They built shanties of straw. A conflagration consumed them, along with all the valuables and many collections of books in Hebrew. But for the survivors, Fez had, at least, the advantages of cosmopolitanism, and a corresponding tolerance of religious diversity and heterodoxy. Vestiges of Christian or pagan ceremonies dappled the culture. Irrespective of their creed, people served pulses at Christmas, and at New Year, Leo Africanus reported, masked children "have fruits given them for singing certaine carols or songs". Divination and necromancy were rife, though proscribed, as Leo pointed out, by "Mahometan inquisitors". Jewish learning had a market niche. Cabbalism was especially popular, its practitioners "never found to erre, which causeth their art of Cabala to be had in great admiration: which although it be accounted naturall, yet never saw I any thing that hath more affinitie with supernatural and divine knowledge". Jews monopolised gold and silver work, forbidden to Muslims because of the usurious profits smiths made on the jewel work they pawned.[16]

To judge, however, from the account of Leo Africanus, the effects of the influx of fugitives from Spain were deleterious for the whole community of Jews in Fez. The Jews occupied one long street in the new city, "wherein they have their shops and their synagogues, and their number is marvellously encreased ever since they were driven out of Spaine". The increase turned them into a minority too big to be welcome. Formerly favoured, now victimised, they paid double the tribute traditionally due. "These Iewes," Leo observed, "are had in great contempt by all men, neither are any of them permitted to wear shooes, but they make them certaine socks of sea-rushes."

Tlemcen, which, like Fez, already had a large Jewish community, was another destination that looked attractive until the expulsees actually arrived. Leo "never saw a more pleasant place", but in Tlemcen, as one of the Spanish refugees recalled, the newly arrived Jews roamed "naked, . . . clinging to the trash-heaps".[17] Thousands of Jews died in a subsequent plague, but enough survived to exacerbate ethnic and religious tension. Though the Jews "in times past" were "all of them exceeding rich", in riots during the interregnum of 1516 "they were all so robbed and spoiled that they are now brought almost unto beggerie".[18] Alarmed citizens accused them of bringing syphilis: "Many of the Jews who came to Barbary . . . carried the disease from Spain. . . . Some unhappy Moors mixed with the Jewish women, and so, little by little, within ten years, one could not find a family untouched by the disease." At first, sufferers were forced to live with lepers. The cure, according to Leo, was to breathe the air of the Land of the Blacks.[19]

Some Jews gravitated towards the Atlantic coast of Morocco, where the kingdom of Fez was crumbling at the edges as herdsmen from the Sahara colonised farmland and reduced the wheat production for export, on which the rulers relied for tolls. In the ports of Safi and Azemmour, the power of Fez was barely felt, and control was in the hands of the leaders of pastoral tribes. But there was still enough arable land to grow some wheat, and the tribal big shots collaborated with Spanish and Portuguese efforts to acquire the surplus cheaply –

and often got bribes and even Iberian titles of nobility in return. In effect, the region became a joint Spanish–Portuguese condominium, or at least protectorate – a kind of free-port zone, exempt both from the control of the sultans in Fez and from the Church's rules against trading with infidels.

The Jewish refugees were the perfect middlemen for this trade. Their expulsion from Spain had a dramatic effect on turnover, making the region Portugal's main source of foreign wheat in the early sixteenth century. They also handled slaves, copper, and iron. The Zamero and Levi families specialised, in addition, in organising the manufacture of the brightly colored woollen cloth that was prized in the gold-bearing regions south of the desert. In partial consequence, from 1492 or 1493, for the rest of the decade, Safi earned more West African gold than the fort of São Jorge.[20]

Yet nowhere in the Maghreb, or even in the Sahel itself, could the Jews find perfect peace. The anti-Semitism of the rabid itinerant preacher al-Maghili pursued and harried them all over the Maghreb. In Tuat he inspired pogroms and acts of arson against Jewish homes and synagogues. He turned the Niger Valley into a danger zone after his preaching mission beyond the Sahara in 1498. In Songhay, Askia Muhammad became "a declared enemy of the Jews. He will not allow any to live in the city. If he hears it said that a Berber merchant frequents them or does business with them, he confiscates his goods and puts them in the royal treasury, leaving him scarcely enough money to get home."[21]

For Jews able to escape Spain via ports on the Mediterranean coast, Italy was an alluring destination. There were so many competing jurisdictions in that patchwork peninsula of many states of varying sizes that it was unlikely ever to be uniformly hostile to any group. Jews would always find a refuge somewhere. Sicily and Sardinia were closed: the king of Aragon controlled them and extended the terms of the expulsion from Spain to cover those islands. Naples was a temporary refuge, where most of the Jews, if plague spared them, fled again when Charles VIII of France conquered the city in 1494.

Meanwhile, as one of the exiles from Spain reported, "Italy and all the Levant became filled with . . . slavers and captives who owed their seamen the cost of their transport." For many refugees, the best hope was to find a sympathetic Jewish community already in place and throw themselves on the mercy of their hosts. In Candia, in Venetian-ruled Crete, the father of the Jewish chronicler Elijah Capsali encountered "many mercies" and collected 250 florins for the relief of Jewish refugees in 1493. After many adventures, Judah ben Yakob Hayyat – whose travels were travails involving imprisonment in Tlemcen, enslavement in Fez, and surviving plague in Naples – found succour in Venice, where fellow Spaniards took pity on him. He also found a welcome in Mantua, where he died at peace among a well-established and secure Jewish community. For those who remained faithful to their religion, their miseries seemed like a trial of faith – a new sacred history of temptation by God, a new exodus leading to a new Canaan, or a re-enactment of the torments of Job.[22]

Among the most hospitable places were Venice and – ironically, perhaps – Rome. The former city was under the rule of a merchant patriciate, who knew better than to exclude potential wealth creators, while in Rome, the papacy had no reason to fear Jews and every interest in having them available to exploit. Like poor immigrants throughout the ages, Jews there adjusted to the jobs no one else would do. Early in the next century, Francisco Delicado, a convert from Judaism who moved between Rome and Venice, wrote one of the first novels of social realism, La Lozana andaluza (The Andalusian Waif), set in the Jewish and converso demi-monde of Rome, where the inmates grubbed inconspicuous lives from brothels and gutters, in a world scarred by syphilis and smeared with filth. Ambiguity, adaptability, and evasion were the only means of survival in this world. It was easy to mistake them for dishonesty. A Roman essayist of the 1530s thought the city's converts were shifty and lying – like Aesop's bat, who represented himself as a mouse to a cockerel and as a bird to a cat. Solomon Ibn Verga was one of these mutable creatures. He masqueraded as a Christian in Lisbon and later returned to practise his faith in

safety in Rome, where he heard one of his fellow deportees exclaim, after
all the sufferings of the journey,

> Lord of the Universe! You have done much to make me forsake my
> religion, so let it be known faithfully, that despite those who dwell in
> heaven I am a Jew and will remain a Jew. And it makes no difference
> what you brought down upon me or bring down upon me![23]

But many of the exiles gave up, returned to Spain, and submitted to
baptism. Andrés de Bernáldez recorded the baptisms of a hundred returnees from Portugal in his own parish at Los Palacios, near Seville.
He saw others struggling back from Morocco, "naked, barefoot, and full
of fleas, dying of hunger".[24]

The most secure destination for exiled Jews, where their communities and culture found a ready welcome and were able to survive and
thrive for centuries to come, was the Ottoman Empire – one of the
world's fastest-expanding states, which covered almost the whole of
Anatolia and Greece and much of south-eastern Europe. Ottoman rulers had long represented themselves as warriors fighting to defend and
strengthen Islam, but they maintained a culturally plural, confession-
ally heterogeneous state in which Christians and Jews were tolerated
but were subject to discriminatory taxation and burdensome forms of
service to the state – the most notorious of which was the annual levy
of Christian children, seized from their families, brought up as Muslims, and enslaved as soldiers or servants of the sultan. On the whole,
the Ottomans preferred Jewish to Christian subjects: they were unlikely to sympathise with the empire's enemies. Among the induce-
ments that made Jews settle in Ottoman lands were fiscal privileges,
free plots for housing, and freedom to build synagogues – in contrast
with Christians, who could use existing churches in land the Ottomans
conquered but who were not allowed to add to them.

An environment hospitable to religious exiles was the product of
two generations of Ottoman expansion. While most other European

states were striving for the kind of strength that emerges from uniform identity, focused allegiance, and cultural unity, the Ottomans embarked on an experiment in empire building among culturally divergent peoples and the construction of unity in diversity. In the thirty years from his accession in 1451, Mehmet II devoted his time as sultan to this project. Before his time, Turks had a reputation as destructive raiders, "like torrential rains", as one of Mehmet's generals recalled in his memoirs,

> . . . and everything this water strikes it carries away and, moreover, destroys. . . . But such sudden downpours do not last long. Thus also Turkish raiders . . . do not linger long, but wherever they strike they burn, plunder, kill and destroy everything so that for many years the cock will not crow there.[25]

After Mehmet's time it was impossible to continue to see Ottoman armies as raiders or Ottoman policies as destructive. Mehmet turned conquest into a constructive force, building the Ottoman state into a culturally flexible, potentially universal empire.

His predecessors had been conscious of a dual heritage: as paladins of Islam, and as heirs of steppeland conquerors with a vocation to rule the world. Without sacrificing those perceptions, Mehmet added a new image of himself as the legatee of ancient Greek civilisation and the Roman Empire. He had Italian humanists at his court, who read to him every day from histories of Julius Caesar and Alexander the Great. He introduced new rules of court etiquette, combining Roman and Persian traditions. In 1453 he conquered Constantinople, where the people still called themselves Romans, and made it his capital. The city was bleak and bare when he conquered it – run down by generations of decline. Mehmet's declared aim was "to make the city in every way the best supplied and strongest city as it used to be long ago, in power, wealth, and glory".[26] To repopulate it and restore its glory, Mehmet was lavish with concessions to immigrants:

The port of Constantinople, with all the tourist sites known to the principal illustrators of the Nuremberg Chronicle, Michael Wohlgemut and Wilhelm Pleydenwurff.

Who among you of all my people that is with me, may his God be with him, let him ascend to Istanbul, the site of my imperial throne. Let him dwell in the best of the land, each beneath his vine and beneath his fig tree, with silver and gold, with wealth and with cattle. Let him dwell in the land, trade in it, and take possession of it.

According to one of the Ottomans' Jewish subjects, Jews "gathered together from all the cities of Turkey" in response. At that time, rabbis in Mehmet's pay circulated among Jewish victims of persecution and local expulsions in Germany the fifteenth-century equivalent of promotional brochures. "I was driven out of my native country," wrote one of them to fellow Jews he had left behind in Germany, "and came to the Turkish land, which is blessed by God and filled with good things. Here I found rest and happiness. Turkey can also become for you the land of peace."[27] Long before the expulsion from Spain, Jewish networks had identified the Ottoman Empire as a suitable place for business and a safe destination for exiles.

Most of Mehmet's other conquests were on his empire's western front, south of the Danube, incorporating an ever-larger Christian subject population. He brought artists from Italy to his court, had himself portrayed in Renaissance style in portraits and medals, learned Greek and Latin, and taught himself the principles of Christianity in order to be able to understand his Christian subjects better. He realised that the key to successful state building lies in turning the conquered into allies or adherents. Oppression rarely works. He won the allegiance of most of the Christians of his empire. Indeed, they supplied many of the recruits to his armies. He opened high office to members of the Greek, Serb, Bulgarian, and Albanian aristocracies, though most of them were converts to Islam. He consciously straddled Europe and Asia. He called himself ruler of Anatolia and Rumelia, sultan and caesar, emperor of Turks and Romans, and master of two seas – the Black Sea and the Mediterranean. He began an intensive programme of investment in his navy, and in 1480 a seaborne Turkish force captured the Italian city of Otranto. Mehmet seemed not only to want to invoke the Roman Empire, but to re-create it. The pope prepared to decamp from Rome, calling urgently for a new crusade.

Mehmet's conquests, however, had been so costly that the empire needed a respite. The state's great institutional weakness, moreover, was an ill-defined system of succession, which tended to plunge the empire into civil war at every sultan's death. So when Mehmet died in 1481, a spell of chaos ensued. Otranto was lost, and when the new sultan, Bayezid II, got hold of power, a reaction against Mehmet's policies

The Temple candelabrum of Jerusalem, reputedly designed by Moses under divine inspiration, symbolised Judaism for the compilers of the Nuremberg Chronicle.

set in. Bayezid exercised more caution, restrained the Ottoman war machine, and repudiated his predecessor's Romanising policy. He restored to mosques the lands Mehmet had secularised to pay for his wars, and – at least at the level of rhetoric – proclaimed a return to Islamic law as the law of the state. He also reframed war as jihad, though his summons to arms, which shows that booty and land were still the main objectives of Ottoman campaigns, was addressed to "[a]ll who wish to join in the sacred conquest, engage in the pleasure of raiding and jihad, and who desire booty and plunder, and all brave comrades who gain their bread by the sword".[28]

Bayezid did not, however, depart from all Mehmet's principles. He saw the expulsion of 1492 as a chance to enrich his own realms and granted Jews unlimited rights to enter and settle. Chroniclers represented this as the result of compassion. Calculation had more to do with it. One of Bayezid's few recorded jokes was a jibe at the supposed

wisdom of the king of Spain, "who impoverishes his country and en-
riches our own" by expelling Jews.[29]

At least as significant for the future of the Mediterranean world was
Bayezid's option in favour of his predecessor's maritime policy. He did
not relax the effort to build up the navy; rather, he pursued it with increased vigour. The transformation of the Ottoman Empire into a great
maritime power was one of the most astonishing episodes in the history of the Mediterranean. No landlubbers had taken to the sea so rapidly or successfully since Rome defeated Carthage. The Turkish vocation
for the sea did not spring suddenly and fully armed into existence. From
the early fourteenth century, Turkish chiefs maintained pirate nests on
the Levantine shores of the Mediterranean. Some allegedly had hundreds of vessels at their command. The greater the extent of coastline
the Ottomans conquered, as their land forces stole west, the greater the
opportunities for Turkish-operated corsairs to stay at sea, with access to
watering stations and supplies from onshore. Throughout the fourteenth century, however, these were unambitious enterprises, limited
to small ships and hit-and-run tactics.

From the 1390s, the Ottoman sultan Bayezid I began to build up a
permanent fleet of his own, but without embracing a radically different
strategy from that of the independent operators who preceded him. But
the winds and currents of the Mediterranean favour warships joining
battle from the north or west, because they tend to have the wind in
their sails. So the Christian powers that lined those shores generally got
the better of adversaries from Islam. Venice, Genoa, and the Spanish
states established a sort of armed equilibrium – a surface tension that
covered the sea and that the Turks could not break. Set-piece battles
usually occurred in spite of Turkish intentions and resulted in Turkish
defeats. As late as 1466, a Venetian merchant in Constantinople claimed
that for a successful engagement Turkish ships needed to outnumber
Venetians by four or five to one. By that date, however, Ottoman investment in naval strength was probably higher than that of any Christian
state. The far-seeing sultan Mehmet II realised that the momentum of

conquests by land had to be supported – if it was to continue – by power at sea.

Bayezid II hoped, at first, to remain focused on investment in a large army, and to rely on an understanding with Venice to keep the empire secure in the Mediterranean. But the Venetians proved unreliable and, in particular, unwilling to place their ports at Ottoman disposal. Even if the empire's expansionist ambitions lay dormant for a while, there were still pirates to deal with and commerce to protect. So Bayezid ordered ships "agile as sea serpents", impressing Christian technicians to help build them. The shadow of a pretender inhibited him. His brother, Djem, whom he had defeated in a contest for the throne, had taken refuge, first with the Mamluks of Egypt, then with the Christians of the West. The Mamluk frontier was hard to hold. On the European front, ferocious campaigns in 1491 and 1492 led to defeat in Austria, though Bayezid strengthened his hold on the western shore of the Black Sea. With Djem out of the way, however, Bayezid's ambitions were loosed. When his chief rival for the throne died in 1495, he felt secure enough to challenge Venice's maritime supremacy in the eastern Mediterranean. In the war of 1499–1502, the effects were dramatic. Bayezid sent three hundred ships against the Venetians in the first year. By the end of the war, his fleet of four hundred vessels included two hundred galleys mounted with heavy guns. No other Mediterranean power could match this might. Venice was humbled, and the Ottomans were elevated to something like superpower status – commanding force greater than that of any conceivable alliance of the empire's enemies. In the new century, Egypt and most of the North African coast as far as Morocco fell under Ottoman dominion.

While the Ottomans took command of the eastern Mediterranean, Spain ascended to something approaching similar control in the western half of the same sea. Once the kingdoms began to recover from the self-inflicted damage of the expulsion of the Jews, the united power of Castile, Aragon, and Granada was insuperable. King Ferdinand had inherited Sicily, Corsica, the Balearic Islands, and Sardinia along with his lands on Spain's eastern shore, as well as a claim to the throne of Naples, which he enforced by conquest early in the new century. The Spanish crown added substantial territories in northern Italy not long after and had acquired Melilla on the North African coast in 1497 – though Spain's many other attempts at conquests in the same region rarely succeeded and never lasted long.

So in the aftermath of 1492, and partly as a result of the events of that year, battle lines were drawn in the Mediterranean for the next century. If neither of the giant powers that faced each other across that sea ever established overall supremacy, it was in part because sailing conditions in the Mediterranean naturally divided it in two halves. The Strait of Messina and the sea around Sicily is like a stopper, corked by the racing current and hazardous whirlpools against shipping in both directions. Though navigable in times of peace, the confluence of the two halves of the Mediterranean is easily policed. Because of the winds and currents, the Turks, despite the numerical superiority of their fleets, remained at a permanent disadvantage. The consequence of the stalemate between Spain and Turkey was that the unity of the Mediterranean world, of which Greek and Phoenician navigators laid the foundations in antiquity, and which the Roman Empire achieved, was never re-established. The shores of the sea have similar climates and ecosystems and many elements of common culture. But they have remained divided, with Islam confined to the south shore and patches of the eastern Mediterranean, while the northern and western ends of the ocean have remained in Christendom. The sea that was once the "middle sea" of Western civilisation became and remained a frontier.

In one further, supremely important way, nature always constrained the Ottomans' naval effort, however much time and investment they put into it. Just as the Strait of Messina squeezed access to the western Mediterranean, so the Turks' approach to the Indian Ocean got trapped in the narrows of the Red Sea and the Persian Gulf, from where easily policed straits guard the way eastward. After 1492, as we shall see, when Europeans began exploring the ocean highways that led them across the Atlantic and on to the wind systems of the world, the disadvantages for Turks would become painfully obvious and ultimately insuperable.

From every rational point of view, the expulsion of the Jews from Spain seems to have been a foolish and disastrous policy. The assumptions on which it was based were false. The evidence cited in its favour was faulty. The arguments used to justify it were unconvincing. The material cost to the Spanish kingdoms in wasted wealth and talent was incalculable. Instead of solving the problem of converso inconstancy, it worsened it by increasing the numbers of insincere or imperfectly instructed converts. In part, however, it has to be understood as a successful episode in a much longer and bigger story: the consolidation and homogenisation of European states. Measures against other communities regarded as foreign were common in the period, both in Spain and throughout Europe. Though the Spanish monarchs did not expel any other groups from the whole of their territories, they did subject foreign communities to arbitrary forms of discrimination, sometimes confiscating property and taking a fairly searching attitude to requests for naturalisation.

Ferdinand and Isabella, like other monarchs of their day and later, wanted subjects with increasingly uniform notions of themselves and uncompromised allegiance to a common identity. They did not want – and probably could not envisage – a politically unified state. Their realms' long, divergent histories and contrasting institutions defined and distinguished Aragon and Castile. When Ferdinand and Isabella called themselves "King and Queen of Spain", they did not mean to erect a new superstate, but to inaugurate a period of close partnership between what would remain distinct countries. But they did want those countries to have consistent cultures and a common creed. In one respect, for Spain, the effect of their policy towards Jews was positive. Spain derived a kind of bonus, in the form of the talents of former Jews who opted for baptism. The numbers of the converts exceeded those of the expelled. So much talent, so much potential had formerly enriched the Jewish community. Now, by effectively compelling conversions, the monarchs garnered that talent, forcing former Jews into the mainstream of Spanish life. Scholars have a tendency to seek converso origins for almost anyone of importance in Spanish culture in the sixteenth and seventeenth centuries; but the scale of the achievements of former Jews and their descendants in letters, learning, science, and the arts was formidable – out of all proportion to their numbers. Converted Jews were the alchemical ingredient that made Spain's golden age.

Chapter 5

"Is God Angry with Us?"

Culture and Conflict in Italy

8 April: Lorenzo the Magnificent dies in Florence.

The portents ranged from the sublime to the ridiculous. By 1492, Lorenzo de' Medici had been Florence's boss for over two decades. Ever since he was twenty years old, he had ruled the city without ever occupying any formal office of state, manipulating its institutions and its wealth, encouraging its writers, scholars, and artists, and ruthlessly suppressing his political enemies. Until the omens appeared, the security he created seemed invulnerable.

On 5 April 1492 a woman leaped from her seat in the church of Santa Maria Novella at early mass and "rushed about with terrible cries", claiming to see a "furious bull, with flaming horns, tearing down this great temple". Shortly afterwards, "the heavens suddenly became black with clouds", and lightning felled the famous dome of the cathedral – the highest in the world at the time. The marble light trap at the summit toppled and crashed into the north wall, "and especially at the side where the Medici palace can be seen, great pieces of marble were wrenched away with awful force and violence. In this portent it more-over happened that one of the gilded balls which also are to be seen upon the roof, was struck by lightning, and fell."[1] That was a peculiarly strong omen, as the balls were the symbols of the Medici and had been added to the skyline at Lorenzo's behest.

Three days later, Lorenzo was dead. Politian, one of the poets in Lorenzo's pay, was anxious that his correspondents should be under no illusion; the heavens had predicted his master's demise: "And on the night on which Lorenzo died, a star, brighter than usual, and larger, hung over the country villa where he lay dying, and at the very moment at which it was ascertained that he breathed his last, it seemed to fall and go out."[2] So Lorenzo's death was attended by a portent as powerful as at Christ's birth. Lightning flashed for three nights following the event, illuminating the vault where the Medici dead lay entombed. As if in anticipation of the civil strife that followed, fighting broke out be-tween the two caged lions kept for the terror and delight of the citizens. Lights glimpsed unnaturally in the sky and the howls of a she-wolf were among other events classed as omens. Even the suicide of a famous phy-sician was interpreted as "an offering to the shade of the Prince" on the grounds that "Medici" literally means "doctors".

Lorenzo died joking that he wished death would wait until he had exhausted the contents of his library. A fellow humanist wrote to Poli-tian with words of partisan consolation: "Is God angry with us, that he has taken from us, in the person of the wisest of men, all hope, all sign and symbol of virtue?" But he continued with a generalisation few would contest: "The evils that befall us in our high places are often like snows, which, as they melt upon the mountain tops, make mighty riv-ers." Lorenzo, the writer correctly affirmed, "maintained the peace of Italy".[3] The king of Naples bewailed the end of a life "long enough for fame but too short for the good of Italy". What chance was there for peace to continue now that he was gone?

"I am not Florence's lord," Lorenzo wrote in 1481, "just a citizen with a certain authority."[4] This was strictly true. To be a lord was not a practi-

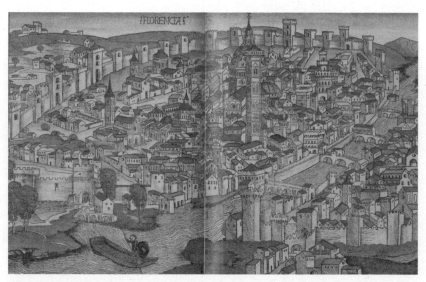

The exceptional majesty with which the Nuremberg Chronicle displays Florence suggests the close links between the humanist scholars of the two cities.

cal aspiration where republican virtue was ingrained. Other Florentine communes had submitted to lords in the course of the late Middle Ages, but not Florence – or so Florentines kidded themselves. Leonardo Bruni, the great ideologue of early-fifteenth-century Florence, was proud that while tyrants triumphed elsewhere, his city had remained true to its heritage as a foundation – so myth sustained – of ancient Roman republicans. Political malcontents who plotted to kill Lorenzo in 1478 saw themselves as embodying the virtues of Brutus, sacrificing Caesar to preserve the purity of the republic. *"Popolo e libertà!"* were rebels' recurrent watchwords – not to be taken too literally, as most rebellions were struggles of excluded families against those the Medici favoured, and few conspirators were willing to sacrifice the blessings of oligarchy: they just wanted the freedom to exploit them for themselves. Alamanno Rinuccini, one of the most thoughtful of the rebels' supporters, secretly denounced Lorenzo in an unpublished *Dialogue on Liberty*, but his main gripe was with the parvenus the Medici raised to eligibility for office.[5]

The "certain authority" Lorenzo admitted to elevated him above all his fellow citizens. He never held any political office. He was never even a member of Florence's executive council, much less head of state – but that did not matter. The Florentine constitution was saturated in republican principles and riven with safeguards against tyranny: in consequence, the nominal officeholders could never get a grip on power. They rotated at two-monthly intervals, selected by a mixture of indirect election and lottery from mercurial lists of eligibly rich or aristocratic families. The key to permanent power lay not in holding office oneself but in managing the system. Lorenzo ruled by stealth.

The first element in his system of management was the dexterous manipulation of institutions and networks. He joined everything, cultivated everybody. Unlike earlier Medici rulers, he chatted with fellow citizens in the cathedral and piazza. He belonged to far more confraternities, guilds, and committees than anyone could hope to attend regularly; but they were a means of extending his network of obligation and of keeping himself informed of what was going on in the city. The formal business of all the organisations he joined was reported to him as a matter of course; more important, perhaps, the gossip transacted at meetings fed back into his system. Ruling a republic was a matter of cybernetics. The key lay in manipulating the system of indirect election and selection by lot that led to membership of the ruling council and other influential committees. Rinaldo Albizzi, for instance, who had briefly forced Lorenzo's father from power and into exile, neglected to fix the elections, with the result that his supporters were ousted and his enemy recalled. The only way to be sure was to be crooked. Lorenzo used bribery and intimidation to fix the rules of eligibility, privilege his own creatures and cronies, and make sure that the final lottery for office was always rigged.

As a result, though he had no formal right of jurisdiction – which, at the time, was considered to be the main attribute of sovereignty – he dispensed justice, in effect, arbitrarily, according to his whim. On a notorious occasion in 1489, he ordered a peremptory public execution – with the scourging of bystanders who had the temerity to object. The only palliation one can offer is that his gout – which always tortured him – was peculiarly painful that day. Effectively, the Medici were monarchs. Lorenzo was the fourth of his line to run the city in succession. When he died, leading citizens lined up to beg his son to take over.

Lorenzo relied on wealth to buy the power he could not get by force or guile. Largesse made him magnificent. The mob that rallied in Lorenzo's support when he survived an assassination attempt in 1478 hailed "Lorenzo, who gives us bread".[6] He milked the state (the evidence, though not conclusive, is too suggestive to discount) and embezzled money from his own cousins when they were his partners in business. He dispensed wealth corruptly to gain and keep power. He never solved the problem of balancing wealth with expenditure; as Lorenzo famously said, "In Florence, there is no security without control." But control cost money, and Lorenzo, like his predecessors, tended to overspend to buy it. He inherited a fortune of over 230,000 florins by his own estimate. This was the biggest fortune in Florence, though depleted from its peak in his grandfather's day. Fraud leached it. A new enterprise – exporting alum – nearly proved ruinous. Lorenzo's personal extravagance made matters worse.[7]

The next element in Lorenzo's system was the exploitation of religion. Though a mere private citizen of ignoble ancestry, he affected sacrality almost as if he were a king. His love poems are justly renowned. His religious poetry was of greater political importance, which is not to say that it was insincere; to become a great saint, it is no bad first step to be a big sinner. Indeed, there is something convincing about Lorenzo's lines, with their yearning for "repose" with God and "relief" for the "prostrated mind": the intelligible longings of a heart bled by business and a conscience stirred by the responsibilities of power. In "The Supreme Good", he confronts this issue:

> How can a heart that avarice infects
> And saturates with such outrageous hopes
> And such unbounded fears discover peace?[8]

Confraternities to which he belonged chanted his calls to repentance. He invested heavily in adorning the religious foundations his family had endowed and boosting their prestige. In particular, he nurtured the Dominican house of San Marco in Florence – a nursery of greatness, where Fra Angelico painted. San Marco struggled to survive financially and recruit postulants until Lorenzo poured wealth into it. His motives were not merely pious. He saw San Marco as a venue for supporters: it was at the heart of the quarter of the city that had the longest associations with the Medici family. He tried to make it the dominant house for the Dominicans of Tuscany and a source of wider influence over the affairs of the Church. He also tried, albeit unsuccessfully, to organise the canonisation of Archbishop Antonino of Florence, the pet churchman of his house in his father's day. When Lorenzo died, his supporters portrayed him as a saint.[9]

Finally, and hardly consistently with saintly aspirations, he made an art of intimidation. Wealth bought power in its crudest form: toughs and bravos to bully fellow citizens within the city; and mercenaries and foreign allies to cow Florence from without. Lorenzo cultivated allies – sometimes the popes, sometimes the kings of Naples, always the dukes of Milan. Invariably, part of the deal was that they would send troops to his aid in the event of an attempted coup or revolution in his city. It was not just that everyone knew he could afford to crush opposition with mercenaries or foreign troops if he wished. He practised the politics of terror to overawe opposition. The city of the Florentine enlightenment was a cruel, savage, bloody place, where the body parts of condemned criminals strewed the streets and revengers mimed ritual cannibalism to round off vendettas. Lorenzo impressed his enemies with horrifying displays of terror and implacable campaigns of vengeance.

The participants in the conspiracy of 1478 suffered the most vicious – but not unrepresentative – violence Lorenzo ever unleashed. Normally, criminals died on gibbets just outside the walls so as not to pollute the city, but Lorenzo had the conspirators tossed screaming from the windows of the palace of the governing council. The crowds in the main square could watch them dangle and twitch, convulsed by their death throes, before slaking their vengeance by literally tearing the bodies to pieces when they hit the ground. Lorenzo made vindictiveness a policy, harrying his victims' survivors into beggary. For a while, the government of Florence even made it an offence to marry one of the conspirators' orphaned or bereft womenfolk: this was equivalent to condemning the women to starve to death.

Lorenzo was magnificent, of course, in art as well as power. As art patrons, the ruling branch of the Medici were never leaders of taste. For them, art was power and wealth. Lorenzo was not, however, the boor modern scholarship has made out. He was a genuine, impassioned aesthete. His poetry alone is ample evidence of a replete sensitivity and a perfect ear. He had, perhaps, a less than perfect eye. His aim was to collect objects of rarity and stunning visual effect: jewels, small-scale antique triumphs of bronze and gold work and gem work. The courtyard of the Medici palace was lined with ancient inscriptions – a display of fashion and wealth.

He was not a builder on the lavish scale of his Medici predecessors. Politics, perhaps, constrained him. He remained actively interested in all public building projects and quietly embellished many of the grand buildings and religious foundations his family traditionally patronised. But there was a touch of vulgarity and ostentation even about the architecture he favoured: the cathedral's golden topknot was a conspicuous reminder of that, especially when the prophetic thunderbolt struck it down. The paintings Lorenzo favoured – it was a trait apparently heritable in the ruling line of the house of Medici – were old-fashioned by Renaissance standards: the hard, gemlike colours of the works of Gozzoli and Uccello, the rich pigments – gilt and lapis lazuli and carmine – that glowed like the fabulous collection of jewels Lorenzo assembled. His taste for battle paintings was part of his pursuit of the cult of chivalry. Tournaments were among his favourite spectacles, and he assembled gorgeous ritual armour in which to appear in the lists. But goldsmiths' work, jewellery and small, exquisite antiquities, constituted his biggest expenditure: wealth that could be handled for tactile satisfaction and moved quickly in case of a change of political fortune – the potential solace of exile, such as befell Lorenzo's father and son.[10]

Still, whatever the deficiencies of his taste or the selectivity of his spending, he was the greatest Maecenas of his day. His death not only brought down his political system; it also threatened with extinction the great artistic and cultural movement we call the Renaissance.

The Renaissance no longer looks unique. Historians detect revivals of antique values, tastes, ideas, and styles in almost every century from the fifth to the fifteenth. The West never lost touch with the heritage of Greece and Rome. Nor did Islam. The culture of classical antiquity and all its later revivals were in any case products of large-scale cultural interaction, spanning Eurasia, reflecting and mingling influences from eastern, southern, south-western, and western Asia. Nor does the reality of the Renaissance match its reputation. Scanning the past for signs of Europe's awakening to progress, prosperity, and values that we can recognise as our own, we respond to the excitement with which Western writers around the end of the fifteenth century anticipated the dawn of a new "golden age". As a result, if you are a product of mainstream Western education, almost everything you ever thought about the Renaissance is likely to be false.

"It was revolutionary." *No:* scholarship has detected half a dozen prior renaissances. "It was secular" or "It was pagan." *Not entirely:* the church remained the patron of most art and scholarship. "It was art for art's sake." *No:* it was manipulated by plutocrats and politicians. "Its art was unprecedentedly realistic." *Not altogether:* perspective was a new technique, but you can find emotional and anatomical realism in much pre-Renaissance art. "The Renaissance elevated the artist." *No:* medieval artists might achieve sainthood; wealth and titles were derogatory by comparison. "It dethroned scholasticism and inaugurated humanism." *No:* it grew out of medieval "scholastic humanism". "It was Platonist and Hellenophile." *No:* there were patches of Platonism, as there had been before, and few scholars did more than dabble in Greek. "It rediscovered lost antiquity." *Not really:* antiquity was never lost, and classical inspiration never withered (though there was an upsurge of interest in the fifteenth century). "The Renaissance discovered nature." *Hardly:* there was no pure landscape painting in Europe previously, but nature got cult status in the thirteenth century, as soon as St Francis found God outdoors. "It was scientific." *No:* for every scientist there was a sorcerer. "It inaugurated modern times." *No:* every generation has its own modernity, which grows out of the whole of the past. If modernity, for us, becomes discernible at around the time Lorenzo de' Medici died, we have to look all around the world to see it stirring.

Even in Florence, the Renaissance was a minority taste. Brunelleschi's designs for the Baptistery doors – the project widely held to have inaugurated the Renaissance in 1400 – were rejected as too advanced. Masaccio, the revolutionary painter who introduced perspective and sculptural realism into his work for a chapel in the church of Santa Maria del Carmine in the 1430s, was only the assistant on the project, supervised by a reactionary master. In Italy generally, the most popular painters of the age were the most conservative: Punturicchio, Baldovinetti, and Gozzoli, whose work resembles the glories of medieval miniaturists – brilliant with gold leaf and bright, costly pigments. Michelangelo's design for the main square of the city – which would have encased the space in a classical colonnade – was never implemented. Much of the supposedly classical art that inspired fifteenth-century Florentines was bogus: the Baptistery was really a sixth- or seventh-century building. The church of San Miniato, which the cognoscenti mistook for a Roman temple, was actually no earlier than the eleventh century.

So Florence was not really classical. Some readers may think that that is too easy to say. By similar logic, after all, one could claim that classical Athens was not classical, for most people there had other values: they worshipped Orphic mysteries, clung to irrational myths, ostracised or condemned some of their most progressive thinkers and

The principal states of Italy in 1492.

writers, and favoured social institutions and political strategies similar to those of today's "silent majority": strait-laced, straight-backed "family values". The plays of Aristophanes – with their lampoons of louche aristocratic habits – are a better guide to Greek morality than the *Ethics* of Aristotle. Florence, too, had its silent majority, whose voice resounded in the 1490s in the blood-and-thunder sermons of the reforming friar Girolamo Savonarola and in the blood-curdling cries of the street revolutionaries his words helped to stir a few years later.

Savonarola was born in 1452 to a life of prosperity, even luxury. Why he turned from it is a mystery – inspired, perhaps, by his pious grandfather, or repelled by his worldly father. There was a hint of reproach or defiance in the language he used when he wrote to his father with the news of his religious vocation.

The reason that moves me to enter a religious order is this: first the great misery of the world, the iniquity of men, the carnal crimes, adulteries, thefts, pride, idolatry, and cruel blasphemies, all present on such a scale that a good man can no longer be found . . . owing to which I prayed daily to my lord Jesus to pull me up out of this slime. . . . I want you to believe that in all my life I have had no greater pain, no greater affliction of mind, than in abandoning my own flesh and blood and going out among people unknown to me, to sacrifice my body to Jesus Christ. . . . I have a cruel struggle on my hands to keep the Devil from jumping on my shoulders, and all the more so the more I think about you. . . . These times with their fresh wounds will soon pass away, and I hope that in time you and I will be consoled through grace in this world, and then in the next one through glory.[11]

Homosexuality and whoredom were the sins that preoccupied him most. He was relatively inexplicit about most others. By the age of twenty, he was convinced that he would be "the enemy of the world". He joined the Dominicans – an order of friars with a strong vocation for preaching and a mission to the poor. He belonged to the strictest tendency in the order, renouncing even the most trivial of personal possessions.

But he was not yet a Bible-thumping thunderer. On the contrary, he was a scholar among scholars, with a distinguished career as a teacher of logic in the schools of his order. The audiences that attended his early sermons consisted of "simpletons and a few little women". He discovered his talent as a popular preacher in the late 1480s. Public adulation began to turn his head. He started believing that "Christ speaks through my mouth". He often vaunted a claim to madness, calling it the folly of God. His views, which were always trenchant, became increasingly fanatical. Rome was a perversion. The true Church was of the poor and known to God alone. His tirades against the sins of the rich became increasingly politically subversive as he established the role of an apostle to the desperate and discontented. "The Devil," he declared, "uses the great to oppress the poor." He denounced the greed and egotism of those who could "buy anything with money". Engravings show what his performances – to call them "sermons" somehow does not capture their function – were like at the time he returned to Florence in 1490 after three years of study in Bologna: the friar flings dramatic, demonstrative gestures at packed audiences, with one hand stretched in rebuke, the other pointing heavenward.[12]

By then, according to his later recollections, he was reading the Bible, beginning with Genesis, "but then I did not know the reason why" – which was tantamount to saying that his readings were inspired by God. "When I came to the Flood," he wrote, "it was impossible to go further." The sense of impending doom, of a new punishment due to a wicked world, was paralysingly strong. He turned to prophecy suddenly. On the second Sunday of Lent, 1491, he gave a sermon that, he said, terrified even him. After a sleepless night, he predicted the end of extravagance and its replacement by a new regime of poverty and charity and "Christ in men's hearts".[13]

Recurrent images began to characterise his visions, recycled in his sermons. He kept seeing swords and knives raining down on Rome, a golden cross above Jerusalem. The hand of God poised to strike the wicked, while angels distributed crosses to those willing to undertake a spiritual crusade to save the Church and the city from corruption. The angels returned with brimming chalices and gave sweet wine to those who took the cross, bitter dregs to those who refused. In an engraving his admirers bought in best-selling numbers, the people of Jerusalem appeared, stripping for baptism, while Florentines averted their gaze. A medal struck to exploit the market for Savonarola memorabilia showed contrasting scenes of divine vengeance and abundance. "I saw," he wrote, in recollections that capture the flavour of the sermons,

> through the power of the imagination, a black cross above Babylonian Rome, on which was written "THE WRATH OF GOD", and upon it there rained swords, knives, lances, and every weapon, a storm of hail and stones, and long, awesome streaks of lightning in dark and murky skies. And I saw another cross, of gold, which stretched from heaven to earth above Jerusalem, and on which was written "THE MERCY OF GOD", and here the skies were calm, limpid and clear as could be; wherefore on account of this vision I tell you that the Church of God must be renewed, and soon, for God is angry. . . . Another image: I saw a sword over Italy, and it quivered, and I saw angels coming who had a red cross in one hand and many white stoles in the other. There were some who took these stoles, others who did not want them. . . . All at once, I saw that sword, which quivered above Italy, turn its point downward and, with the greatest storm and scourge, go among them and flay them all. . . . Be converted, Florence, for there is no other remedy for us but penitence. Clothe yourselves with the white stole while you still have time. . . . for later there will be no room for penitence.[14]

Critics of his fanaticism levelled predictable charges. "I am not mad," Savonarola retorted. At first, he refused to say where he got his prophecies from, because "in the past I, too, would have laughed at such things. . . . I am not saying, nor have I ever told you, that God speaks to me. I say neither yes or no. You are so far from the faith that you do not believe. You would rather believe in some devil who spoke with men and foretold future things." Nor did Savonarola make the mistake of claiming any personal merit or pretending, blasphemously, that God's favour was evidence of God's grace. "This light," he admitted, referring to the gift of prophecy, "does not justify me." By January 1492, however, he was getting less cautious. "It is God," he began to claim, "not I, who says these things."[15]

In as far as they referred to Florence rather than to the Church, Savonarola's rages against wealth and corruption and the general moral state of the city seem unmistakably directed against Lorenzo the Magnificent. Lorenzo, however, showed no resentment or anxiety. He had expelled Bernardo da Feltre, another tub-thumper whom he suspected of political subversion, but he treated Savonarola with indulgence. Lorenzo cherished much devotion for the Dominicans. He regarded their house in Florence as a special project of his dynasty. He hoped to use reformers' programmes and arguments to augment his own family's influence over the Church.

Nevertheless, it was becoming obvious that Savonarola was shaping up to defy Lorenzo openly. The ground he chose was not solely or even chiefly that of politics, but rather matters of philosophy and taste, and he bid for the support of intellectuals as well as the mob. He prefaced his own prophecies with an anatomisation of the falsehood of astrology – which was one of the esoteric enthusiasms of Lorenzo's circle. Another ground of conflict concerned the usefulness of reason and science. One of the most powerful books to appear in print in 1492 was Savonarola's ruthlessly masticated digest of logic (*Compendium Logicae*), in which he denounced reason as diabolical. The idea that pagans like Aristotle and Plato had anything to teach readers of scripture was, to him, revolting. He denounced the specious arguments of classically inspired theologians who had tried to fit the ancient Greeks and Romans into God's scheme of salvation. He pointed out how dodgy their etymologies were that linked Jove and Jehovah. He deplored the way classical scholars made pagan deities double as personifications of Christian virtues, and he lampooned their solemn invocations of Virgil as a supposed prophet of Christianity. He scorned

Savonarola denounced astrology, the humanists' favoured means of political forecasting, as "contrary not only to holy scripture but also to natural philosophy".

humanists' cherished notion that ancient Greeks had experienced a partial revelation from God.

In November, Politian hit back with *Lamia*. The title alluded to a classical commonplace – a mythical queen who, thwarted in love, lost her reason and turned into a child-murdering monster. In Renaissance scholars' learned code, she represented hypocrisy: Politian was accusing Savonarola of abusing learning against learning. At a time when Europe was convulsed by fear of witches, he likened his adversary to hags who reputedly plucked out their eyes at night in a diabolic ritual, or to old men who remove their spectacles along with their false teeth and become blind to self-criticism. Philosophy, Politian insisted, is the contemplation of truth and beauty. God is the source of our soul and our mind. He gives them to us for the scrutiny of nature, which in turn discloses God.

Savonarola also differed bitterly from Lorenzo's circle on the subject of poetry. Lorenzo and his followers loved it and practised it. Savonarola claimed to see it as an abomination. On 26 February 1492, Politian published an outline of knowledge, which he called the *Panepistemon* – the Book of Everything. He made what at first glance seem extraordinary claims for his own favourite art of poetry. The poet's was a special kind of knowledge, which owed nothing to reason or experience or learning or authority. It was a form of revelation, divinely inspired. It was almost the equal of theology – a means of revealing God to man. Politian was speaking for most of his fellow scholars. He was uttering a commonplace among Florence's academicians. Shortly afterwards, in the summer of the same year, after the death of Lorenzo the Magnificent, Savonarola's reply appeared in print. The idea that poets could write in praise of God was sickeningly presumptuous. "They blaspheme," he declared, "with vile and stinking lips. For not knowing Scripture and the virtue of God, under the name of the most loathsome and lustful Jove and other false gods and unchaste goddesses and nymphs, they censure our omnipotent and ineffable Creator whom it is not at all permitted to name unless he himself allows it in Scripture." Poetry "wallowed among the lowest forms" of art.[16] Botticelli painted his enigmatic allegory of Calumny to defend the theology of poetry from Savonarola's imprecations.[17]

In sermons, meanwhile, the friar began calling for the books of poets and Platonists to be burned. A couple of years later, when his supporters seized power in Florence and drove out Lorenzo's heir, they made a bonfire of Medici vanities and outlawed the pagan sensuality of classical taste.

The Florentine engraver of the 1500 edition of Savonarola's *Truth of Prophecy* imagines him debating the topic with the learned of all religions.

1492

In retrospect, Savonarola came to see Lorenzo's death as a kind of showdown with the values he hated and a kind of divine validation of his own views. He claimed to have predicted it. The night before lightning struck the cathedral he had another of his fits of sleeplessness. It was the second Sunday of Lent, and the lectionary called for a sermon on the subject of Lazarus, but Savonarola could not concentrate on the text. God seemed to take over. "This saying," the friar later recalled, "came out of my mind at that time, 'BEHOLD THE SWORD OF THE LORD, SUDDEN AND SWIFT, COVERING THE EARTH.' So I preached to you that morning and told you that God's wrath was stirred up and that the sword was ready and near at hand."[18]

Another death Savonarola claimed to predict occurred on 25 July: that of Pope Innocent VIII. To understand the significance of his death, a retrospective of his life is necessary. Innocent never impressed anyone very favourably. The Florentine ambassador, Guidantonio Vespucci, summed up common opinion diplomatically when he said the pope was "better suited to receive advice than give it".[19] Innocent became pope at a stalemated conclave in 1484, allegedly by signing petitioners' claims for favours in his cell at night during the voting. He was renowned for affability and good intentions. But – even in his rare intervals of good health – he was hardly equal to the job.

Most of his pontificate was dominated by violent quarrels with the king of Naples, who scorned the papacy's historic rights to jurisdiction in his kingdom and incited rebellions in the papal states. The throne of Naples, and that of Sicily, which was tied to it, had been disputed between rival claimants from Spain, France, and England for over two hundred years – ever since Spanish conquerors installed the ruling Aragonese dynasty and displaced the French House of Anjou, whose descendants never ceased to assert their claims and who were still plotting coups and launching raids. The Angevin claim was a subject of dispute in its turn between the houses that descended from the line: those of the dukes of Lorraine, who had a strong claim but little power with which to enforce it; the kings of England, who had long abandoned interest in Sicily; and the kings of France, who – because of their growing power, if for no better reason – were increasingly realistic claimants.

Another of Savonarola's prophecies was that France would invade Italy in order to seize the Angevin inheritance. France was the sword that pierced his many visions. But you did not need to be a prophet to know that an invasion was only a matter of time. As Innocent's pontificate unfolded, everyone could see it coming.

Expectations focused on the king of France, Louis XI, who united Angevin claims to Naples and Sicily because he was the residuary legatee of the previous claimant. Louis, however, was too prudent and practical to risk launching long-range wars. Louis was not made for glory. His mind was calculating, his methods cautious, his ambition worldly. "I will not say I ever saw a better king," wrote his secretary, "for although he oppressed his subjects himself, he would not allow anyone else to do so." By a mixture of astuteness and good fortune, he had a glorious reign. His great rival, Charles the Bold of Burgundy, fell at the Battle of Nancy, in 1477, in an attempt to re-create the ancient kingdom of Lorraine. The English, who had carved an empire in France by violence early in the century, had been expelled from the mainland by 1453, their former dominions firmly attached to the crown. Louis was free to assert royal power in parts of France that had formerly been merely nominal parts of the kingdom, including Languedoc in the south and Brittany in the north. France was the fastest-expanding realm in Christendom. Success nourished ambitions, excited envy, and attracted the eyes of outsiders in need of allies.

Louis' son and heir, Charles, had an upbringing that might have been calculated to turn him away from the paths his father followed. Louis was a neglectful father, but when he did take a hand in his son's education, he was full of uncharacteristically high-minded counsel.

God our creator has given us many great favours, for it has pleased him to make us chief, governor, and prince of the most noteworthy region and nation on earth, which is the kingdom of France, whereof several of the princes and kings who preceded us were so virtuous and valiant that they gained the name of Very Christian King, by reducing many great lands and divers nations of infidels to the good Catholic faith, extirpating heresies and vices from our realm, and preserving the Holy, apostolic See and the holy Church of God in their rights, liberties, and prerogatives, as well as by doing various other good deeds worthy of perpetual memory and in such a way that a certain number of them were held to be saints living forever in the very glorious company of God in his paradise.[20]

This rhetoric was traditional in the French royal house, as was the doctrine that the king was the servant of the people. But like most rhetoric, it tended to be honoured more in the breach than in the observance. Charles's values – his frameworks of understanding his role as a Christian king – were drawn more from stories of knights than of saints, more chivalry than clerisy. He ascended the throne as Charles VIII in 1483 at the age of thirteen, resolved to be as unlike his father as possible. Their personalities were at odds. Where Louis had been worldly, Charles was woolly; whereas the father was a realist, the son was a romantic. He spent most of his childhood in his mother's company, reading her books. He became immersed in what we would now classify as chick-lit: romantic tales of chivalry, much the same kind of stuff that turned Columbus's head – the medieval equivalent of cheap novels, in which, typically, heroes undertook perilous journeys to conquer distant kingdoms and marry exotic princesses. In the *Histoire de Mélusine*, Charles read of a queen's sons – young men like himself – who launched adventures of conquest in Cyprus and Ireland.

Lady, if you please, it seems the time has come for us to undertake a journey, so as to learn of foreign lands, kingdoms, and places and win honor and good renown on distant frontiers. . . . There we shall learn what is different about distant lands and what they have in common with our own. And then, if fortune or good luck is willing to befriend us, we would dearly like to conquer lands and realms.[21]

It would be hard to imagine a programme that more exactly fore-shadowed Charles's ambitions. Taking her leave of her adventurous sons, Mélusine grants them leave to do "what you wish for and what you see as being to your profit and honour". She advises them to follow all the rules of a chivalrous life, adding counsel that seems to anticipate Charles's methods as a conqueror:

And if God gives you good fortune and you are able to conquer land, govern your own persons and those of your subjects according to each person's nature and rank. And if any rebel, be sure to humble them and make clear that you are their lords. Never lose hold of any of the rights that belong to your lordship. . . . Take from your sub-jects your rents and dues without taxing them further, save in a just cause.[22]

In one aspect, however, the successors of Mélusine's sons failed to follow her advice. "Never," said the heroine, "tell of yourselves what is not reasonable or true." Writers of chivalry, by contrast, filled their chronicles with marvels and fables, improbable episodes, fantastic mon-sters, and impossible deeds. People treated them as true, much as mod-ern TV addicts relate to their soap operas. Scenes from fictional pilgrimages adorned stained-glass windows at Sable and Chartres. Charles VIII was among the many readers take in by chivalric tales.

Even more relevant to Charles's own prospects was *The Book of the Kings' Three Sons*, in which young heirs to the thrones of France, En-gland, and Scotland quit their homes secretly to fight for the king of Naples and his beautiful daughter, Yolande, against the Turks. "If you undertake the journey," urged the knights who sought the princes' help, "you will learn knowledge of all the world. Everyone will be happy to be your subject. Neither Hector of Troy nor Alexander the Great ever had the renown you will gain after your death." In August 1492, when he was planning his own expedition to Naples, he read the book afresh. His moral education was largely based on a book of chivalric examples drawn from stories of the Trojan War and presented in the form of dialogues between Prince Hector and the Goddess of Wisdom.[23]

Historians have tried to discard the traditional view that tales of chivalry besotted Charles VIII and filled him with romantic notions. But none of the alternative explanations for his behaviour works. There was no economic or political advantage to be gained from invading Italy, whereas the conclusion that story-book self-perceptions jostled in the king's mind seems inescapable. As heir of René of Anjou, he succeeded to a great romantic lost cause. Beyond Naples and Sicily lay the lure of Jerusalem, the long-lost crusader kingdom. The title of King of Jerusalem, though disputed by other monarchs, went with the Sicilian throne. Charles's accounts show that he remained an avid collector of chivalric books throughout his life. He identified with a former conqueror of Italy, his namesake Charlemagne, whom many writers reworked as a fictional hero. He called his son Charles-Orland, after Roland, Charlemagne's companion, who, in fictions his legend spawned, supposedly roamed southern Italy performing deeds of love and valour and who, in an equally false and venerable fiction, died fighting Muslims. Charlemagne was more than a historical figure: legends cast him as a crusader and included a tale of a voyage to Jerusalem, which he never made in reality. He was a once and future king who, in legend, never died but went to sleep, to reawaken when the time was ripe to unify Christendom. The legend blended with prophecies of the rise of a Last World Emperor, who would conquer Jerusalem, defeat the Antichrist, and inaugurate a new age, prefatory to the Second Coming.

Italians with their own agendas encouraged Charles's fantasies. When he entered Siena, the citizens greeted him with paired effigies of himself and Charlemagne, his supposed predecessor. In the violently divided politics of Florence, some citizens wanted him as an ally against others. Venetians and Milanese wanted him on their side in their wars against Naples and the pope. When popes had quarrels with Naples, they wanted him to fight on their behalf. When Charles was still a small boy, Sixtus IV had sent him his first sword as a Christmas gift.

If Charlemagne's road through Naples led – at least in fiction – to Jerusalem, it was conceivable at the time that Charles VIII could follow him all the way. The prospects for renewing the crusade against the Turks seemed genuinely promising. The internecine squabbles of the Ottoman dynasty had driven the pretender to the sultanate, Prince Djem or Zizim, into the arms of the Knights of Rhodes, who had sent him to France for safe keeping in 1482. *The Book of the Kings' Three Sons* featured a Turkish prince who embraced Christianity and converted his people: to Charles, it must have read like a prophetic text. The sultan of Egypt, who put politics above religion, offered a million ducats in support of a new crusade. Meanwhile, the menace of Turkish power in the Mediterranean grew as raids spread as far as Italy and a Turkish task force seized Otranto. In 1488, a Venetian publicist visited France to canvas support. "Today," he complained, "faith has fallen, zeal is dead. The Christian cause has tumbled to a point so low that it is no longer for the sake of Jerusalem, or Asia, or even Greece that the Holy See has sent us to your Majesty, but it is for Italy herself, for the very towns of the holy Roman Church, her cities and people, that we have come to beg your aid."[24]

On the way to Jerusalem and the lands of the Turks, the crown of Naples and Sicily gleamed. As early as 1482, the pope – Sixtus IV at that time – trailed the possibility before the unresponsive eyes of Louis XI, suggesting explicitly that young Charles could be the beneficiary. If France wanted to conquer Naples, "now is the acceptable time. . . . This realm belongs by hereditary right to his royal Majesty. . . . The pope's will is that his Majesty or the lord dauphin be invested with this kingdom."[25]

In the late 1480s, dissensions within the kingdom of Naples seemed to make the project increasingly practicable. In 1489, Charles received a group of dissident Neapolitan nobles at his court. Their numbers grew over the next three years. During 1490, they laid out plans for the conquest at repeated meetings of Charles's council. The pope's envoys reported – with some cautious qualifications – that the French at last seemed to be steeled for the invasion. Charles prepared his route southward by alliance with Milan and covered his northern flank by marrying Anne of Brittany and attaching that dangerously independent duchy firmly, at last, to France. The news of the fall of Granada in January 1492 came like a call to compete for glory. A few weeks later, Innocent made his peace with Naples. Broadly speaking, the terms were that the pope would continue to dispense justice in Naples – but only according to the king's wishes – while Naples would support the papacy with force of arms. To seal the bargain, the Neapolitans presented the pope with their most precious relic – the tip of the lance that was supposed to have pierced Christ's side at the Crucifixion. Ironically, the settlement excited French interest as the dispute never had. French lust for the Neapolitan crown began to increase, with consequences that would prove fatal in the future. From March to May 1492, a Milanese embassy was in Paris, enticing the king into a final decision. Their machinations infuriated Peter Martyr, who from his vantage point at the court of the king of Aragon thought it "folly to place a viper or scorpion in one's own bed in the hope that it may poison one's neighbour. . . . You will all see. Charles, if he has any sense, will know how to exploit his chance."[26]

While they were at work, news of Lorenzo the Magnificent's death arrived. A major obstacle disappeared. Florence, weakened by Lorenzo's death and awestruck by Savonarola's preaching, would be unable to put up much resistance to a French advance. Meanwhile, almost as soon as Innocent fixed matters with Naples and took solemn possession of the Holy Spear, a new, protracted illness overcame him, which proved to be his last. His physicians grew desperate. One of them allegedly offered to succour his patient with his son's blood, which the pope refused to drink. By July, Innocent's stomach pains were becoming unbearable, the sores on his legs unsightly. The shadow of his impending death seemed visible. The mob grew restive. The cardinals began to manoeuvre in preparation for the conclave. By 19 July, according to the Florentine ambassador, the pope's body was effectively dead and only his soul remained to him. He yielded it up five days later. Before an invasion could begin, however, another obstacle arose. Innocent VIII had already decided to back a rival contender for the throne of Naples; but between indecision and infirmity he is unlikely to have offered serious opposition to Charles's hopes, had he lived.

The conclave that followed his death took place in an atmosphere redolent of corruption. Moralists loved to find fault with Rome. According to the most anticlerical and sententious of the diarists of the time, the city housed sixty-eight hundred harlots "not counting those who practised their nefarious trade under the cloak of concubinage and those who practised their arts in secret". The front-runner to succeed Innocent VIII seemed representative of all that was rotten in Rome. Rodrigo Borgia had been the favourite and runner-up at the last conclave, when Innocent VIII was elected, but his reputation, as a Florentine ambassador recorded, was already unsavoury: false and proud. People excused his notorious womanising, and the three children he fathered, on the grounds that he was fatally attractive. The wealth he piled up by accumulating benefices and offices of profit quenched all his disadvantages. "He possesses," as a diarist who knew him observed, "immense quantities of silver plate, pearls, hangings, and vestments embroidered in gold and silk, and all of such splendid quality as would befit a king or a pope. I pass over the sumptuous adornments of his litters and trappings for his horses, and all his gold and silver and silks, together with his magnificent wardrobe and his hoards of treasure."[27]

To win the new election, Borgia supposedly bought Cardinal Sforza's vote with four mule loads of silver – on the pretext that they would go to his house for safe keeping. He got most of the rest of the votes he needed without compromising his own fortune – by promising to reward his supporters from the Church's stock of profitable jobs. Stefano Infessura, a humanist diarist with a talent for satire, explained how on his election the new pope began his reign "by giving his goods to the poor" – by paying for the votes he had bought with promises. The cardinals elected him Pope Alexander VI on the night of 10 August.

It was a scandalous choice but not – for the times – an inappropriate one. Borgia was an accomplished and indefatigable man of business. His flagrant nepotism dominates historical traditions about him. He heaped honours and titles on his children. "Ten papacies," according to the ambassador of Ferrara, would not have yielded enough to satisfy all the Borgia cousins who thronged the curia. Abuses, however, did not doom the Church. The problems that proved intractable were diplomatic.

From the pope's point of view, a French invasion, which his predecessors had sought so ardently, would now be a disaster. The arrangements Innocent VIII made with Naples were perfectly satisfactory. The new heir to the Neapolitan throne bettered them and paid Alexander handsomely for his support. Charles VIII, the pope knew, would spread ruin and scatter ban. As Alexander strove to uphold the royal house of Naples, Charles took the offensive, igniting the pope's deepest fear by impugning the validity of his election. In effect, Alexander had bribed his way into the papacy, and the legitimacy of his position was questionable. Charles recalled the French cardinals and banned all payments of Church dues to Rome. He bid for a higher source of legitimation than even the pope could confer. He took a crusading oath and vowed that he would not stop at Naples, but use it as a launching point for the conquest of Jerusalem.

While Charles secured his flanks and rear by treaties with his enemies the rulers of England and the Netherlands, the invasion was postponed until 1494. When the king of Naples died in January 1494, the French were almost ready to invade. On 3 September 1494, Charles left the French frontier and marched on Naples with an army of some forty thousand men. Peter Martyr, watching events unfold, raged in frustration: "What Italian can take up his pen without crying, without dying, without being consumed by pain?" The invader's progress south was like a triumph, as cities and duchies capitulated and the pope's partisans defected or fled. Along the way, Charles picked up fortunes in ransoms

– the price communities paid to avoid pillage. Pope Alexander, seeming to accept the inevitable, surrendered Rome into the king's hands, counting himself lucky to escape deposition. Rome emptied of notables and valuables. "People are in terror," wrote the Milanese envoy in May 1495, "not only for their property, but for their lives also. Rome has never been so entirely cleared of silver and valuables of all sorts. Not one of the cardinals has enough plate to serve six persons. The houses are dismantled."[28] Refusing to anoint Charles as king of Naples, Alexander fled.

But Charles was the victim of his own success. He occupied the kingdom of Naples with such ease that all Europe's neutrals, and even some of his former friends, became as alarmed as his enemies at the growth of his power. The pope put together a coalition of Venice, Spain, England, and the Duke of Milan, ostensibly to fight the Ottomans but really to reverse Charles's achievements. It was not, at first, militarily active, but it was effective in encouraging local opposition to Charles. When the king returned to France with his booty in July, Milanese forces ambushed him and seized almost all the treasures he had gathered. Over the next couple of years, Spanish-led forces chased out the garrisons he left behind in Naples.

"1494: Charles VIII invades Italy. Beginning of modern times." I can still recall the list of memorable dates my history teacher wrote on the blackboard when I was at my first school. The idea behind what at the time was a conventional way of dating the dawn of modernity was that until the French invasion, the Renaissance was confined to Italy. Charles unlocked it and took Italian arts and ideas back with him across the Alps, making it possible for the initiatives that made our world to spread around Europe.

No one still thinks anything of the sort. The Renaissance no longer looks like a new departure in the history of the world; rather, it was just more of the same, or an intensification of medieval traditions of humanistic learning and reverence for classical antiquity. New ideas were not all of Italian origin, and humanism and classicism had independent origins in other parts of Europe – especially in France, the Netherlands, and Spain. Italian learning and technical and artistic savoir-faire were already sought after in much of Europe. In Spain, the fall of Granada did most to introduce Italian taste, for the conquered city cried out for new churches and palaces in a classicising spirit. Charles VIII, in any case, did little to spread Italian taste even in France. The year 1492 was at least as decisive as 1494 in the history of his involvement in Italy, for it was then that he made up his mind to invade.

In combination, the death of Lorenzo the Magnificent and the invasion of Charles VIII constituted a crisis in the history of the Renaissance. Ficino thought Plato's fortunes had collapsed with Lorenzo's death.[29] After the Bonfire of the Vanities, even Botticelli gave up painting erotic commissions and reverted to old-fashioned piety. The Renaissance seemed in abeyance. But the greatest age was long over. By the mid-fifteenth century, the generation of Brunelleschi (d. 1446), Ghiberti (d. 1455), Donatello (d. 1466), Alberti (d. 1472), and Michelozzo (d. 1472) was ageing, dead, or dying. The institutions of the republic had fallen under the control of a single dynasty. But the tradition of excellence in arts and learning lived on. The sculptor Andrea Verocchio and the incomparable painter Sandro Botticelli (1445–1510) lived next door to the house of the explorer Amerigo Vespucci, whose writings popularised knowledge of the continent that came to be named after him. In the church of Ognissanti, Botticelli and Ghirlandaio (1448–96) worked on commissions from Vespucci's family.

Although the revolution that was to overthrow the Medici in 1494 caused a temporary loss of opportunities for patronage, the careers of the next generation – including Michelangelo, who was Ghirlandaio's apprentice – were already under way. At the time, Machiavelli was an unknown twenty-something. Florence's fertility in the production of genius seemed inexhaustible. Leonardo da Vinci had left the city in 1481 and gone to Milan, where he struggled to get paid for his paintings and worked hard glorifying the local tyrant in bronze or designing engineering works. Michelangelo was just eighteen years old when the death of Lorenzo forced him from the security of the Medici court back to his father's home. He worked hard to regain favour and in January 1494 was commissioned by the new head of the Medici family to produce a snow statue. The snow seemed hardly to have melted when political upheaval forced the Medici out. Michelangelo (among other artists) went with them and took refuge in Venice.

Nor is it fair to say that Lorenzo's death, or even the revolution that followed it, seeded Florentine talent throughout Italy. There had long been a lively market for skills in artistry and eloquence. Rome was the most important focus, for the popes had a long tradition as collectors of antiquities, patrons of art, and employers of high achievers not only in sacred learning but also in law, diplomacy, rhetoric, and the formulation of propaganda. To the frustration of believers in the exemplary value of ancient republican virtues, the rise of dictators and despots in Italian cities actually stimulated the markets in learning and art. Autocrats needed rhetoricians to advocate their merits, justify their usurpations of power, and excuse their wars. Tyrants needed sculptors and archi-tects to design and erect their monuments and perpetuate their images. Courts needed artists to paint their personnel and design their theatres of power – the masques and jousts, the processions and parades that awed enemies and enthused followers. Because artists often doubled as engineers, and sculptors skilled in bronze casting could transfer their talents to making guns, the growing political tensions in Italy also cre-ated opportunities for artists all over the peninsula.

Even in combination with the events of 1494, those of 1492 did not stimulate the Renaissance, liberate it from the confines of Flor-ence, or disseminate it around the world. Lorenzo the Magnificent and Charles VIII no longer look like harbingers of modernity. The mental world they shared was chivalric. They looked back for their values: Lorenzo to antiquity, Charles to a fictional version of the clas-sical and medieval past. Savonarola, perhaps, was a more important or representative figure for the future of the world. At first glance, he seems an even more regressive type than his chivalrically minded contemporaries, sunk in the ostentatiously austere late-medieval piety that most people nowadays find baffling or irksome. His addiction to millenarianism, his confidence in visions, his prophetic stridency, his hatred of art, and his mistrust of secular scholarship align him with aspects of the modern world most moderns reject: religious obscurantism, extreme fanaticism, irrational fundamentalism. In some ways, the conflicts he brought to a head – the confrontation of worldly and godly moralities, the uncomprehending debate between rational and subrational or suprarational mind-sets, the struggle for power in the state between the partisans of secularism and spirituality or of science and scripture – are timeless, universal features of history. Yet they are also, in their current intensity and ferocity, among the latest novelties of contemporary politics. The culture wars of our own time did not begin with Savonarola, but he embodied some of their most fearsome features.

In his prescriptions for Christendom, Savonarola was not an innovator, but he seemed "swollen with divine virtue", according to Machiavelli, who, as a youngster, heard the friar's sermons as he huffed and puffed in the pulpit. He brought unique force to the expression of some long-standing priorities of the reforming prophets of the late-medieval Church: revulsion from the Church's involvement in the world and the corrupting effects of wealth and secular power; denunciation of the overweening power of the popes over clergy and the clergy over laypeople; horror at the way pharisees seemed to have taken over the Church, binding and laming the search for salvation with obedience to formulaic rules and meaningless rituals. He was convinced that Scripture contained the whole of God's message, universally accessible, and that readers of Scripture needed no other knowledge except of prayer and mortification. His condemnation of Roman excess – though perhaps not quite as colourfully insulting as Luther's, with its rich language of the lavatory and the whorehouse – anticipated in tone and content the invective of the founder of Protestantism:

Go to Rome and see! In the mansions of the great prelates there is no concern save for poetry and the oratorical art. Go thither and see! Thou shalt find them all with the books of the humanities in their hands, telling one another that they can guide men's souls by means of Virgil, Horace, and Cicero. . . . The prelates of former days had fewer gold miters and chalices, and what few they possessed were broken up and given to relieve the needs of the poor. But our prelates, for the sake of obtaining chalices, will rob the poor of their sole means of support. Dost thou not know what I would tell thee? . . . O Lord, arise, and come to deliver thy Church from the hands of devils, from the hands of tyrants, from the hands of iniquitous prelates.[30]

Savonarola prefigured Luther, too, in his insistence on the doctrine of salvation by the free grace of God, which – except in the hands of reformers who used it to denounce the Church's rules of charity and piety – was perfectly innocent, orthodox Catholicism, but which became the slogan of the Reformation:

God remits the sins of men, and justifies them by his mercy. There are as many drops of compassion in heaven as there are justified men upon earth; for none are saved by their own works. . . . And if, in the presence of God, we could ask all these justified sinners, "Have you been saved by your own strength?" all would reply as with one voice, "Not unto us, O Lord! not unto us; but to thy name be the glory!" Therefore, O God, do I seek thy mercy, and I bring not unto thee my own righteousness; but when by thy grace thou justifiest one, then thy righteousness belongs unto me; for grace is the righteousness of God.[31]

An anonymous painting from 1498 shows what became of Savonarola, and how Florentines wanted the rest of us to remember his fate. Here, in place of the "vanities" the prophet had kindled in the same place a few years before, the flames consume Savonarola himself. It is a depiction of his death at the stake: the pyre is gigantic, towering, more like a ship than a scaffold, with its skyward, mast-like reach, topped with a cross. A high causeway links it to the municipal palace, from where the preacher was led to public execution. But the man who once turned heads and sparked ardour in the hearts of the people is now strangely ignored. Children play, merchants pass through; it is business as usual in the Piazza della Signoria. Only those who carry wood to the pyre are engaged in Savonarola's reckoning. The message of the image is obvious: Florence spared no pains or expense to burn the heretic, but did not want to appear to have taken any notice of him.

A few years after Savonarola's immolation, Luther visited Florence. But he did not need to experience the place to adopt the martyred friar as a hero or succumb to his influence. Savonarola's popularity with his followers, and the informal power he exercised in the Florentine republic after the fall of the Medici, ensured that almost every word he uttered from the pulpit found its way into print. Luther knew his sermons well, reprinted two of them, with an admiring preface of his own, and acknowledged him as a forerunner. "The Antichrist of that time made the memory of that great man perish," he complained, "but see! He lives. And his memory is blessed."[32]

Chapter 6

Towards "the Land of Darkness"

Russia and the Eastern Marches of Christendom

*7 June: Casimir IV, king of Poland and Grand Prince
of Lithuania, dies.*

The messengers turned back. They were on their way from Moscow, the capital or courtly centre of Muscovy – an upstart state that had become, in twenty years of aggressive dynamism, the fastest-expanding empire in Christendom. Their destination was the court of Casimir IV, king of Poland and sovereign – "Grand Prince" or "Grand Duke" in the jargon of the time – of Lithuania. Casimir was, by common assent, the greatest ruler in Christendom. His territory stretched from the Baltic Sea to the Black Sea. Its eastern frontier lay deep inside Russia, along the breakwater between the Dnieper and Volga valleys. Westward, it unfolded as far as Saxony and the satellite kingdoms of Bohemia, and Hungary, which Casimir more or less controlled. On the map, it was the biggest and most formidable-looking domain in the Latin world since the fall of the Roman Empire.

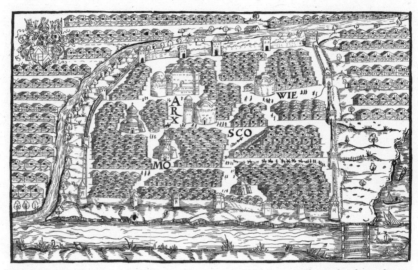

The Kremlin, the "citadel of Moscow", as it appeared to an ambassador from the Holy Roman Empire in 1517, with the stone structures conspicuous among the wooden houses.

The envoys from Moscow, however, were undaunted. They were carrying breathtakingly defiant demands for the surrender of most of Casimir's Russian dominions, which Muscovites had been infiltrating for years, into the hands of their own prince. They turned back, not because the power of Poland and Lithuania deterred them, nor because the summer roads were hot, boggy, and mosquito-ridden, but because the world had changed.

By rights, the world should have been close to ending. According to Russian reckoning, 1492 marked the close of the seventh millennium of creation, and prophets and visionaries were getting enthusiastic or apprehensive, according to taste. Calendars stopped in 1492. There were sceptics, but they were officially disavowed, even persecuted. In 1490, the patriarch of Moscow conducted an inquisition against here-tics, torturing his victims until they confessed to injudicious denuncia-tions of the doctrine of the Trinity and the sanctity of the Sabbath. Among the proscribed thoughts of which the victims were accused was doubt about whether the world was really about to end.

The news that made the Muscovite messengers backtrack reached them in the second week of June. Casimir IV had collapsed and died while hunting in Trakal, not far from Vilnius, where they had been hoping to meet for negotiations. For Russia, the prospects defied the prophecies. Casimir's death improved Muscovy's outlook. The messengers rode hard for Moscow. It was time for new instructions and even more outrageous ambitions.

Between the Carpathian Mountains and the Balkan uplands in the south and the Baltic Sea in the north, eastern Europe's geography is hostile to political continuity. Cut and crossed by invaders' corridors, it is an environment in which – with its flat, open expanses, good communications, and dispersed populations – states can form with ease, survive in struggle, and thrive only with difficulty. There are forty thousand square miles of marshland in the middle of the region, covering much of what is now Belarus, around the upper Dnieper. Around this vast bog, the steppeland curls to the south and the bleak, ridgeless North European plain – choked with dense, dark forests – stretches uninterruptedly westward from deep inside Siberia. The lie of the land favours vast and fragile empires, vulnerable to external attack and internal rebellion. Armies can shuttle back and forth easily. Rebels can hide in the forests and swamps. Volatile hegemonies have come and gone in the region with bewildering rapidity. In the fifth century the Huns extended their sway from the steppelands to the east around the marshes and into the northern plain. In the ninth century a state the Byzantines called Great Moravia reached briefly from the marshes to the Elbe. In the late tenth and eleventh centuries a native Slav state occupied most of the Volga Valley. The most spectacular empire makers to unify the region arrived sweating from the depths of Asia in the thirteenth century, driving their vast herds of horses and sheep. The Mongols burst into Western history – like a scourge, as some chroniclers said, or, said others, like a plague.

The earliest records of Mongol peoples occur in Chinese annals of the seventh century. At that time, the Mongols emerged on to the steppes of the central Asian land now called Mongolia, from the forests to the north, where they lived as hunters and small-scale pig breeders. Chinese writers used versions of the name "Mongols" for many different communities, with various religions and competing leaderships, but their defining characteristic was that they spoke languages of common origins that were different from those of the neighbouring Turks. On the steppes they adopted a pastoral way of life. They became horse-borne nomads, skilled in sheep breeding, dairying, and war.

The sedentary peoples who fringed the steppelands hated and feared them. They hated them because nomadism and herding seemed savage. Mongols drank milk – which the lactose-intolerant sedentarists found disgusting. They drank blood – which seemed more disgusting still, though for nomads in need of instant nourishment it was an entirely practical taste. The sedentarists' fear was better founded: nomads needed farmers' crops to supplement their diet. Nomad leaders needed city dwellers' wealth to fill their treasure hoards and pay their followers. In the early twelfth century, the bands or alliances they formed got bigger, and their raids against neighbouring, settled communities became more menacing. In part, this was the effect of the growing preponderance of some Mongol groups over others. In part, it was the result of slow economic change.

Contact with richer neighbours gave Mongol chiefs opportunities for enrichment as mercenaries or raiders. Economic inequalities greater than the Mongols had ever known arose in a society in which blood relationships and seniority in age had formerly settled everyone's position. Prowess in war enabled particular leaders to build up followers in parallel with – and sometimes in defiance of – the old social order. They called this process "crane catching", like caging valuable birds. The most successful leaders enticed or forced rival groups into submission. The process spread to involve peoples who were not strictly Mongols, though the same name continued to be used – we use it still – for a confederation of many peoples, including many who spoke Turkic languages, as the war bands enlarged.

The violence endemic in the steppes turned outwards, with increas-ing confidence, increasing ambition, to challenge neighbouring civili-sations. Historians have been tempted to speculate about the reasons for the Mongols' expansion. One explanation is environmental. Tem-peratures in the steppes seem to have fallen during the relevant period. People farther west on the Russian plains complained that a cold spell in the early thirteenth century caused crops to fail. So declining pas-tures might have driven the Mongols to expand from the steppes. Pop-ulation in the region seems to have been relatively high, and the pastoral way of life demands large amounts of grazing land to feed rela-tively small numbers of people. It is not a particularly energy-efficient way to provide food because it relies on animals eating plants and people eating animals, whereas farming produces humanly edible crops and cuts out animals as a wasteful intermediate stage of production. So perhaps the Mongol out-thrust was a consequence of having more mouths to feed.

Yet the Mongols were doing what steppelanders had always sought to do: dominate and exploit surrounding sedentary peoples. The differ-ence was that they did it with greater ambition and greater efficiency than any of their predecessors. In the late twelfth or early thirteenth century a new ideology animated Mongol conquests, linked to the cult of the sky, which was probably a traditional part of Mongol ideology but which leaders encouraged in pursuit of programmes of political unifica-tion of the Mongol world. Earth should imitate the universal reach of the sky. Mongol leaders' proclamations and letters to foreign rulers are explicit and unambiguous in their claims: the Mongols' destiny was to unify the world by conquest.

Wherever the Mongol armies went, their reputation preceded them. Armenian sources warned Westerners of the approach of "precursors of the Antichrist . . . of hideous aspect and without pity in their bowels, . . . who rush with joy to carnage as if to a wedding feast or orgy". Rumours piled up in Germany, France, Burgundy, Hungary, and even in Spain and England, where Mongols had never been heard of before. The invaders looked like monkeys, it was said, barked like dogs, ate raw flesh, drank their horses' urine, knew no laws, and showed no mercy. Matthew Paris, the thirteenth-century English monk who, in his day, probably knew as much about the rest of the world as any of his countrymen, summed up the Mongols' image: "They are inhuman and beastly, rather monsters than men, thirsting for and drinking blood, tearing and devouring the flesh of dogs and men. . . . And so they come, with the swiftness of lightning to the confines of Christendom, ravaging and slaughtering, striking everyone with terror and with incomparable horror."[1]

When the Mongols struck Russia in 1223, the blow was entirely unexpected: "No man knew from whence they came or whither they departed."[2] Annalists treated them as if they were a natural phenomenon, like a briefly destructive bout of freak weather or a flood or a visitation of pestilence. Some Russian rulers even rejoiced at the greater destruction the Mongols visited on hated neighbours. But the first Mongol invasion was no more than a reconnaissance. When the nomads returned in earnest in 1237, their campaign lasted for three years. They devastated and depopulated much of the land of southern and north-eastern Russia and ransomed or looted the towns.

The Mongols' vocation for world rule, however, was theoretical. They demanded submission and tribute from their victims, but they were not necessarily interested in exercising direct rule everywhere. They had no wish to adapt to an unfamiliar ecosystem, no interest in occupying lands beyond the steppe, and no need to replace existing elites in Russia. They left the Christian Russian principalities and city-states to run their own affairs. But Russian rulers received charters from the khan's court at Saray on the lower Volga, where they had to make regular appearances, loaded with tribute and subject to ritual humiliations, kissing the khan's stirrup, serving at his table. The population had to pay taxes directly to Mongol-appointed tax gatherers – though as time went on, the Mongols assigned the tax gathering to native Russian princes and civic authorities. They passed their gleanings on to the state, centred at Saray, where the Mongols came to be known as the Golden Horde, perhaps after the treasure they accumulated.

The Russians tolerated this situation, partly because the Mongols intimidated them by selective acts of terror. When the invaders took the great city of Kiev in 1240, it was said, they left only two hundred houses standing and strewed the fields "with countless heads and bones of the dead".[3] Partly, however, the Russians were responding to a milder Mongol policy. In most of Russia, the invaders came to exploit rather than to destroy. According to one chronicler, the Mongols spared Russia's peasants to ensure that farming would continue. Ryazan, a Russian principality on the Volga, south of Moscow, seems to have borne the brunt of the Mongol invasion. Yet there, if the local chronicle can be believed,

> the pious Grand Prince Ingvary Ingvarevitch sat on his father's throne and renewed the land and built churches and monasteries and consoled newcomers and gathered together the people. And there was joy among the Christians whom God had saved from the godless and impious khan.[4]

Many cities escaped lightly by capitulating at once. Novgorod, that famously commercial city, which the Mongols might have coveted, they bypassed altogether.

Moreover, the Russian princes were even more fearful of enemies to the west, where the Swedes, Poles, and Lithuanians had constructed strong, unitary monarchies capable of sweeping the princes away if they ever succeeded in expanding into Russian territory. Equally menacing were groups of mainly German adventurers, organised into crusading "orders" of warriors, such as the Teutonic Knights and the Brothers of the Sword, who took monastic-style vows but dedicated themselves to waging holy war against pagans and heretics. In practice, these orders were self-enriching companies of professional fighters, who built up territorial domains along the Baltic coast by conquest. In campaigns between

1242 and 1245, Russian coalitions fought off invaders on the western front, but they could not sustain war on two fronts. The experience made them submissive to the Mongols.

Muscovy hardly seemed destined to dominate the region. The principality owed its existence to the Golden Horde. Muscovite princes proved that they could manipulate Mongol hegemony to their own advantage, but they remained the Mongols' creatures. Indeed, it was hard to imagine Muscovy unless backed by Mongol power. In the mid-thirteenth century, Alexander Nevsky, prince of Novgorod, showed the way to make use of the Mongols. He created the basis of his own myth as a Russian national hero by submitting to the Golden Horde and turning west to confront Swedish and German aggressors. His dynasty levered Muscovy to prominence by stages. His son Daniel (1276–1303), who became ruler of Moscow, proclaimed the city's independence from other Russian principalities and ceased payment of tribute, except to the Mongols. Daniel's grandson became known as Ivan the Moneybag (1329–53) from the wealth he accumulated as a farmer of Mongol taxes. He called himself "Grand Prince" and raised the see of Moscow from a bishopric to an archbishopric.

Muscovy still depended on the Mongols. The principality's first challenge to Mongol supremacy, in 1378–82, proved premature. The Muscovites tried to exploit divisions within the Golden Horde in order to avoid handing over taxes. They even beat off a punitive expedition. But once the Mongols had re-established their unity, Muscovy had to resume payment, yield hostages, and stamp coins with the name of the khan and the prayer "Long may he live". In 1399 the Mongols fought off a Lithuanian challenge to their control of Russia. Over the next few years they asserted their hegemony in a series of raids on Russian cities, including Moscow, extorting promises of tribute in perpetuity. Thereafter, the Muscovites remained meekly deferential, more or less continuously, while they built up their own strength.

They could, however, dream of pre-eminence, under the Mongols, over other Christian states in Russia. Muscovy's great advantage was its central location, astride the upper Volga, controlling the course of the river as far as the confluence of the Vetluga and the Sura. The Volga was a sea-wide river, navigable almost all along its great, slow length. Picture Europe as a rough triangle, with its apex at the Pillars of Hercules. The corridor that links the Atlantic, the North Sea, and the Baltic forms one side; the linked waters of the Mediterranean and Black Sea form another. The Volga serves almost as a third sea, overlooking the steppes and forests of the Eurasian borderlands, linking the Caspian Road and the Silk Roads to the fur-rich Arctic forests and the fringes of the Baltic world. The Volga's trade and tolls helped fill Ivan's money bags and elevate Muscovy over its neighbours.

Rulership was ferociously contested, because the rewards made the risks seem worthwhile. In consequence, political instability racked the state and checked its ascent. For nearly forty years, from the mid-1420s, rival members of the dynasty fought each other. Vasily II, who became ruling prince at the age of ten in 1425, repeatedly renounced and recovered the throne, enduring spells of exile and imprisonment. He blinded his rival and cousin and suffered blinding in his turn when his enemies captured him: as a way of disqualifying a pretender or keeping a deposed monarch down, blinding was a traditional, supposedly civilised alternative to murder. When Vasily died in 1462, his son, Ivan III, inherited a realm that war had rid of internal rivals. Civil wars seem destructive and debilitating. But they often precede spells of violent expansion. They militarise societies, train men in warfare, nurture arms industries, and, by disrupting economies, force peoples into predation.

Thanks to the long civil wars, Ivan had the most efficient and ruthless war machine of any Russian state. The wars had ruined aristocrats already impoverished by the system of inheritance, which divided the patrimony of every family with every passing generation. The nobles were forced to serve the prince or collaborate with him. Wars of expansion represented the best means of building up resources and accumulating lands, revenues, and tribute for the prince to distribute. For successful warriors, promotions and honours beckoned, including an enduring innovation: gold medals for valour. Nobles moved to Moscow as offices of profit at court came to outshine provincial opportunities of exploiting peasants and managing estates. Adventurers and mercenaries – including many Mongols – joined them. By the end of Ivan's reign, an aristocracy of service over a thousand strong surrounded him.

A permanent force of royal guards formed a professional kernel around which provincial levies grouped. Peasants were armed to guard the frontiers. Ivan III set up a munitions factory in Moscow and hired Italian engineers to improve what one might call the military infrastructure of the realm – forts, which slowed adversaries, and bridges, which sped mobilisation. He abjured the traditional ruler's role of leading his armies on campaign. To run a vast and growing empire, ready to fight on more than one front, he stayed at the nerve centre of command and created a system of rapid posts to keep in touch with events in the field. None of his other innovations seemed as important, to him, as improved internal communications. At his death, he left few commands to his heirs about the care of the empire, except for instructions about the division of the patrimony and the allocation of tribute; but the maintenance of the post system was uppermost in his mind: "My son Vasily shall maintain, in his Grand Princedom, post stations and post carts with horses on the roads at those places where there were post stations and post carts with horses on the roads under me." His brothers were to do the same in the lands they inherited.[5]

Backed by his new bureaucracy and new army, Ivan could take the step so many of his predecessors had longed for. He could abjure Mongol suzerainty. In the event, it was easy, not only because of the strength Ivan amassed but also because internecine hatreds shattered the Mongols' unity. In 1430, a group of recalcitrants split off and founded a state of their own in the Crimea, to the west of the Golden Horde's heartland. Other factions usurped territory to the east and south in Kazan and Astrakhan. Russian principalities began to see the possibilities of

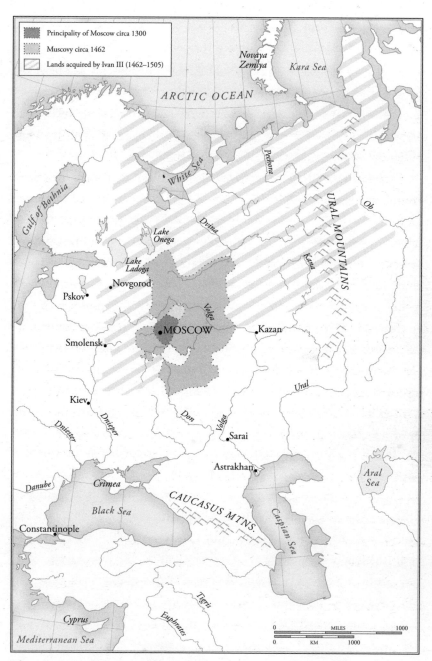

Novaya
Zemlya   *Kara Sea*

ARCTIC OCEAN

Pechora

Gulf of Bothnia

White Sea

URAL MOUNTAINS

Ob

Dvina

Lake
Onega

Kama

Lake
Ladoga

•Novgorod

Pskov•

Volga

•MOSCOW   •Kazan

Smolensk•

Ural

Kiev•   *Don*   *Volga*

Dnieper

Dniester

•Sarai

Danube   Crimea

Astrakhan•

*Aral
Sea*

Black Sea   CAUCASUS MTNS.

*Caspian
Sea*

Constantinople•

Tigris

Cyprus   *Euphrates*

0   MILES   1000

Mediterranean Sea   0   KM   1000

The expansion of Muscovy under Ivan III.

independence. Formerly, once the shock of invasion and conquest was over, their chroniclers had accepted the Mongols, with various degrees of resignation, as a scourge from God or as useful and legitimate arbitrators, or even as benevolent exemplars of virtuous paganism whom Christians should imitate. Now, from the mid-fifteenth century, they recast them as villains, incarnations of evil, and destroyers of Christianity. Interpolators rewrote old chronicles in an attempt to turn Alexander Nevsky, who had been a quisling and collaborator on the Mongols' behalf, into a heroic adversary of the khans.[6]

Ivan allied with the secessionist Mongol states against the Golden Horde. He then stopped paying tribute. The khan demanded compliance. Ivan refused. The horde invaded, but withdrew when menaced with battle – a fatal display of weakness. Neighbouring states scented blood and tore at the horde's territory like sharks at bloodied prey. The ruler of the breakaway Mongol state in the Crimea dispersed the horde's remaining forces and burned Saray in 1502. Russia, the chroniclers declared, had been delivered from the Mongol yoke, as God had freed Israel from Egypt. The remaining Mongol bands in the Crimea and Astrakhan became Ivan's pensioners, for whom he assigned one thousand gold rubles at his death.

The Mongols' decline liberated Ivan to make conquests for Muscovy on other fronts. From his father, Vasily II, he inherited the ambition, proclaimed in the inscriptions on Vasily's coins, to be "sovereign of all Russia". His conquests reflect, fairly consistently, a special appetite to rule people of Russian tongue and Orthodox faith. His campaigns against Mongol states were defensive or punitive, and his forays into the pagan north, beyond the colonial empire of Novgorod, were raids. But the chief enemy he seems always to have had in his sights was Casimir IV, who ruled more Russians than any other foreigner. How far Ivan followed a systematic grand strategy of Russian unification is, however, a matter of doubt. No document declares such a policy. At most, it can be inferred from his actions. He may equally well have been responding pragmatically to the opportunities that cropped up. But medieval rulers rarely planned for the short term – especially not when they thought the world was about to end. Typically, they worked to re-create a golden past or embody a mythic ideal.

To understand what was in Ivan's mind, one has to think back to what the world was like before Machiavelli. The modern calculus of profit and loss probably meant nothing to Ivan. He never thought about realpolitik. His concerns were with tradition and posterity, history and fame, apocalypse and eternity. If he targeted Muscovy's western frontier for special attention, it was probably because he had the image and reputation of Alexander Nevsky before his eyes, refracted in the work of chroniclers who turned back to rewrite their accounts of the past, to burnish Alexander's image, after a spell of neglect, and re-idealised him as "the Russian prince" and the perfect ruler. Ivan did not initiate this rebranding, but he paid for chroniclers to continue it in his own reign.

Therefore, when Ivan began turning his wealth into conquests, he first tackled the task of reunifying the patrimony of Alexander Nevsky. Ivan devoted the early years of the reign to suborning or forcing Tver and Ryazan, the neighbouring principalities to Muscovy's west, into subordination or submission, and incorporating the lands of all the surviving heirs of Alexander Nevsky into the Muscovite state. But thoughts of Novgorod, where Alexander's career had begun, were never far from his mind. Novgorod was an even bigger prize. The city lay to the north, contending against a hostile climate, staring from huge walls over the grain lands on which the citizens relied for sustenance. Famine besieged them more often than human enemies did. Yet control of the trade routes to the River Volga made Novgorod cash rich. It never had more than a few thousand inhabitants, yet its monuments record its progress: its kremlin, or citadel, and five-domed cathedral in the 1040s; in the early twelfth century, a series of buildings that the ruler paid for; and, in 1207, the merchants' church of St Paraskeva in the marketplace.

From 1136, communal government prevailed in Novgorod. The revolt of that year marks the creation of a city-state on an ancient model – a republican commune like those of Italy. The prince was deposed for reasons the rebels' surviving proclamations specify: "Why did he not care for the common people? Why did he want to wage war? Why did he not fight bravely? And why did he prefer games and entertainments rather than state affairs? Why did he have so many gyrfalcons and dogs?" Thereafter, the citizens' principle was: "If the prince is no good, throw him into the mud!"[7]

To the west, Novgorod bordered the small territorial domain of Russia's only other city-republic, Pskov. There were others again in Germany and on the Baltic coast, but Novgorod was unique in eastern Europe in being a city-republic with an extensive empire of its own. Even in the West, only Genoa and Venice resembled it in this respect. Novgorod ruled or took tribute from subject or victim peoples in the boreal forests and tundra that fringed the White Sea and stretched towards the Arctic. Novgorodians had even begun to build a modest maritime empire, colonising islands in the White Sea. The evidence is painted on to the surface of an icon, now in an art gallery in Moscow but once treasured in a monastery on an island in the White Sea. It shows monks adoring the Virgin on an island adorned with a golden monastery with tapering domes, a golden sanctuary, and turrets like lighted candles. The glamour of the scene must be the product of pious imaginations, for the island in reality is bare and impoverished and surrounded, for much of the year, with ice.

Pictures of episodes from the monastery's foundation legend of the 1430s, about a century before the icon was made, frame the painter's vision of the Virgin receiving adoration. The first monks row to the island. Young, radiant figures expel the indigenous fisherfolk with angelic whips. When the abbot, Savaatii, hears of it he gives thanks to God. Merchants visit. When they drop the sacred host that the holy monk Zosima gives them, flames leap to protect it. When the monks rescue shipwreck victims, who are dying in a cave on a nearby island, Zosima and Savaatii appear miraculously, teetering on icebergs, to drive back the pack ice. Zosima experiences a vision of a "floating church", which the building of an island monastery fulfils. In defiance of the barren environment, angels supply the community with bread, oil, and salt. Whereas Zosima's predecessors as abbots left because they could not endure harsh conditions, Zosima calmly drove out the devils who tempted him. All the ingredients of a typical story of European imperialism are here: the more than worldly inspiration; the heroic voyage into a perilous environment; the ruthless treatment of the natives; the struggle to adapt and found a viable economy; the quick input of commercial interests; the achievement of viability by perseverance.[8]

Outreach in the White Sea could not grasp much or get far. Novgorod was, however, the metropolis of a precocious colonial enterprise by land among the herders and hunters of the Arctic region, along and across the rivers that flow into the White Sea, as far east as the Pechora. Russian travellers' tales reflected typical colonial values. They classed the native Finns and Samoyeds of the region with the beast men, the *similitudines hominis*, of medieval legend. The "wild men" of the north spent summers in the sea lest their skin split. They died every winter, when water came out of their noses and froze them to the ground. They ate each other and cooked their children to serve to guests. They had mouths on top of their heads and ate by placing food under their hats; they had dogs' heads or heads that grew beneath their shoulders; they lived underground and drank human blood.[9] They were exploitable for reindeer products and fruits of the hunt – whale blubber, walrus ivory, the pelts of the Arctic squirrel and fox – that arrived in Novgorod as tribute from the region and were vital to the economy.

Ivan coveted this wealth, and even sent an expedition to the Arctic in 1465 in an attempt to grab a share of the fur trade. But in the 1470s an opportunity arose to seize Novgorod itself. A dispute over the election of a new bishop rent the city. Partisans on both sides looked for protectors or arbitrators in neighbouring realms. Should Novgorod submit to Ivan's overlordship by sending the bishop-elect to Moscow for consecration? Or should the city try to perpetuate its independence by sending to Kiev, which was safely distant, in the realm of Casimir of Lithuania? For the city's incumbent elite, Casimir was the less risky bet.

He could be invoked in Novgorod's defence, as a deterrent against a Muscovite attack. But he was so busy on other fronts that he was most unlikely ever to interfere with Novgorod's autonomy. The city fathers voted to make Casimir their "sovereign and master" and send their bishop to Kiev.

Ivan called their bluff and prepared to attack. He justified war by sanctifying it. The people of Novgorod were, he claimed, guilty of punishable impiety – abandoning Orthodoxy and bowing to Rome. The accusation was false. While encouraging Catholicism, Casimir tolerated other creeds among his subjects, and a bishop consecrated in Kiev would not necessarily be compromised in his Orthodoxy. Ivan, however, claimed to see Novgorod's bid for independence as a kind of apostasy, whoring after false gods – like the Jews, he said, breaking their divine covenant to adore a golden calf. By conquering them he would save them.[10]

Ivan's propaganda also besmirched Novgorod with denunciations, on more secular grounds, as a nest of habitual recalcitrants. "The habit" of the citizens, a chronicler in Ivan's pay complained, was to

> disagree with a great prince and dispute with him. They will not pay respect to him, but instead they are taciturn, obstinate, and stubborn, and do not adhere to the principles of law and order. . . . Who among the princes would not become angry with them . . . ? For even the great Alexander [Nevsky] did not tolerate such behavior.[11]

Ivan's enemies in the Novgorod elite appealed to Casimir IV to rescue them. But they sought to put intolerable restrictions on him, demanding of the Catholic prince that he build no Roman churches, appoint only Orthodox governors, and allow bishops of Novgorod in future to seek consecration outside his realms. They even demanded that he settle territorial disputes between Novgorod and Lithuania in favour of "the free men of Novgorod".[12] Casimir remained aloof. There seemed no point in spilling blood and spending treasure for such obstreperous allies. Novgorod's citizen army of "carpenters, coopers and others, who from birth had never mounted a horse" was on its own.[13] When Ivan invaded, he crushed resistance within a few weeks. Simultaneously, with an army of mercenaries and tributaries, he occupied the remote provinces of Novgorod's colonial frontier.

The terms of the peace were full of face-saving formulas, but the upshot was clear. "You are free to do as you please," said Ivan, "provided you do as I please." After a few years, he did away with all pretence of respect for Novgorod's autonomy. He moved in another army, abolished residual privileges, and annexed the territory to Muscovy. The great bell that had summoned the "free men" to assemble ended up in Moscow in the belfry of the Kremlin. Ivan had, as he wrote to his mother, "subjected Novgorod the Great, which is part of my inheritance, to my entire will and I am sovereign there just as in Moscow".[14]

The conquest of Novgorod shocked Ivan's most powerful neighbours – Casimir in the west and Khan Ahmed of the Golden Horde in the south. Had they joined in attack, they could have matched Ivan's power, but Casimir – distracted as ever by rival concerns, and sanguine, as ever, in evaluating the Muscovite threat – relied on Ahmed as a surrogate. When the khan invaded Russia in 1480, Ivan, as we have seen, was free to concentrate his forces and repudiate the Golden Horde's historic claims to tribute.

Rather as Sonni Ali did in Timbuktu, Ivan dispersed Novgorod's elite. The first purge came in 1484, when a large force of mailed Muscovites tramped into the city and rounded up suspected foes. In 1487, when Ivan launched the first of a series of border raids against Lithuania, he secured Novgorod by expelling thousands of inhabitants – members of the families of leading citizens – on the alleged grounds that they were plotting against the authorities. Another one thousand expulsions followed in 1489. The expulsees' property went to some two thousand loyal colonists whom Ivan introduced.[15] Meanwhile, the historic principalities that fringed Muscovy's ancient patrimony to the West – all of which were already under Ivan's control – were formally annexed.

Muscovy's sudden and vertiginous rise took all Europe by surprise. The Saxon traveller and diplomatist Nikolaus Poppel, who arrived in Moscow in 1486, thought Ivan must be Casimir's vassal. He was astonished to find that the Russian ruler had more power, more wealth, and possibly, by that date, more territory than the master of Poland and Lithuania. Fascinated, he contemplated the vast, open, exploitable lands that stretched to the Arctic, full of sable and copper and gold. But Ivan would not let him, or his successor as imperial ambassador in 1492, go there. In the Latin West, Russia assumed the mysterious renown of a fantasy land, an icy Eldorado full of strange wealth, with monster-haunted frontiers reaching towards the unknown. In the circumstances, Casimir might be forgiven for underestimating his eastern neighbour and neglecting the threat from Russia. He was always juggling conflicting responsibilities on other fronts, squeezing Prussia into submission, insinuating his brothers or sons into power in Hungary and Moldova, duelling with the Habsburgs for control of Bohemia.

Ivan could therefore go on provoking Casimir with impunity. As soon as Novgorod fell to the Muscovites, Ivan forbade Lithuanian enclaves within Novgorod's territory from paying the taxes they owed to Casimir. In the 1480s, complaints lodged by Casimir's envoys accumulated in Moscow: "thieves" from Muscovy were raiding across the border, burning and pillaging villages, sowing terror. Ivan professed ignorance and claimed innocence, but clearly the raids had his backing. They were part of a systematic strategy for destabilising the border. Towards the end of the decade they escalated outrageously. In 1487, one of Ivan's brothers occupied a slice of borderland on the Lithuanian side, and Ivan appointed a governor in districts traditionally part of Lithuania. A raid in 1488 carried off seven thousand of Casimir's subjects. Many border towns reported repeated raids between 1485 and 1489.

Border warfare was effective. Casimir's subjects, when he was unable to protect them, transferred their allegiance to the aggressor as the price of peace. Orthodox Russian lords, who had long lived under Lithuanian rule without resentment, began to defect to Muscovy, declaring their lands to be under Ivan's "jurisdiction and protection".[16] When Casimir died, Ivan suspended negotiations and adopted the title "Sovereign of all Russia" – an explicit avowal of his intention of stripping Lithuania of all its Russian and Orthodox subjects. He launched full-scale invasions on two fronts, gobbling up the valley of the upper River Oka and advancing through the uplands of the Vyazma region, as far as the headwaters of the Dnieper. Almost everywhere his forces went, local rulers who submitted were reinvested with their rights as subjects of Muscovy. In two decades, Lithuania lost control of seventy administrative districts, twenty-two forts, nineteen towns, and thirteen villages.

The frontier that emerged was both linguistic and religious. Russian identity was measurable in Russian speech. But religious orthodoxy was the identifier Ivan preferred. Doctrinally, Russia was close to Rome. The difference that meant a lot to theologians concerned the emanation of the Holy Spirit: "from the Father and the Son," said the Western creed; "from the Father," said Orthodox Russians. This was too arcane a dispute to mean much to most laymen, but the culture and liturgy of the two churches were mutually offensive. Westerners found married, compulsorily bearded clergy alarming and the Slavonic language indecorous in church. Russians felt the same way about clean-shaven celibates spouting Latin. It is tempting to dismiss as mere posturing Ivan's self-proclaimed role as a crusader for Orthodoxy. But it really seems to have meant a lot to people at the time and to have influenced many defectors from Lithuanian allegiance. Though Ivan had occasional disputes with the Turks, Russian propagandists almost never denounced the Ottomans as "infidels". They generally reserved that insult for Catholics, and for Orthodox who were in communion with Rome.

1492

To understand the power of anti-Catholic language in Ivan's rhetorical armoury, awareness of the sense of threat that loomed over the Orthodox world is essential. Even when 1492 came and went without provoking the apocalypse, fear that the end of the world could not be far off persisted. Even after two generations, the events of 1453, when the Turks wrenched Constantinople from Christendom and extinguished an empire sanctified by Christian tradition, still disturbed and challenged Orthodox thinkers. Orthodoxy seemed beleaguered. Theologically informed minds in Russia naturally thought of the trials of faith in ancient Israel and regarded stubborn, uncompromising adherence to every peculiarity of their faith as the only way to restore divine favour.

Catholic gains, meanwhile, exacerbated the centuries-old enmity between the churches. Catholic diplomacy and evangelisation had seduced many Orthodox communities on the fringes of the Latin world back into communion with Rome. Theological debate, meanwhile, gradually resolved most of the credal issues between the two churches. The main outstanding disagreement was – on the face of it – too arcane to matter to any but the subtlest and most disputatious minds: towards the end of the eighth century, the Western churches added a phrase to the creed, proclaiming that the Holy Spirit "proceeded" not from the Father alone, as the Easterners continued to say, but also from God the Son. Each church regarded the other's formula as an offence against the unity of God. Westerners said the Eastern formula degraded the Son. Easterners said the Westerners were relegating the Holy Spirit to a sort of second-rank Godship.

In the 1430s, on Byzantine initiative, the leaders of the churches of Rome and Constantinople agreed to leave the controversy unresolved and to patch up their differences in order to collaborate against the Turks. Russian sees, including that of Moscow, had representatives among the seven-thousand-strong Eastern contingent at the Council of Florence in 1439, where the deal was clinched and the reunion of Christendom proclaimed. But outstanding issues remained. When the archbishop of Moscow returned to his see, the local clergy and citizens were outraged at what they denounced as betrayal. They flung the newcomer into prison and elected a successor who would stand up for the independent traditions of Orthodoxy. Most other churches in the Greek tradition also reneged on the deal, but in Byzantium, the emperors adhered to it. The monarchs who, more than all others, bore the responsibility of defending Orthodoxy seemed to have sold out to heresy.

What happened in the Byzantine empire mattered in Moscow, because even when the Russians emerged from the Mongols' thrall, they remained under the spell of Constantinople. Towards the end of the tenth century, the founder of the first documented Russian state applied to Constantinople for his religion and his wife. In politics and aesthetics Russians' models remained Byzantine for the rest of the Middle Ages. It is not surprising that the Russians, who owed so much to Byzantine culture, revered the Byzantine emperors. The Turks, who owed Byzantium nothing, and reviled Christianity, revered them, too. By the time Ivan III ruled in Muscovy, the Turks had Byzantium surrounded. The empire was reduced to a rump. The city was at the sultan's mercy. But the victors held back, unwilling to break the traditions of the people who still called themselves Romans. Of course, there were solid reasons for keeping Byzantium independent. The Turks could control the city's elites with threats and promises. The emperor and patriarch could guarantee the loyalty of the Ottomans' Christian subjects. But whenever the Turks contemplated the extinction of the empire, there was something numinous about Byzantium that stayed their hands.

When they finally lost patience, the blow came quickly and inevitably. The accession as sultan of Mehmet II in 1451 at the age of nineteen marked the end of counsels of prudence. He resented foreign control of a stronghold that dominated the Dardanelles – a strait vital for the communications of his empire. He fancied himself in the Roman emperors' place. Every contrivance of the siege engineer's craft prepared the fall of the city. Huge forts, known respectively as the castles of Europe and Asia, rose on either shore to command access to the Bosporus. The heaviest artillery ever founded arrived to batter the walls. Ships came overland in kit form to outflank the defenders' boom. The Byzantine church made submission to Rome in order to secure Latin help, which came reluctantly and too late. In the end, sheer weight of numbers proved decisive. The attackers climbed the breaches over the bodies of dead comrades. The corpse of the last Constantine was identified only by the eagle devices on his foot armour.

Formerly, there had been other contenders for the role of the third Rome, but they had all dropped out of the running. In the middle of the thirteenth century, the recently Christianised Serbian kingdom already housed, in monasteries founded by kings at Sopocani and Mileseva, some of the most purely classical paintings – modelled, that is, on those of ancient Greece and Rome – of the Middle Ages. About a century later, the Serbian monarch Stefan Dusan dreamed of beating the Turks to the conquest of Constantinople, and described himself with pride – if a little exaggeration – as "lord of almost the whole of the Roman Empire". His younger contemporary the Bulgarian czar John Alexander claimed lordship over "all the Bulgarians and Greeks" and had himself painted in boots of imperial scarlet – a fashion exclusive to emperors – with a halo of gold. A translator at his court, working on a version of a Byzantine chronicle, substituted for "Constantinople" the name of John Alexander's capital at Trnovo, and called it "the new Constantinople".[17] Serb and Bulgarian bids for empire, however, proved too ambitious. Both states fell to the Turks.

Even at Byzantium's last gasp, in 1452, when the Russian church reluctantly transgressed its tradition of deference to the see of Constantinople – defying the Byzantine rapprochement with the Latin communion by electing a patriarch of its own – Vasily II felt obliged to apologise to the emperor: "We beseech your sacred majesty not to blame us for not writing to your Sovereignty beforehand. We did this from dire necessity, not from pride or arrogance."[18] When the imperial city fell, Russia felt bereft. What did God mean by allowing it to happen? How did he want the Orthodox faithful to respond? One obvious answer began to gain acceptance in Muscovy: responsibility for safeguarding Orthodoxy must move from Constantinople to Moscow.

Ivan staked a claim to a Byzantine inheritance when he married a Byzantine princess. Surprisingly, perhaps, the idea was the pope's. In 1469, when the marriage was first mooted, Ivan was a twenty-nine-year-old widower. Zoe – or Sophia, as Russians called her – was a twenty-four-year-old spinster, plump but pretty, who was, as her tutor reminded her, "a pauper", but who embodied the prestige of the Byzantine imperial dynasty and legacy. She was the niece of the last Byzantine emperor. She lived in Rome, as the ward and guest of the pope, a fugitive from the Turkish conquest. Pope Paul II offered Ivan Sophia's hand. This shows that Rome was relatively well informed about Russia. The pope knew that Ivan would find a Byzantine pedigree hard to resist. He hoped that Sophia would make Ivan an ally in a new crusade against the Ottomans and would provide the Russians with a shining example of conversion from Orthodoxy to Catholicism. But for Sophia the long journey to Russia was a spiritual homecoming that reunited her with the church of her ancestors. As she travelled across country, through Pskov and Novgorod to Moscow, she worshipped with reverence wherever she went. She did not jib at rebaptism in the Orthodox rite, before her marriage in 1472, or at the orders Ivan gave her entourage forbidding them to display their crucifixes in public.

In the 1470s – hesitantly and unsystematically at first – Ivan began to call himself "Czar" of all Russia, in allusion to the title of "Caesar" that Roman emperors had affected.[19] Previously, the monarch of Constantinople and the khan of the Golden Horde were the only rulers Muscovites had flattered with so resounding a title. In the next decade Ivan's escalating pretensions became obvious during his sporadic negotiations with the Holy Roman Empire. When Frederick III offered to elevate Ivan from the rank of Grand Prince and invest him as a king, Ivan replied disdainfully.

By God's grace we have been sovereigns in our own land since the beginning, since our earliest ancestors. Our appointment comes from God, as did that of our ancestors, and we beg God to grant to us and our children to abide forever in the same state, namely as sovereigns in our own land; and as before we did not seek to be appointed by anyone, so now do we not desire it.[20]

When Nikolaus Poppel offered to arrange for Ivan's daughter to marry Frederick's nephew, the margrave of Baden, Ivan's response was equally peremptory. "It is not fitting," read the instructions he gave to his own ambassador. The lineage of the rulers of Muscovy was more ancient than that of the Habsburgs. "How could such a great sovereign hand over his daughter to that margrave?"[21] When, in answer to the prophets who foresaw the imminent end of the world, Patriarch Zosima of Moscow recalculated the calendar in 1493, he took the opportunity to reinvent "the pious and Christian-loving Ivan" as "the new Czar Constantine", in allusion to the first Christian emperor, who founded Constantinople. Moscow, he continued, was "the new city of Constantinople, that is to say, The New Rome". Soon after, a false genealogy circulated in Muscovy, tracing the dynasty back to a mythical brother of Augustus, first emperor of Rome. In a work addressed to either Ivan III or his son, a pious monk, Filofei by name, in the frontier-state of Pskov proclaimed Moscow "the Third Rome" after Rome itself and Constantinople. The first had fallen through heresy. The Turks

used their scimitars and axes to cleave the doors of the second Rome, ... and here now in the new, third Rome, your mighty empire, is the Holy Synodal Apostolic Church, which to the ends of the universe in the Orthodox Christian faith shines more brightly than the sun in the sky. Pious czar, let your state know that all Orthodox empires of the Christian faith have now merged into one, your empire. You are the only czar in all the Christian universe.[22]

Filofei called Orthodoxy "synodal" to distinguish it from Catholicism, which exalted the pope above other bishops.

In endorsing the notion of the third Rome, Ivan appropriated what seems originally to have been a propaganda line spun in Novgorod to exalt that city's bishop as a rival to Moscow's. In 1484, the clergy of Novgorod elected a bishop whom Ivan rejected, and claimed that Novgorod had received a white cowl from Rome at the behest of Constantine, the first Roman emperor, as a sign that "in the third Rome, which will be Russia, the Grace of the Holy Spirit will be revealed".[23] Towards the end of his reign Ivan adopted a new seal: a double-headed eagle, which, whether he copied it from the Byzantines or from the Holy Roman Empire, was an unmistakably imperial motif.

He rebuilt Moscow to clothe it in grandeur befitting its new imperial status and, perhaps, to array it for the apocalypse expected in 1492. The new palace chapel of the archbishop of Moscow was dedicated to Our Lady's Robe – a holy relic that had protected Constantinople many times before the failure of 1453. There could be no clearer symbol that Moscow had taken over Constantinople's former sanctity. Other buildings contributed to the general embellishment of what was still a modest-looking city, built mainly of wood. The Kremlin acquired formidable brick walls. Agostino Fioravanti – one of Ivan's imported Italian engineers – made the Cathedral of the Assumption rise over the city in gleaming stone in celebration of the conquest of Novgorod. In the 1480s the Cathedral of the Assumption followed to provide a space for the czar to worship in, while the archbishop's palace acquired a sumptuous new chapel. Other Italian technicians built a new audience chamber for Ivan, the Palace of Facets.

By taking his wife from Rome and architects from Italy, Ivan tugged the Renaissance eastward. He set a trend that reached Hungary in 1476, when King Mathias Corvinus married an Italian princess, abandoned the gothic plans for his new palace, and remodelled it on Italian lines in imitation of one of the most famous architectural texts of antiquity: the younger Pliny's description of his country villa. One of the Italian humanists the king employed was explicit about the building's inspiration. "When you read," he told Mathias, "that the Romans created gigantic works that proved their magnificence, you do not permit, invincible prince, that their buildings should surpass yours, . . . but you revive once again the architecture of the ancients."[24] The king also compiled a much envied classical library. Over the next couple of generations, Renaissance taste would dominate the courts of Poland and Lithuania. Revulsion from Catholicism made Russia a tough environment for Latin culture of any sort, but Ivan showed at least that the cultural frontier was permeable.

Ivan turned Russia into the uncontainable, imperial state that has played a major role in global politics ever since. In his reign, the extent of territory nominally subject to Moscow grew from fifteen thousand to six hundred thousand square kilometres. He annexed Novgorod and wrenched at the frontiers of Kazan and Lithuania. His priorities lay in the West. He defined Russia's championship of Orthodoxy. He drew a new frontier with Catholic Europe, but, while excluding Catholicism, he opened Russia to cultural influences from the West. He discarded the Mongol yoke and reversed the direction of imperialism in Eurasia. From his time on, the pastoralists of the central Asian steppes would usually be victims of Russian imperialism rather than empire makers at Russian expense. In all these respects the influence of his achievements has endured and helped shape the world in which we live, in which Russia seems to teeter on the edge of the West, never utterly alien but maddeningly unassimilable. But the most striking effect of his reign on the subsequent history of the world has usually gone unremarked: the opening of Russia's way east, towards what contemporaries called "The Land of Darkness" – Arctic Russia and Siberia, which, of all the colonial territories European imperialists conquered in the sixteenth and seventeenth centuries, is the only land where empire endures today.

Here, to the north-east, Ivan's armies ventured into little-known territory, along a route explored by missionaries in the previous century, following the River Vym towards the Pechora. The object of this thrust into the Land of Darkness was the effort to control the supply of boreal furs – squirrel and sable – for which there was enormous demand in China, central Asia, and Europe. Sable was black gold, and fur was to the Russian empire what silver was to Spain's and spices to Portugal's. In 1465, 1472, and 1483, Ivan sent expeditions beyond the reach of Novgorod's empire, to Perm and the Ob, with the aim of imposing tribute in furs on the tribespeople who lived there. The biggest invasion was that of 1499, when the city of Pustozersk was founded at the mouth of the Pechora. Four thousand men crossed the Pechora on sleds in winter and made for the Ob, returning with a thousand prisoners and many pelts. Ivan's ambassador in Milan claimed that his master received a thousand ducats' worth of fur in annual tribute. The region remained occluded by myth. When Sigmund von Herberstein served as the Holy Roman Emperor's envoy to Moscow in 1517, he picked up some of the stories of monstrously distended giants, men without tongues, "living dead", fish with men's faces, and "the Golden Old Woman of the Ob". Nonetheless, by comparison with the previous state of knowledge, Russian acquaintance with the boreal north and with Siberia was transformed by the new contacts.

Something of the feel of this new adventure is detectable in the testament Ivan left at his death. The laws of succession of Muscovy were vague. That is why Ivan's father had fought long wars against his cousins. Ivan imprisoned two of his own brothers. In an attempt to pre-empt rebellions, every ruler of Muscovy left a testament, bequeathing his lands and revenues to his heirs. Ivan's conquests made his testament especially long, brimming with the names of exotic communities and distant frontiers. After pages devoted to the many communities gained from Lithuania, and among lists of the appurtenances and possessions of the independent Russian principalities Muscovy had absorbed, with the territories Ivan confiscated from his brothers, the document turns to the eastern borderlands and the strange, vast empire acquired with the conquest of Novgorod. The Mordvins appear – pagan forest dwellers, speakers of a Finnic tongue, who occupied the slopes of the Urals and the strategic frontier along the northern border of Kazan. The lands of their neighbours the Udmurts are listed, which Ivan seized in 1489. The "Vyatka land" is mentioned – but not its once indomitable people. These herdsmen of the northern plains had tried to remain independent by shifting allegiance between the Russians and the Mongols. When Ivan lost patience with them, he invaded with overwhelming force, put their leaders to death, carried off thousands of Vyatkans into captivity, and resettled their territory with reliable Russians. Novgorod's territories are painstakingly enumerated, with eighteen places dignified as cities, and the five provinces into which the territory was divided, stretching north to the White Sea and, beyond Novgorod's colonial lands, the valley of the northern Dvina, and the savage tributaries known as the Forest Lop and the Wild Lop. Pskov is bestowed, even though it remained a sovereign city-state, allied with Ivan but outside his empire.

And from the pages of Ivan's testament, the sources and rewards of his success gleam. After bestowing sealed coffers of treasure to various heirs, and the residue of his treasury to his successor, Ivan listed the small change of empire:

> rubies, and sapphire, and other precious stones, and pearls, and any articles of dress decorated with precious stones, and belts, and golden chains, and golden vessels, and silver ones, and stone ones, and gold, and silver, and sables, and silk goods, and divers other belongings, whatever there is, as well as whatever is in the treasury of my bedchamber – icons and golden crosses, and gold, and silver, and other belongings – and whatever is in the custody of my major-domo . . . and my palace secretaries – silver vessels and money, and other belongings

and similar hordes in the care of other officials and in provincial palaces, "my treasure and my treasures, wherever they shall be".[25]

The year 1492 was the decisive one for the reign, not only because the world failed to end but also because a new world began for Russia when Casimir IV died. His sons divided his inheritance. The only power capable of challenging Muscovy in the vast imperial arena between Europe and Asia dissolved. The frontier between Orthodoxy and Catholicism wavered a great deal in future centuries, but it never strayed far from the lines laid down in the treaties Ivan and his son made with Casimir's heir. Muscovy became Russia — recognisably the state that occupies the region today. Russia was able to turn east towards the Land of Darkness and begin to convert the great forests and tundra into an empire that has remained Russia's ever since.

Chapter 7

"That Sea of Blood"

Columbus and the Transatlantic Link

12 October: Columbus lands in the New World.

The story is incredible but irresistible. As Ferdinand and Isabella rode into Granada, only one of the followers who thronged their camp was unable to enjoy the triumph. After years of striving for the monarchs' patronage, Christopher Columbus had just learned that a committee of experts had rejected his proposal for an attempted crossing of the Western Ocean. He turned his back on the celebrations and rode off disconsolately, knowing that his suit had finally failed.

After a day on the road, a royal messenger overtook him and demanded his immediate return to the royal tent outside the fallen city. A change of heart had come suddenly, like all the best miracles. Columbus made the first leg of his transatlantic journey on the back of a mule, bound for Granada.

It sounds like a romanticised version of the real story. But history has all the best stories, which fiction can never excel. What really happened to Columbus is far more interesting than any of the heroic myths his life has generated.

Columbus's proposal was unoriginal. Several attempts were made during the fifteenth century to explore Atlantic space, but most doomed themselves to failure by setting out in the belt of westerly winds, presumably because explorers were anxious for a guaranteed route of return. You can still follow the tiny gains in the slowly unfolding record on rare maps and stray documents. In 1427, an otherwise unknown voyage by a Portuguese pilot called Diogo de Silves was recorded on a map: Silves established for the first time the approximate relationship of the islands of the Azores to one another. Between 1452, when the westernmost islands of the Azores were discovered, and 1487, when the Fleming Ferdinand van Olmen was commissioned to seek, like Columbus, "islands and mainlands" in the ocean, at least eight Portuguese commissions survive for voyages into the recesses of the Atlantic. None, however, is known to have made any further progress. They departed from the Azores, where the westerlies beat them back to base. In 1492 in Nuremberg, Martin Behaim's friends and supporters were advocating the same point of departure for their own dreamed-of Atlantic crossing, which never materialised.

Not only was an Atlantic crossing impracticable, to judge from these precedents; until very recently, it had also seemed unlikely to be profitable. Until the 1480s, exploitation of the Atlantic yielded few returns, outside Madeira, which became a major contributor of taxation to the Portuguese crown thanks to sugar planting in the mid-fifteenth century. Explorers' hope of establishing direct contact with the sources of West African gold proved illusory, though access to gold at relatively low prices improved as a result of increased trade with native kingdoms. This trade produced other saleable articles for European markets – especially, from 1440, increasing numbers of slaves, whom Portuguese desperadoes also obtained by raiding. But even for these, markets were limited, because great slave-staffed plantations of the sort later familiar in parts of the Americas hardly existed in Europe, where slaves' roles were still largely in domestic service. The Canary Islands, meanwhile, attracted a good deal of investment because they produced large amounts of natural dyestuffs and seemed potentially exploitable for sugar: but their inhabitants fiercely resisted European encroachments, and the conquest was long and costly.

In the 1480s, however, the situation changed. The sugar trade of Madeira boomed, carried by sixty or seventy ships in a single year. Meanwhile, in 1484, sugar refining began in the Canary Islands. In 1482, thanks to the new port at São Jorge da Mina, on West Africa's underbelly, large amounts of gold now began to reach European hands. In the same decade, Portuguese contact with the kingdom of Kongo began; voyages towards and around the southernmost tip of Africa encountered unremittingly adverse currents, but they also showed that there were westerly winds in the far South Atlantic, which might at last lead to the Indian Ocean. For the same decade, the port records of Bristol in England show an increasing throughput of North Atlantic commodities, including salt fish, walrus ivory, and products of whaling. English and Flemish merchants in Bristol and the Azores became alert to the investment opportunities. By the end of the decade it was obvious that Atlantic investment could yield dividends. Now it became easier to raise money for new enterprises, chiefly among Italian bankers in Lisbon and Seville.

But if the business climate was increasingly favourable to a new assault on the problems of Atlantic navigation, it was hard to find the right man for the job. Only a foolhardy or greenhorn explorer could make headway in Atlantic navigation. To get much beyond the Azores, you had to take a risk no previous adventurer had been willing to face: you had to sail with the wind at your back.

One of the extraordinary facts about the history of maritime exploration is that most of it has been done against the wind. To modern sailors it seems so strange as to be counter-intuitive, but it made perfect sense for most of the past – simply because explorers of the unknown needed to be sure of their route home. An adverse wind on the outer journey promised a passage home. To break the mould and sail outwards with the wind, an explorer would need to be very ignorant or very desperate.

Christopher Columbus was both. He was a Genoese weaver's son with a large, clamorous, and exigent family. The Catalan, French, Galician, Greek, Ibizan, Jewish, Majorcan, Polish, Scottish, and other increasingly silly Columbuses concocted by historical fantasists are agenda-driven creations, usually inspired by a desire to arrogate a supposed or confected hero to the cause of a particular nation or historic community – or, more often than not, to some immigrant group striving to establish a special place of esteem in the United States. The evidence of Columbus's origins in Genoa is overwhelming: almost no other figure of his class or designation has left so clear a paper trail in the archives. The modesty of his background makes his life intelligible. For what motivated him to become an explorer was a desire to escape from the world of restricted social opportunity in which he was born.

Only three routes of upward mobility were available to socially ambitious upstarts such as Columbus: war, the Church, and the sea. Columbus probably contemplated all three: he wanted a clerical career for one of his brothers, and fancied himself as "a captain of cavaliers and conquests". But seafaring was a natural choice, especially for a boy from a maritime community as single-minded as that of Genoa. Opportunities for employment and profit abounded.

Columbus's reading helped to put plans for seaborne adventure in his mind. The geographical books his biographers usually dwell on played little or no part. Columbus hardly began reading geography until he was middle-aged, and most evidence of his perusal of geographical texts dates from after he had begun exploring. Instead, as a young man and during the formative years of his vocation as an explorer, he read the fifteenth-century equivalent of pulp fiction: seaborne knightly romances and some of the more sensational saints' lives. The saints' lives included the old tale of St Brendan the Navigator, who set out in his curragh from Ireland and found the earthly paradise, and the legend of St Eustace, who suffered nobly while searching the seas for his sundered family. The typical chivalric story line started with a hero down on his luck – which was just how Columbus depicted himself in the self-indulgent pleas for sympathy that streamed from his pen. Usually the hero was the victim of some unfair derogation – a royal foundling or a noble scion stripped of his birthright. Columbus's frequent fantasies about noble ancestors whom he imagined for himself and his absurd claim that "I am not the first admiral of my line"[1] recall the tradition.

In many chivalric romances popular at the time, the hero's escape route into the world of acceptance was by way of seaborne derring-do, in the course of which he would sail to exotic lands, find an island or a remote realm, battle for it against giants and monsters and pagans, and become its ruler. The usual fade-out featured the hero marrying a princess. Cervantes satirised the tradition in *Don Quixote* when he made Sancho Panza ask the Don to make him "governor of some island, with, if possible, a little bit of the sky above it".[2]

Real lives sometimes reflected this kind of art. Earlier in the fifteenth century, the Portuguese prince the infante Dom Henrique, whom we inappropriately call Henry the Navigator, even though he never made more than a couple of short trips by sea, was a reader of chivalric and astrological literature – a combination fatal to a rational self-perception. He was a cadet of his dynasty but longed to be a king, and he assembled, at a cost he could ill afford, an entourage of lowlifes and desperadoes, whom he called his "knights and squires". They sustained their way of life mainly by piracy, at first, and increasingly by slave raiding along the African coast, where they called their adversaries "wild men of the woods" – the savage, hairy creatures who typically opposed knights in chivalric stories, paintings, and sculptures. They made repeated but always unsuccessful efforts to conquer a kingdom for Dom Henrique in the Canary Islands, most of which at the time remained in the hands of pelt-clad, goat-herding aboriginals, whose way of life was tribal and whose only weapons were literally sticks and stones. Through these shabby endeavours, Dom Henrique's followers kept up a chivalric pantomime, affecting such names from romance as Lancelot or "Tristram of the Isle", exchanging vows, and sometimes achieving admission to the order of chivalry, the Order of Christ, of which their leader was Grand Master, appointed by the Portuguese king.

The thug who called himself Tristram of the Isle was a paladin of the island of Madeira, which had been the *mise-en-scène* of a popular chivalric love story for about a hundred years before Dom Henrique ordered his men to colonise it. There Tristram lived the romance implied by his Arthurian name, exacting oaths of vassalage from the cutthroats who came to his island. No incident better captures the tenor of his life than a curious abuse of chivalric conventions in 1452. Diogo de Barrados, a knight of Henry's service, had been exiled to Madeira, where he served Tristram in his household like a knightly retainer, performing "honour and vassalage". Ever since Arthur and Lancelot, lords had tended to encounter sexual trouble with their ladies and household knights. In the present case, Diogo abused his status to seduce Tristram's daughter. The scene – laconically recounted in a royal pardon – in which Tristram chopped off the offender's pudenda and flung him into a dungeon, takes us into a strange world of mingled chivalry and savagery.

Among Henrique's followers, Bartolomeo Perestrello was one whose real life followed the trajectory of a chivalric novel. His grandfather was a merchant-adventurer from Piacenza, who followed the sort of advice that flowed from how-to business gurus in the Italy of his day. "Go west, young man," the career consultants of the day advised – to the underdeveloped, burgeoning Iberian Peninsula. Once established in Portugal, the Perestrello family climbed to the court when Bartolomeo's elder sisters clambered into the bed of the archbishop of Lisbon, who kept both of them as mistresses simultaneously. Service in Dom Henrique's household led Bartolomeo to a seaborne career and captaincy of the uninhabited little island of Porto Santo, near Madeira, which Henrique colonised, partly as a base for his operations in Africa and the Canaries, and partly in the hope of developing sugar plantations. To be "governor of some island" was, perhaps, not much of a career path from the margins of social acceptability in Portugal. But it brought Bartolomeo status in his own little world and nominal membership in the nobility.

Columbus knew Bartolomeo's story well, because he married his daughter. In the 1470s, Columbus was working as a sugar buyer for a family of Genoese merchants, shuttling between the eastern Mediterranean and the African Atlantic. When he frequented the island of Porto Santo, he picked up gleanings from the world of Dom Henrique, and he met Doña Felipa – who was probably one of the few noblewomen poor enough, marginal enough, and, by the time of their marriage, sufficiently ageing to contemplate such a miserable match. At the same time, Columbus made the acquaintance of the winds and currents of the African Atlantic. He acquired enough experience of Atlantic sailing to know two key facts: there were easterly winds in the latitude of the Canaries, and westerlies to the north. The makings of a successful round trip were therefore available.

If one discounts legends spun after his death, and his own self-aggrandizing account, it becomes possible to reconstruct the process by which Columbus formulated his plan. There is no firm evidence that he had any sort of plan before 1486; only pious deference to unreliable sources makes most historians date it earlier. Nor was the plan ever very clear in his own mind. Like any good salesman, he changed it according to the proclivities of his audience. To some interlocutors, he proposed a search for new islands; to others, a quest for an "unknown continent" presumed, in some ancient literature, to lie in the far Atlantic; to others, he argued for a short route to China and the rich trades of the Orient. Historians have got themselves into a tangle trying to resolve the contradictions. Really, however, the solution to the "mystery" of Columbus's proposed destination is simple: he kept changing it. The tenacious certainty most historians attribute to him was a myth he created and his earlier biographers enshrined. The adamantine Columbus of tradition has to be rebuilt in mercury and opal.

Indeed, what mattered to Columbus was not so much where he was going as whether, in a social sense, he would arrive. When he wrote – as we would now say – to "confirm the terms of his contract" with his patrons, he was clear about the objectives that mattered to him:

> so that from thenceforth I should be entitled to call myself Don and should be High Admiral of the Ocean Sea and Viceroy and Governor in perpetuity, of all the islands and mainland I might discover and gain, or that might thereafter be discovered and gained in the Ocean Sea, and that my elder son should succeed me and his heirs thenceforth, from generation to generation, for ever and ever.[3]

The Sancho Panza syndrome, the pursuit of vainglory in imitation of chivalric fiction, resounds in these lines. Outrageous claims for noble status and lavish rewards accompanied his negotiations with potential princely patrons for leave and means to make an attempted Atlantic crossing.

Social ambition crowded out other objectives. There was little room for the motives biographers have traditionally assigned him – scientific curiosity and religious fervour. He did show – not much at first, and hardly at all before his first voyage, but increasingly as he got older – some pride in how experience acquainted him with facts inaccessible from books. This is hardly evidence that he prefigured the empirical values of modern science; rather, it shows the effects of his tussles with learned sceptics who dismissed his generally wild theories about geography. Religion grew on him. The extraordinary, gruelling experiences of transatlantic exploration turned him – as traumas often do – towards God. And he found refuge from the embitterment and disillusionment that overcame him later in life in prophecy, mysticism, and such extremes of affected piety as appearing at court in chains and in the rough

habit of a friar. But the young Columbus evinced no particular religiosity. His head was hard and full of calculations.

He did come under the influence of the Franciscan friars who be-
friended him at their house in Palos, on Castile's Atlantic coast. They
belonged to the so-called spiritual wing of the order, valuing the spirit
of St Francis more than the order's rules and regulations. Their eager-
ness to evangelise and their urgent belief, which drove their vocation,
that the world would soon come to an end planted growing notions in
Columbus's mind. By the early 1490s, Columbus was beginning to incorporate one or two of their favourite images into his own rhetoric in
support of his schemes. He began to advocate encounter with and conversion of pagan peoples as part of the purpose of Atlantic exploration.
And – if his later recollections were right – he suggested to Ferdinand
and Isabella that the profits of his proposed voyage could be diverted to
the conquest of Jerusalem, which, according to the Franciscans' prophecies, would be the work of the "Last World Emperor" and one of the
events with which God would prepare the world for the apocalypse. The
monarchs, he said, smiled when he said it. Historians have usually supposed that theirs was a smile of scepticism, but really it was a smile of
pleasure. Ferdinand, as heir to the apocalyptic prophecies that had surrounded the kings of Aragon for centuries, rather fancied himself as the
Last World Emperor.

Going to sea made a critical difference to Columbus's religious life.
To medieval people, the sea was God's arena, where the winds were his
breath and the storms were his bolts and arrows. In the midst of the
ocean, Columbus was, like St Francis in his poverty, utterly dependent
on God. His references to religion then began to take on a solemnity
and profundity they never had before. Until then, Columbus seems
rather to have exploited other people's religiosity than to have felt it
himself.

In the late 1480s, his failure to attract patronage was not solely the
result of his egregious demands. None of the objectives he advocated

seemed convincing to most experts. New Atlantic islands might well exist. So many had been found that it was reasonable to suppose that others might await discovery. But new islands remoter than the Canaries and Azores would be less profitable to exploit, even supposing that they were suitable for the cultivation of sugar or of some other product in high demand. The possibility of finding an unknown continent – the Antipodes, as geographers called it – seemed remote. The balance of antique geographical lore was against it. And even if it existed, it was hard to see what good could come of it, compared with explorations that opened a new route to the rich pickings of Asia and the eastern seas. Finally, the idea that ships could reach Asia by crossing the Atlantic seemed strictly impossible. The world was too large. Ever since Eratosthenes had worked out the maths around the end of the third century BC, savants in the West had known roughly how big the world is. Asia was so far from Europe by the westward route that no ship of the day would be capable of making the journey. Supplies would be exhausted and drinking water would go foul while many thousands of miles remained to be traversed.

Yet during the 1470s and 1480s a minority of experts began to entertain the possibility that Eratosthenes was wrong and that the earth was a smaller planet than previously supposed. Readers will recall the story of Martin Behaim, the Nuremberg cosmographer who, in 1492, made the world's oldest surviving globe to capture the smallness of the world. And among his circle of correspondents was Paolo Toscanelli, whose reputation as a cosmographer shone in his native Florence, and who wrote to the Portuguese court urging an attempt to reach China via the Atlantic. Antonio de Marchena, a Franciscan astronomer who was prominent at the Castilian court, and who became one of Columbus's best friends and supporters, shared the opinion.

Under the influence of these theorists, Columbus began to turn from the fiction of chivalry to scour geographical books for evidence that the world is small. By misreading much of the data and misrepresenting the rest, he came up with a fantastically small estimate: at least

20 per cent smaller than in reality. He also argued that the eastward extent of Asia had traditionally been underestimated. It would be possible, he concluded, to sail from Spain to the eastern rim of Asia "in a few days".[4]

So, after many failures and shifts of pitch, the project he eventually succeeded in selling was for a westward voyage to China, possibly breaking the journey at Japan, or "Cipangu", as people called it then, which Marco Polo had located, with exaggeration, some fifteen hundred miles into the ocean beyond China. According to his own account of the final negotiations with his patrons, he stressed historical evidence that long-past rulers of China – whom he called by the title of "Grand Khan" affected by a dynasty dethroned in 1368 – had written to the popes expressing interest in Christianity. Piety cloaked the promise of the commercial and political advantages Columbus advertised at other times. Using "India" to mean "Asia", according to the usage of the time, he went on:

> And Your Highnesses decided to send me . . . to the said regions of India to see the said princes and their peoples and lands and how they were disposed and the manner whereby their conversion to our holy faith might be effected; and you ordered that I should not travel eastwards by land, as is customary, but rather only by way of the west, where, to this day, as far as we know for certain, no one has ever gone.[5]

Did Ferdinand and Isabella go along with this scheme? No document committed them to the goal Columbus set for himself. His commission referred only to "islands and mainlands in the Ocean Sea". The monarchs gave him letters addressed vaguely to "the most Serene Prince our dearest friend", which Columbus firmly intended to present to the ruler of China. The monarchs were, however, anxious about the gains Portugal was making as a result of Atlantic exploration. Portugal had access to gold from beyond the Sahara and was investigating routes into the Indian Ocean. Castile had gained no new offshore resources beyond the Canary Islands. When it became apparent that Columbus's project could be financed at no direct cost to the king and queen (the old non-sense about Isabella pawning her jewels to meet Columbus's costs is another myth), there seemed no reason not to let Columbus sail and see what would happen.

The key investors in the voyage – a group of Italian bankers in Se-ville and court officials in Castile and Aragon – had already collaborated in financing a series of expeditions of conquest in the Canary Islands, and were in a position to monitor the improving yields of Atlantic en-terprise. The three little ships and the men to crew them came from the port of Palos, thanks to the collaboration of the local fixer Martín Alonso Pinzón, who was, in effect, Columbus's co-commander and po-tential rival on the voyage. Martín Alonso commanded the *Niña*; his brother, Vicente Yáñez, was captain of the *Pinta*, leaving the flagship, *Santa María*, to Columbus – who henceforth rather grandiloquently called himself "the Admiral". By fitting the *Niña* with an all-square rig to match the other two vessels, the leaders of the expedition demon-strated their confidence that they would sail with following winds throughout the journey ahead.

They chose the Canaries as their point of departure. The reasons – though Columbus never explicitly declared them – are obvious. The ar-chipelago included the port of San Sebastián de la Gomera, the most westerly harbour at the disposal of a Spanish fleet. The latitude matched what most cartographers estimated to be that of Guangzhou, the most famed port in the Chinese world. From Gomera, on 6 September, they set their course due west. The plan was to keep going until they struck land.

It was more easily said than done. In the Northern Hemisphere, practised navigators could maintain their course by celestial navigation with the naked eye, keeping the noon sun by day and the Pole Star by night at a constant angle of elevation. Columbus claimed to be able to do this himself – but he was routinely, mendaciously self-congratulatory, and it would be rash to believe any of his claims. A story that probably originates in one of his own accounts of his exploits captures the way he used navigational instruments. On 24 September, after a series of phoney landfalls, malcontents among the crew murmured to each other that it was "great madness and self-inflicted death to risk their lives to further the crazy schemes of a foreigner who was ready to die in the hope of making a great lord of himself".[6] If crewmen did think that, they were right. "To be a great lord" was Columbus's driving force. Some of them argued that "the best thing of all would be to throw him overboard one night and put it about that he had fallen while trying to take a reading of the Pole Star with his quadrant or astrolabe". The story brilliantly evokes the outlandish boffin, practising in ungainly isolation his newfangled techniques while struggling on a rolling deck with unmanageable astronomical gadgets.

In principle, quadrant and astrolabe are easy to use to establish latitude. You fix on the Pole Star through a narrow sighting on a rod linked to an armature and read your latitude from the corresponding point on the attached scale. In practice, the technique is maddeningly unreliable on an unstable surface. Defeated – like everyone else at the time who tried to use navigational instruments – by the pitch and roll of the ship, Columbus never used his precious technology accurately. Instead, he relied on a less glamorous and more traditional way of keeping his course. He had a copy of a common navigator's almanac, which tabulated latitude according to hours of daylight. He kept track of time at night by a traditional method, observing the passage around the Pole Star of the Guard Stars in the constellation of the Little Bear. On 30 September, for instance, he counted nine hours for the duration of the night, which gave him a figure of fifteen hours of daylight. He then plucked the corresponding latitude from his table. Over the voyage as a whole, the errors he recorded exactly matched misprints in the table. The instruments were mere flummery, wielded like a conjurer's wands, to distract his audience from what was really going on.

An engraving illustrating one of the earliest editions of the first printed report of Columbus's voyage captures the image he wanted to convey: he appears alone on his ship, manipulating the rigging, as if there were no one else there to share his burden; he represents the epitome of solitary, friendless heroism, and a triumph of self-generated resource. Columbus was prey to anxieties about isolation, and fears – verging on paranoia – of the perfidy of those around him. He was an outsider in all company, a foreigner excluded from the almost ethnic loyalties that divided his crews: the Basques, who rioted together; and the men of Palos, who owed allegiance to the Pinzón clan.

Four further themes dominated Columbus's later memories of the voyage: phoney landfalls, which undermined the men's morale; fear, as the winds carried them westward, that they would never find a wind to take them home; increasing tension between co-commanders and between commanders and crew; and Columbus's own barely perceptible doubts, which afflicted him increasingly as the expedition spent longer and longer out of sight of land.

He searched for signs – the swirl and fall of songbirds – and began implicitly to liken the journey to the voyage of Noah's ark, recording or perhaps imagining visits of "singing landbirds" to his ship. The biblical allusions multiplied. On 23 September he reported "a high sea, the like of which was never seen before except in the time of the Jews when they fled from Egypt behind Moses".[7] Columbus's growing conviction that he had a sort of personal covenant with God was beginning to emerge; by the time he got back to Spain he had become a visionary, subject to periodic delusions in which a divine voice addressed him directly.

Columbus soon half-revealed to himself his own doubts of the distance to the Indies: a few days out from Gomera, he began to falsify the log, undercutting the number of miles in the figures he passed on to his men. Since his approximations of distance tended to be overestimates, the false log was more accurate than the one he kept for himself. His weakness for wishful thinking and his assumption that the ocean must be strewn with islands constantly excited hopes of land in the offing. The slightest indication – a chance shower, a passing bird, a supposed river – aroused expectations doomed to be dashed. On 25 September he declared himself certain he was passing between islands. He did not feel confident enough to turn aside to look for them, but he inscribed them on his chart. Meanwhile, he grew so alarmed at the crew's anxieties that he was glad of an adverse wind. "I needed such a wind," he wrote, "because the crew now believed that there were winds in those seas by which we might return to Spain."[8]

By the end of the first week in October, when patience must have been at a premium throughout the fleet, Columbus and Pinzón met for an acrimonious interview. They ought to have found land by now, if Columbus's calculations were right. Martín Alonso demanded a change of course to the south-west, where he expected Japan to lie. At first, Columbus refused on the grounds that it was "better to go first to the mainland". But his resistance was short-lived. On 7 October, attracted by those standbys of lost sailors – the flight of birds and the forms of clouds – or deflected, perhaps, by fear of mutiny, he altered course for the south-west. By 10 October, the men "could endure no more". That very night the crisis passed. The following day sightings of flotsam multiplied, and as night fell everyone seems to have been excitedly anticipating land. During the night, Columbus later claimed, he "had it for certain that they were next to land. He said that to the first man to call that he had sighted land he would give a coat of silk without counting the other rewards that the king and queen had promised."[9]

At two o'clock on the morning of Friday, 12 October, five weeks into their journey, a seaman straining from the rigging of Martín Alonso's ship set up the cry of "Land!" The agreed signal – a shot from a small cannon – rang out, and all three ships answered with praises to God. To the presumed chagrin of the lookout, Columbus claimed the reward for himself on the grounds that he had seen a light from land the previous night. Cupidity can hardly explain this stunningly unfair egotism. Columbus – in his self-appointed role as chivalric type – had to be the first to spy land, like the model hero of a Spanish version of the Alexander romance, in which Alexander sails to India and "Thus spake Alexander, the first of all his crew, / That he had seen the land ahead ere any seaman knew."[10]

What with unrecorded drift, the distortions of magnetic variation, and the untrustworthiness of the surviving fragments of his log, it is impossible to reconstruct Columbus's course with absolute confidence. Therefore, we do not know exactly where he made landfall. His descriptions of places and courses generally are too vague and too riven with contradictions to be reliable. His accounts of his travels are highly imaginative – almost poetic – and readers who take them literally crucify themselves in struggling to make sense of them. All that is certain about the first island he touched when he reached the Caribbean is that it was small, flat, fertile, dotted with pools, and largely protected by a reef, with what Columbus calls a lagoon in the middle, and a small spit or peninsula on the eastern side: this formed an exploitable natural harbour. It could have been almost any of the islands of the Bahamas and Turks and Caicos. The natives, according to Columbus, called it Guanahani. He christened it San Salvador. The island now called Watling is the least-bad match for his description.

To judge from the surviving materials, what impressed Columbus most were the natives. This does not necessarily reflect his own priorities, for his first editor, whose extracts from Columbus's papers are almost all we have of the explorer's account of his first voyage, was obsessed with the "Indians" of the New World. He selected what concerned them and, perhaps, left out much that did not. Four themes emerge from the narration of the encounter as we have it.

First, Columbus stressed the nakedness of the people he confronted. For some readers at the time, nakedness had negative connotations, rather as it might in the United States today, where it seems inseparable from lurid fears of sexual excess. Some late-medieval clerics were obsessed by fears of heretics whom they called "Adamites" and who supposedly believed that they were in a permanent state of innocence, which they signified by going naked, at least in their own congregations, where they were said to practise orgies of promiscuity. The sect seems to have existed only in overexcited minds. Hang-ups of this kind were not, how-ever, as common then as they are now. Most of Columbus's contempo-raries would have thought well of nakedness. For classically inclined humanists, it signified the sort of sylvan innocence ancient poets associ-ated with the "Age of Gold". For Franciscans, who were the source of the most marked religious influences on Columbus, nakedness was a sign of dependence on God: it was the state to which St Francis himself stripped to proclaim his vocation. Most readers at the time would probably have inferred that the people Columbus met were "natural men", free of the accomplishments and corruptions of civilisation.

Second, Columbus repeatedly compared the islanders with Canari-ans, blacks, and the monstrous humanoid races that were popularly supposed to inhabit unexplored parts of the earth. The purpose of these comparisons was not so much to convey an idea of what the islanders were like as to establish doctrinal points: the people were comparable with others who inhabited similar latitudes, such as Canarians and black Africans, in conformity with a doctrine of Aristotle's; they were physically normal, not monstrous, and therefore – according to a com-monplace of late-medieval psychology – fully human and rational. This qualified them as potential converts to Christianity.

Third, Columbus insisted on their natural goodness. He portrayed them as innocent, unwarlike creatures, uncorrupted by material greed – indeed, improved by poverty – and with an inkling of natural religion undiverted into what were considered "unnatural" channels, such as idolatry. By implication, Columbus's "Indians" were a moral example to Christians. The picture was strongly reminiscent of a long series of exem-plary pagans in medieval literature, whose goodness was meant to be a reproach to wicked Christians.

Finally, Columbus was on the lookout for evidence that the natives were commercially exploitable. At first sight, this seems at odds with his praise of their moral qualities, but many of his observations cut two ways. The natives' ignorance of warfare establishes their innocent credentials but also makes them easy to conquer. Their nakedness might evoke an idyll, but to sceptical minds it could also suggest savagery and similarity to beasts. Their commercial inexpertise showed that they were both uncorrupted and easily duped. Their rational faculties made them both identifiable as humans and exploitable as slaves. Columbus's attitude was ambiguous but not necessarily duplicitous. He was genuinely torn between conflicting ways of perceiving the natives.

Columbus spent the period from 15 October to 23 October reconnoitring small islands. His observations of the natives show that he felt – or wanted to convince himself – that they were, in his eyes, becoming more civilised or, at least, more astute. In one place, they knew how to drive a bargain. In another, the women wore a sketchy form of dress. In another, the houses were well and cleanly kept. Through sign language, or interpreted from the utterances of the natives, indications multiplied of mature polities, headed by kings. Though we cannot know where to place these islands on a map of the Caribbean, they occupy an important place in the map of Columbus's mind: serially aligned, leading onwards towards the imagined "land which must be profitable". In Columbus's imagination, the first big piece of gold reported to him, on 17 October, became an example of the coinage of some great prince.

The same tension of mounting expectations affected Columbus's perceptions of the natural world. He claimed to see hybrid plants that cannot have existed. He noted the abundance of mastic where none grew. He speculated about dyes, drugs, and spices, which, he admitted, he could not identify. He got around the Caribbean by kidnapping or cajoling native guides to accompany his vessels. The islands were linked by canoe-borne trade, and the local navigators had complete mental maps at their disposal, which some of them supplemented, on a later voyage, by laying out a scheme for Columbus, using beans and pebbles.

From Columbus's point of view, however, the trading prospects seemed desperately unpromising. One of the engravings accompanying his first printed report shows what he was after: in the lee of one of his island discoveries, a rich merchant galley lies, while merchants in oriental headgear and robes exchange rarities with natives onshore. The scene was fantastic, but Columbus was hoping to find such prospects opening in reality before his eyes, as proof that he was close to the prosperous economies of Asia. Instead, it seemed he had stumbled on a Stone Age obstacle course, where no one produced anything for which he would be able to find a market.

In his own mind at least, Columbus was approaching civilised lands and profitable trades. As he approached Cuba on 24 October, he assumed he was about to find Japan or China. When he got there, he took refuge in vague descriptions unrelated to reality. Everything was of the sweetest and fairest. As it became increasingly obvious that the inhabitants were poor and improbable trading partners, he began to advocate their evangelisation as an alternative justification for his enterprise. He adumbrated a vision of a purified Church peopled by unsullied innocents. Alternatively, the thought that the people could be enslaved to make up for the lack of other marketable goods kept obtruding. This was typical of Columbus, who never found it hard to simultaneously entertain incompatible thoughts.

Dissatisfied with Cuba, he tried to get away from the island, but adverse winds frustrated several attempts. Martín Pinzón, however, succeeded in making off on his own, and remained out of touch until the expedition was almost over. True to form, Columbus suspected his co-commander of disloyalty and seeking private gain. On 4 December, Columbus at last escaped from Cuba and stumbled upon Hispaniola. For two reasons, it was the most important island he was ever to find. In the first place, it produced fair quantities of gold. This was the making of Columbus's mission; without it, he would almost certainly have returned home to ridicule and obscurity. Second, the island housed an indigenous culture of sufficient wealth and prowess to impress the Spaniards. With some of the natives, Columbus could establish friendly relations – or so he thought – and fix in their territory the intended site of a future colony.

In what survives of his account, Columbus made little mention of the superior material civilisation of the islands. But the elaborate stonework

Natives' nudity and timidity symbolise innocence, while the king of Spain beholds Columbus's landfall. From a versified version of Columbus's report (1493).

and woodwork, the ceremonial spaces, the stone-lined ball courts, the stone collars, pendants, and stylised statues, the richly carved wooden thrones, the elaborate personal jewellery all combined to convince him that Hispaniola was his best find so far, with the most promising environment and the most ingenious inhabitants. "It only remains," he wrote to the monarchs, "to establish a Spanish presence and order them to perform your will. For . . . they are yours to command and make them work, sow seed, and do whatever else is necessary, and build a town, and teach them to wear clothes and adopt our customs."[11] In Columbus's changed perceptions of the people, all the agonies of Spain's future in the

New World were foreshadowed. A long-term colonial vision crowded out the quick pickings he formerly imagined – the exotic products, the commercial gain. In the unequal Arcady he now envisaged, the natives would be "civilised" in the Spaniards' image, and the colonists would be teachers as well as masters. The Spaniards could suck like leeches, build like bees, or spread an inclusive web like spiders. Neither Columbus nor any of his successors ever resolved the contradictions.

To understand the febrile mental condition that now overtook him, a leap of imagination is needed: what must it have been like to be isolated on what he called "that sea of blood", thousands of miles from home, surrounded by unknown perils, baffled by an unfamiliar environment, for which neither reading nor experience equipped Columbus or any of his men, and surrounded by the unintelligible babble and gestures of captive guides? Not surprisingly in these circumstances, his grip on reality wavered. At first, for instance, he was disinclined to believe the natives' stories of how they were hunted by cannibal enemies (though those stories were, in essence, true). Within a few weeks, however, he was entertaining far more bizarre fantasies: of islands populated respectively by Amazon women and bald men, of the enmity of Satan, "who desired to impede the voyage", of the proximity of the fabled Prester John (according to medieval legend, a Christian potentate, dwelling supposedly in the depths of Asia, who longed to join a Western crusade).

In these circumstances, he claimed to have a sudden revelation. On Christmas Eve, his flagship ran aground. At first he was inclined to blame the negligence of a lazy seaman, who, against orders, left a boy in charge of the tiller. On reflection, the next day he saw the outcome rather differently, as the result of treachery by "the men of Palos", who had begun by giving him a dud ship and ended by failing to ease it off the rocks. The wickedness of the crew seemed providentially ordained, as surely as that of Judas. "It was a great blessing," he wrote, "and the express purpose of God that the ship should run aground there." The event obliged him to leave some of his men behind – a garrison, which, he hoped, would become the kernel of a colony. The debris of the ship and the dregs of the crew would supply the needs of the moment. As if by a miracle, the ruin of the ship provided "planks to build the fort with and stocks of bread and wine for more than a year and seed to sow and the ship's boat and a caulker and a gunner and a carpenter and a cooper".[12]

The disaster turned Columbus's thoughts homeward. He had collected many samples of gold, pods of pungent chilli, rumours of pearls, and some human specimens in the form of kidnapped natives to show off back at court. He had discovered the pineapple, tobacco – "some leaves which must be highly esteemed among the Indians",[13] though he did not yet know what it was for – the canoe, and the hammock, a gift of Caribbean technology to the rest of the world and to seamen in particular. If he had not reached China or Japan, he had, he reflected, at least found "a marvel" – the realm of Sheba, perhaps, or the land from which the Magi bore their gifts of gold and aromatics.

On 15 January, he encountered a fair wind for home. Curiously, he began by setting a course to the south-east, but he quickly reverted to what had surely always been his plan: heading north, combing the ocean in search of the westerlies familiar to him from his early experiences of Atlantic navigation. All went fairly well until 14 February, when he ran into a terrible storm, which provoked the first of a long series of intense religious experiences that recurred at every major crisis of Columbus's life. He expressed a sense of divine election so intense that nowadays it would be regarded as evidence of suspect sanity. God had spared him for divine purposes; he had saved him from the enemies who surrounded him; "and there were many other things of great wonder which God had performed in him and through him".[14] After taking refuge in the Azores he arrived home, congratulating himself on a miraculous deliverance, via Lisbon. There he had three interviews with the king of Portugal – a curious incident that has aroused suspicions of his intentions. Martín Pinzón, from whom the storm had parted him, arrived at almost the same time, exhausted by the exertions of the voyage. He died before being able to present a report to the monarchs. Columbus had the field to himself.

Opinion was divided on Columbus's achievement. One court cosmographer called it a "journey more divine than human". But few other commentators endorsed Columbus's opinions. Columbus had to insist he had reached or approached Asia: his promised rewards from the monarchs depended on his delivering on his promises in that respect. In the opinion of most experts, however, he clearly could not have reached Asia, or got anywhere near it: the world was too big for that. Most likely, Columbus had just encountered more Atlantic islands, like the Canaries. He might have stumbled on "the Antipodes" – an opinion many humanist geographers entertained with glee. "Lift up your hearts!" wrote one of them, "Oh, happy deed! That under the patronage of my king and queen the disclosure has begun of what was hidden from the first creation of the world!"[15]

As it turned out, this was close to the truth: there really was a formerly unknown hemisphere out there. On a subsequent voyage, Columbus realised that he had indeed found what he called "another world". But his contract with the monarchs was linked to his promise of a short route to Asia, and he was obliged to insist he had delivered on that promise, in order to claim his rewards. The explorers who followed up his voyages later in the decade proved that his route led to a vast area of continuous land without any of the characteristics, peoples, or products Europeans expected to find in Asia. But they went on looking for a westward route to the East. Maps of the sixteenth century generally underestimated the breadth both of the Americas and of the Pacific Ocean. Only very gradually in the course of the sixteenth and seventeenth centuries did their true dimensions emerge.

Most of the gifts Columbus brought home had a certain exotic allure – captive natives, parrots, specimens of previously unknown flora – but no obvious exploitability. He did, however, have a small quantity of gold obtained from the natives by trade. And he claimed to have got near to its source. That alone made a return voyage worthwhile from the monarchs' point of view. He departed on 24 September 1493.

Columbus's course this time led sharply south of his former track to Dominica in the Lesser Antilles, along what proved to be the shortest and swiftest route across the Atlantic. Once he was back in the Caribbean, his picture of his discoveries crumbled. First, the stories of cannibals proved gruesomely true when the explorers stumbled on the makings of a cannibal feast on the island Columbus named Guadalupe. Then, more grisly still, he found on arrival on Hispaniola that the natives had massacred the garrison he left there; so much for the innocuous, malleable "Indians". Then, as he struggled to build a settlement, the climate proved deadly. What Columbus had praised as ideally salubrious turned out to be unbearably humid. His men grew first restive, then rebellious. There were reports – or were they later embellishments? – of ghostly wailings by night and of shadowy processions of headless men grimly greeting the famished colonists in the streets.

The disappointments masked a stunning achievement. Between them, Columbus's ocean crossings of 1492–93 established the most practical and most exploitable routes back and forth across the Atlantic, linking the densely populated belt of the Old World, which stretched from China cross southern and south-western Asia to span the Mediterranean, with the threshold of the richest and most populous regions of the New World.

Other explorers rushed to exploit the opening. In consequence, the 1490s were a breakthrough decade in Europe's efforts to reach out across the ocean to the rest of the world. In 1496 another Italian adventurer, backed by merchants in Bristol and the English crown, discovered a direct route across the North Atlantic, using variable springtime winds to get across and the westerlies to get back: his route, however, was imperfectly reliable and remained little developed, except for access to the cod fisheries of Newfoundland, for over a hundred years. Meanwhile, Portuguese missions to the Indian Ocean by traditional routes investigated whether that ocean was genuinely landlocked. In 1497–98, a Portuguese trading venture, commissioned by the crown and probably financed by Florentine bankers, attempted to use the westerlies of the South Atlantic to reach the Indian Ocean. Its leader, Vasco da Gama, turned east too early and had to struggle around the Cape of Good Hope. But he managed to get across the Indian Ocean anyway and reach the pepper-rich port of Calicut. The next voyage, in 1500, used the direct route without a serious hitch. Meanwhile, despairing of Columbus's increasingly erratic behaviour, Ferdinand and Isabella repudiated his monopoly and opened Atlantic navigation to his rivals. In 1498 Columbus effectively demonstrated the continental nature of his discoveries; before the decade was over, follow-up voyages by competitors confirmed the fact and traced the coastline of the New World from the narrows of the Central American isthmus to well south of the equator – probably at least to about thirty-five degrees south.

This breakthrough of the 1490s, which opened direct, long-range routes of maritime trade across the world between Europe, Asia, and Africa, seems sudden; but it is intelligible against the background of the slow developments in European technology and knowledge, and the acceleration of the benefits of Atlantic exploration in the previous decade. Was there more to it than that? European historians have long sought to explain it by appealing to something special about Europe – something Europeans had that others lacked, which would explain why the world-girdling routes, which linked the Old World to the New and the Indian Ocean to the Atlantic, were discovered by European enterprise and not by that of explorers from other cultures.

Technology is inescapably an area to search. It would, for instance, have been impossible for explorers to remain long at sea or return home from unfamiliar destinations without improved water casks and suitable navigational techniques. Most of the technical aids of the period, however, seem hopelessly inadequate to these tasks. Navigators relied on the sheer accumulation of practical craftsmanship and lore to guide them in unknown waters. Columbus's failure with the quadrant and astrolabe suggests a further conclusion: if such technology had been decisive, Chinese, Muslim, and Indian seafarers, who had access to similar tools centuries earlier, would have got farther faster than any of their counterparts from Europe.

The shipwright's was a numinous craft, sanctified by the sacred images with which ships were associated: the ark of salvation, the storm-tossed bark, and the ship of fools. In partial consequence, it was a traditional business, in which innovation was slow. Little by little, during the fourteenth and fifteenth centuries, Atlantic and Mediterranean schools of shipbuilding exchanged methods of hull construction. Atlantic and northern shipwrights built for heavy seas. Durability was their main criterion. Characteristically, they built their hulls plank by plank, laying planks to overlap along their entire length and then fitting them together with nails. Mediterranean shipbuilders preferred to begin with the frame of the ship. Planks were then nailed to it and laid edge to edge. The Mediterranean method was the more economical. It demanded less wood and far fewer nails: once the frame was built, most of the rest of the work could be entrusted to less-specialised labour. Frame-first construction therefore spread all over Europe until by the sixteenth century it was the normal method everywhere. For ships expected to bear hard pounding, however, in wars or extreme seas, it remained worthwhile investing in the robust effect of overlapping planks.

The ships that carried the early explorers of the Atlantic were round-hulled and square-sailed – good for sailing with the wind, and therefore for tracing the routes outwards from Iberia with the north-east trades and back via the Azores with the westerlies of the North Atlantic. Gradual improvements in manoeuvrability helped, as a result of tiny incremental improvements in rigging. In the fifteenth century, ships with at least one triangular sail appeared in the African Atlantic with increasing frequency – and sometimes with two or three, suspended on long yards attached by ropes to masts raked at an acute angle to the deck. These craft, usually called caravels, could sail close to the wind, tacking within much narrower confines than a conventional vessel when trying to beat their way across the path of the trade winds without being forced too far to the south: typically, caravels could maintain a course only thirty degrees off the wind. They were useful along the African coast but made no contribution to transatlantic sailing. Columbus scrapped the triangular rig of one of his ships in favour of the traditional square sails.

If technology cannot explain what happened, then most of the cultural features commonly adduced remain unhelpful, either because they were not unique to the western European seaboard, because they are phoney, or because they were not around at the right time. The political culture of a competitive state system was shared with South-east Asia and with parts of Europe that contributed nothing to exploration. The explorers of the modern world operated among expanding states and emulous competitors in every continent. Christianity was less conducive to commerce than Islam or Judaism, among other religions that value the merchant life as a means to virtue. The tradition of scientific curiosity and empirical method was at least as strong in Islam and China in what we think of as the late Middle Ages (though it is true that a distinctive scientific culture did become discernible later in Europe and in the parts of the Americas settled from Europe). Missionary zeal is a widespread vice or virtue, and – though most of our histories ignore the fact – Islam and Buddhism both experienced extraordinary expansion into new territories and among new congregations, at the same time as Christianity, in what we think of as the late Middle Ages and early modern period. Imperialism and aggression are not exclusively white vices. We have seen evidence of only one feature of European culture that did make the region peculiarly conducive to breeding explorers. They were steeped in the idealisation of adventure. Many of them shared or strove to embody the great aristocratic ethos of their day – the "code" of chivalry. Their ships were gaily caparisoned steeds, and they rode the waves like jennets.

The Atlantic breakthrough is part of a huge phenomenon: "the rise of the West", "the European miracle" – the elevation of Western societies to paramountcy in the modern history of the world. Thanks to the displacement of traditional concentrations of power and sources of initiative, the former centres, such as China, India, and parts of Islam, became peripheral, and the former peripheries, in western Europe and the New World, became central. Yet Europeans' leap into global maritime prominence was not, it seems, the outcome of European superiority, but of others' indifference and the withdrawal of potential competitors from the field. The Ottoman seaborne effort was stunning by the standards of the day. But straits stoppered it in every direction. In the central Mediterranean, the Persian Gulf, and the Red Sea, access to the oceans was through narrow channels easily controlled by enemies.

In other parts of the world to which we must now turn, opportunities were limited or neglected. Russia – overwhelmingly and inevitably in the face of an icebound ocean, despite the heroism of monks who colonised islands in the White Sea in the fifteenth century – was focused on expanding to landward. Chinese naval activity was aborted in the fifteenth century, probably as a result of the triumph at court of Confucian mandarins, who hated imperialism and despised trade. Civilisations in most other parts of the world had reached the limits of seaborne travel with the technology at their disposal, or were pinioned by winds or penned by their own diffidence. To understand Europe's opportunity, we have to explore potentially rival regions. We can start by following Columbus's imaginary trajectory, to China and the world of the Indian Ocean, and see what was happening there in and around 1492.

Chapter 8

"Among the Singing Willows"

China, Japan, and Korea

Jen-tzu — fifteenth day of the seventh month: Shen Zhou
paints a mystical experience.

Usually, when he could not sleep, the painter lit his lamp and read. But reading could never bring rest to his mind. One summer's night in 1492, he fell asleep to the sound of the rain. Suddenly, a cold gust nipped him into wakefulness.

The rain had ceased. He rose and dressed and spread a book, as usual, under the flickering candlelight. But he was too tired to read. So he just sat there in unrelieved silence, under an almost lightless moon, with the shutters drawn back to let in the rain-freshened air. Squatting on a low bench, he spent the rest of the night gazing vaguely into the darkness of the narrow courtyard of his house. He sat, as he recalled the next morning, "calmly doing nothing".

Gradually, he began to notice sounds. Wind breathed somewhere in clumps of faintly rustling bamboo. Occasionally, dogs growled. The watchmen's drumbeats marked the passage of hours. As the night lifted and faint daylight spread, the painter heard a distant bell. He became aware of senses he usually repressed, and of little life-enhancing experiences you cannot find in books. He began to get from the world the insights he strove to convey in painting: true perceptions, which penetrate appearances and reach the heart and nature of things. All sounds and colours seemed new to him.

"They strike the ear and eye all at once," he said, "lucidly, wonderfully, becoming a part of me."

Not only did he make a written record of the experience. He also painted it, in ink and colours, on a scroll of paper designed to be weighted and hung on a wall. The painting survives. In the centre of the composition, the painter is a tiny, hunched figure, wrapped in a thin robe, with a knot of hair gathered on his balding head. His low-burned light is beginning to get smoky on the table beside him. All around, the hazy light of dawn discloses immensities of nature that dwarf the painter and his flimsy house. Tall, great-rooted trees reach up, craggy cliffs rise, with mountains bristling in the background. But all their power seems to flow into the little man in the middle, without disturbing his tranquillity.

When he finished the scroll, he signed it with his name: Shen Zhou. He was sixty-five years old, and one of China's most celebrated painters. Because he was rich in his own right, he was almost uniquely privileged among the painters of the world in his day. He could resist the lures of patrons, and paint what he wanted.[1]

Meanwhile, on the other side of the world, another individual with mystical inclinations, and a habit of staying up late at night, was struggling to imagine what China was like. Christopher Columbus was on his way there. At least, that was what he hoped. Or at least, that was what he said.

While Shen Zhou strove for calm and meditated in serenity, Columbus could not resist restlessness and operated in a violent and unstable part of the world. Readers of the last chapter will recall his story. Poor but ambitious, of modest means and few prospects, he had tried every

Shen Zhou recorded his
nocturnal vigil in this sketch,
in which he portrays himself
dwarfed by nature, as well as a
long prose account.

available means of escape into a world of wealth and grandeur: he had
tried enlisting in war; he had thought of embracing a career in the
Church; he had striven unsuccessfully to accumulate a fortune as a
small-time merchant, shipping sugar and gum around the Mediterranean and the eastern Atlantic. We have seen how he had married –
lovelessly, it seems – a minor aristocrat's daughter, without achieving
much social elevation as a result. He had modelled his life on fiction,

trying to live like the hero of the fifteenth-century equivalent of a popular novel – a seaborne tale of chivalric romance.

At last, in the attempt to get someone rich to back him to undertake a voyage of discovery, he hit on the idea of proposing a shortcut to China, westward, across the ocean, "where", he said, "as far as we know for certain, no one has ever gone". Doubts tortured him. No one knew how far away China was, but Europe's geographers were almost united in the knowledge that the world was too big to be easily encompassed by the feeble ships available at the time, with their limited means of stowing fresh food and water. China was so far away, consensus averred, that Columbus and his crew, if they ever got there, would be dead on arrival. For an escapee from failure and poverty, though, the risk seemed worth taking. The bankers in Seville – Spain's Atlantic-side boomtown – who backed Columbus did not have to risk much. And if he pulled off the feat he promised, the profits might be dazzling.

One of the inspirers of Columbus's enterprise, the Florentine geographer Paolo Toscanelli, had pointed out the possibilities: "[T]he number of seagoing merchants in China is so great that in a single noble port city they outnumber all the other merchants of the world. . . . Westerners should seek a route there, not only because great wealth awaits us from its gold and silver, and all sorts of gems, and spices such as we never obtain, but also for the sake of China's learned sages, philosophers, and skilled astrologers."[2]

Europeans did not know much about China, but they knew it was the biggest, richest market, the most productive economy, and the most powerful empire in the world. Beyond that, their detailed information was all out of date. Until about a hundred years before, contact with China had been fairly extensive. Merchants and missionaries shuttled back and forth along the Silk Roads that crossed the mountains and deserts of central Asia, spreading commodities and ideas through the continent and the world. For a while, in the thirteenth and early fourteenth centuries, it had even been possible to take a fast-track route on horseback across the Eurasian steppe – the great, arid, windswept prairie that arcs from the Hungarian plain, almost without interruption, across Mongolia to the Gobi and the threshold of China. Mongol imperialists united the entire route, conquered China, policed the Silk Roads, and facilitated communications throughout the breadth of the lands they ruled.

But in 1368 a revolution in China expelled the heirs of the Mongols and ruptured the roads. The last recorded European mission to China had made its way through in 1390. Since then, silence had enshrouded the distant empire. The only detailed description still available in Europe was even more antiquated – compiled towards the end of the thirteenth century by Marco Polo. As we have seen, Columbus and his contemporaries still thought of the emperor of China as the Great Khan – a Mongol title no Chinese ruler had borne since the revolution of 1368. Much as they longed for Chinese goods, they knew virtually nothing – yet – of porcelain or tea, the Chinese exports that would transform European taste in succeeding centuries.

They were right, however, about one thing: contact with China could provide unprecedented opportunities for Europeans to get rich. Ever since Roman times, Europeans had longed to break into the world's wealthiest arena of exchange but had always laboured under apparently insuperable disadvantages. Even when they could get to China, or to the other fabulously opulent markets around the Indian Ocean and on the shores of maritime Asia, they had nothing to sell. Their remote, peripheral corner of Eurasia was too poor. As a fourteenth-century Italian guide to the China trade complained, European merchants bound for China had to take silver with them – at the risk of impoverishing Europe further by draining bullion eastward – because the Chinese would accept nothing else. At the frontier, they had to hand the silver over to imperial customs officials and accept paper money in exchange. This, for the backward Europeans, was a novelty that demanded explanation and reassurance.

By the fifteenth century, although Europeans did not yet know it, changes in the economic situation in China, and in East Asia generally, were creating new opportunities, for silver was rising spectacularly in value in China relative to other Asian markets as people's confidence in paper and copper currency wavered. Anyone who could shift silver from India and Japan, where it was relative cheap, to China, where it could be exchanged for gold or goods on favourable terms, stood to make a fortune. If Europeans could get their ships to Eastern ports, they could profit from the differentials.

These new circumstances created conditions in which the history of the world could unfold in new, unprecedented ways. Columbus's scheme for reaching China was part of a potentially world-transforming outreach that would, eventually, put the economies of East and West in touch and integrate them into a single, global system. Access to Eastern markets would unlock riches Westerners had formerly only dreamed of and enable them to begin to catch up with the richer economies and more powerful states that, previously, had dominated the world.

Columbus, however, never made it to China. On his first voyage, he stumbled on Caribbean islands where he warped the locals' name, "Caniba", into "people of the khan" and fantasised about his presumed proximity to the Orient. When he got home, engravers illustrated his reports of the poor, naked people he encountered with pictures of Chinese traders doing business offshore. When Columbus returned in 1493, he sailed around part of Cuba and made his crew swear that it was no island but a promontory of the Chinese mainland. On subsequent voyages, though he realised he was in "another world", he continued to hope that China was nearby – through an undiscovered strait, or around some cape that lay just beyond his reach.

If he had got to his objective, what would he have found?

China was the nearest thing to a global superpower the world then knew: bigger and richer than all its possible competitors combined. The disparity of population was decisive. The statistics accumulated at the time were fragmentary and delusive, as millions of people successfully concealed themselves from the state in order to avoid taxes and forced labour. China had the most sophisticated census-making methods in the world, but the figure of less than sixty million people reported by the empire's statisticians in 1491 is certainly a serious underestimate. China had perhaps one hundred million people, whereas the whole of Europe mustered only about half that number. The size of the market and the scale of production matched the level of population. China's giant economy dwarfed that of every other state in the world. The empire's huge surplus of wealth distorted the economies of all the lands that looked to China to generate trade, from Europe, across Asia and the Indian Ocean, to Japan. China produced so much of everything that there was little demand for imported goods. The luxuries China did import, however, especially spices, aromatics, silver, and (more problematically) the warhorses of which China could never get enough, commanded prices that left buyers from elsewhere in the world marginalised.

A snapshot view of China at the time is available – but not, of course, from Western sources. A Korean official shipwrecked on the Chinese coast in 1488, and detained in the country while state officials investigated his status, wrote up his experiences and observations. Contemporaries in Korea disbelieved his account, which he was obliged to defend at court in 1492. His education in the Confucian classics and admiration for Chinese culture certainly influenced him. Still, the diary Ch'oe Pu compiled on his long journey by canal from the coast to the capital, and back to Korea by road, is a unique and vivid record by a keen observer, describing – as a sixteenth-century editor put it – "the ever-changing ocean, mountains, rivers, products, people, and customs all along the way".[3] The Chinese, he found, recognised Korea as "a land of protocol and morality"[4] – a land like theirs, producing people they could deal with. But the unfamiliarity of strangers evoked surprise and suspicion. In almost every encounter Ch'oe Pu had, his hosts began by thinking evil of him: he was, they assumed, a Japanese pirate or a foreign spy. At times during his struggles to prove his identity, "it would have been easier to die at sea".[5] He clearly did not speak Chinese, but he made himself understood by writing everything down in the characters the Korean language had borrowed from China. Even learned interlocutors found his strangeness puzzling. "Why," asked one of them in a typical conversation, "when your carriages have the same axle-width and your books the same writings as those of China, is your speech not the same?"[6]

Even so, Ch'oe Pu was disposed to admire China and found plenty to justify his admiration. He encountered robbers mild enough to return his saddle. When he displayed his certificates, officials showed due respect for the high place he had attained in Korea's civil-service examinations.[7] As his party trekked northward from the remote spot on the Chekiang coast where his ship came to grief, Chinese officials hustled and hurried them along with extraordinary efficiency, even a touch of officiousness. In eight sedan chairs at first, and then by boat along China's great network of rivers and canals, with a military escort, they struggled through, regardless of weather. "The laws of China are strict," the guard commander told Ch'oe Pu, who wanted to halt in the teeth of a storm. "If there is the slightest delay, we will be punished" – and he was right. When they arrived at Hangchow, after less than a fortnight on the road and with only one day's rest, his zeal was rewarded with a flogging for having made poor time. It was unjust, but it was law. In China, laws served as deterrents, to fulfil a Confucian principle: punishments should be so severely deterrent that they need never be enforced.

Ch'oe Pu approved of this principle, and, in general, of the well-regulated nature of the state. Western historians have long engaged in pointless conflict in an attempt to identify the "first modern state" – some locating it in England, others in France or the Spanish empire, or the Netherlands or even Lithuania. China had already exhibited the key characteristics for centuries: internal sovereignty; central government; centrally appointed administrators; a uniform system of administration; uniform laws, currency, weights, and measures; rapid internal

communications; and a bureaucracy, chosen by merit, that made it unnecessary to devolve power locally or regionally into aristocratic hands.
Candidates for provincial magistracies – the officials who represented
the emperor and dispensed justice, enforced law, collected taxes, and
supervised security measures – were selected by examination in knowledge of the Confucian classics, writing essays that tested their powers
of marshalling arguments for and against various propositions and
choosing between them on moral and practical grounds. In the late fifteenth century, officials had to send in self-evaluations every six years,
and the lower ranks were winnowed by inspection by their superiors,
who collected complaints from any subject who claimed to have been
unfairly treated.

Above all, the wealth of China impressed Ch'oe Pu. Even in the
jungly, malarial region he first had to cross, he found that "the people
were thriving and the houses splendid". His description of Suzhou exudes the envy of a goggle-eyed window-shopper, awed by "all the treasures of the land and sea, such as thin silks, gauzes, gold, silver, jewels,
crafts, arts, and great and rich merchants". Markets multiplied like
stars; ships billowed like clouds. Life was luxurious. South of the Yang-
tze, where "towers look out on other towers, and boats ply stem to
stern", Ch'oe Pu found incomparable wealth and a model civilisation,
where "even village children, ferrymen, and sailors can read".[8] Parts of
the north and west of the country seemed less prosperous, with many
low, thatched dwellings and thinner settlement. To Ch'oe Pu's preju-
diced eyes, there was more barbarian influence in those zones, detectable in the violent dispositions of some of the inhabitants. Overall,
however, China fulfilled the visitor's hopes: his picture is of a land pros-
pering under the benign rule of an altruistic Confucian elite.

He was right about the power of the bureaucracy. China was already
a modern state, with an official class recruited – in theory – from all
ranks of society, on merit tested by examination in knowledge of the
Confucian classics. The emperor could not do without them. At intervals in the late fourteenth and fifteenth centuries, emperors tried to

dispense with them, ignore them, or replace them with rival elites: eunuch courtiers, for instance; army top brass; or Buddhist or Taoist
clergy. But the mandarins won every contest for power. Sometimes they
went on strike; sometimes they intimidated emperors with their sheer
intellectual superiority. They emerged from every crisis with a reinforced sense of their own indispensability.

Despite the power of the bureaucracy, other sources show that the
state was not easily able to tax China's wealth efficiently or turn that
wealth into effective military power. No province ever fulfilled its tax
quota. In the late fifteenth century, some provinces could not raise enough
revenue to pay their garrisons. From 1490 a series of famines struck the
tea-producing region of Xenzi, and the farmers devoted their wares to the
purchase of grain. By the 1490s, many military units were at less than 15
per cent of their nominal strength. While the army wilted for lack of
money, shortage of horses rendered it relatively immobile.

By long-standing custom, the state traded tea for horses with herdsmen in central Asia. The finest specimens came from beyond the deserts and mountains, from the land of Fergana, now spread across
Uzbekistan, Kyrgyzstan, and Tajikistan beyond the deserts and mountains. Meanwhile, wars in central Asia for control of Fergana interrupted the horse trade and threatened the security of China itself. In
1492 the Chinese thought they had brokered peace between the warring states, but the Chinese-nominated candidate for Fergana's disputed
throne was kidnapped en route to take up his position. Laboriously,
China had to muster strength for a punitive expedition. By 1497 they
had installed their candidate, but the warfare rumbled on, and China's
capacity for effective intervention slowly dwindled.

On the southern frontier, too, Ming imperialism faltered: early in the
history of the dynasty, China had not hesitated to intervene in the politics of South-east Asian states to ensure that power stayed in the hands of
regimes the Chinese approved of. But in the 1480s, when the ruler of
Vietnam launched an effort to turn South-east Asia into an empire of his
own, China did no more than issue a mild admonition to uphold Confu-

cian values, respect countries that paid tribute to China, care for his own people, and "act righteously". Military show played an important role in compensating for real strength. Ch'oe Pu was treated to "thousands of arms and shields" lining the walls of Yueh-ch'i (Xunjiang) with "masses of pennants" and the rumble of gongs and drums.[9]

Reading between the lines, moreover, we see that the political system Ch'oe Pu described had glaring imperfections. On the face of it, China looked like an exemplary modern state, with a bureaucracy and judiciary selected by merit, qualified by education and examination, and appointed and salaried by the government. In practice, there was never enough money to finance the system. The imperial family was a terrible burden on the exchequer. Every living descendant of the founder of the dynasty, by wives and official concubines who were often numerous, lived on a pension from the state, and the first Ming emperor had twenty-six sons. The numbers of imperial dependants grew exponentially. One prince had ninety-four children. Officials were paid in grain, and by the time shortfalls and conversion costs turned their appropriations into cash, they rarely received more than a tiny proportion – sometimes as little as 5 per cent of their nominal entitlement. Not that the salaries were fixed at generous rates anyway. In practice, officials had to be rich or corrupt or both. Ch'oe Pu sometimes had to bribe his way out of police custody. His diary shows how officials manipulated the reports they transmitted to court in order to spare the emperor from bad news. Data on piracy, banditry, and rural unrest and bureaucratic negligence were all edited out of documents the Korean saw compiled. Some officials deliberately misrepresented castaways as Japanese pirates in order to get the bounty money.

So the Chinese ideal of keeping political power out of the hands of the rich was unrealised in practice. Moreover, although the Confucian elite was supposedly a meritocracy, it had many of the pockmarks with which vices scar aristocracies. The examination system ensured that officials shared the same formation and outlook. The fact that most of them had to ascend through the same categories of service to the throne gave them a strong esprit de corps. They were united in veneration of Confucian values. They shared a conviction that the conduct of state business was their privilege as well as their responsibility. They joined in defence of their traditional social and economic advantages, which the emperors periodically tried to limit – especially exemption for themselves and their families from some forms of taxation. They formed a class, ten thousand strong, with a remarkably uniform set of self-perceptions and a profound jealousy of any outsiders who presumed to contend for power. They particularly resented the religious minorities who contended for power and influence at court: Buddhists, whom they suspected of amassing wealth in order to seize power, and Taoists, whose ancient religion they despised as magical mumbo-jumbo.

There were philosophical issues at stake: for Confucians, the gods were a remote and unintrusive influence, as long as the emperor performed the rites that supposedly kept heaven and earth in harmony. Buddhists and Taoists did not believe that the universe was so easily manageable, struggling for virtue and even for survival against a natural world that teemed with contentious spirits. Islam, which had arrived in China soon after the death of the prophet Muhammad, was still numerically insignificant, but it had a relatively large following among the court eunuchs. Eunuchs rivalled the bureaucratic mandarins for powerful posts at court, because they were dependants of the emperor and had none of the conflicts of interest that posterity brings.

Although eunuchs, Buddhists, and Taoists remained at loggerheads with the Confucian establishment, other parts of the elite were collaborating in exceptional ways. In the past, merchants and mandarins had often been at odds because of the scholars' contempt for commercial values. Now, however, there were signs of rapprochement. Strictly speaking, merchants were not allowed commemorative inscriptions on their tombs, because they constituted the lowest class of society, below peasants and artisans. "The gentry," according to a maxim of the early sixteenth century, "know how to orient themselves to study, the peasantry know to devote themselves to agriculture, and the merchants, while adept at trading, do not go beyond their station."[10]

But wealth circumvents conventions, as the case of Wang Zheng shows. He was one of the richest men in China, who inherited a fortune and made another of his own in the grain business. He had the privilege of a long and adulatory – but still informative – epitaph when he died, seventy years old, in 1495. To designate him as a merchant would be opprobrious, so he went down as "unemployed scholar", since he had studious habits from childhood. "His most cherished matters of heart," said the tombstone, "were ancient and contemporary calligraphy and paintings in ink." Though he claimed to detest his calling, and to have deserted it when he could for altruistic duties – philanthropic work or official employment as a magistrate's clerk – he was deft enough in business to acquire an art collection in which "the top paintings were truly priceless". His aspirations were focused on his sons, all of whom took civil-service examinations and pursued official careers.[11] Similar cases are known among salt merchants in Yangzhou. When one of the most successful of them, Fan Yenfu, retired in the mid-1490s, local officials presented him with a collection of scholarly writings – a sign of equality of eminence in the values that they all thought stamped the elite.

In some ways, confronting the Confucian establishment, the emperors of the Ming dynasty had long been the foremost outsiders. As they strove to balance the contending religious factions, the ruling dynasty chose to be called "Ming" in defiance of Confucianism, for the name was a Buddhist epithet. It denoted the "Brightness" anticipated in the fabled deity Lord Maitreya, who, according to one strand in Buddhism, would preside over the end of the world. Although successive emperors could hardly escape Confucian values during their education at court, the tension present at the foundation of the Ming dynasty remained. Emperors frequently tried to break the hold of the official class on power, but always failed. At different times, they tried empowering Buddhist or Taoist clergy to offset the influence of the mandarins. By 1486 there were 1,120 monks in official positions at court.

1492

Emperors employed thousands of eunuchs, to the disgust of the official class; there were as many eunuchs as mandarins in the service of the empire by the 1480s. Ch'oe Pu expressed surprise at eunuchs in power; in his country, he protested, they would be allowed only to sweep the palace and carry messages.[12] In China, they ran many departments of government, including the dreaded internal security agency, the so-called Western Depot, established in 1477 to seize and punish suspected traitors. But reliance on the mandarins to staff the provincial administration and the courts of law proved inescapable. Generally in the fifteenth century, moreover, emperors tended to be short-lived, and inherited "greybeard" mandarin counsellors from their fathers and grandfathers.

In the late fifteenth century, the Chinese imperial court was in the grip of a reaction in favour of the political power of the mandarin class – something like a Confucian revolution. In large part, this was because of a change of power at the top: the accession of an emperor thoroughly educated in Confucian pieties and deep in cahoots with the Confucian elite. Partly, however, it was a reaction against the spectacular growth, in preceding reigns, of the numbers, wealth, and power of the Confucians' enemies. Confucians traded hatred with Buddhists and Taoists. A judge who denounced the previous emperor's favourite monk as "a good-for-nothing vagabond from the marketplace" was beaten, demoted, and exiled. Other Confucian critics of the monks got the same treatment. A hundred thousand Buddhist and Taoist clergy were ordained in 1476. The following year, the emperor decreed that in the future, ordination ceremonies would take place only once every twenty years. The government also tried to tighten the qualifications for ordination in the Buddhist and Taoist hierarchies. Scandal broke out over the sale of ordination certificates – ten thousand of them, for instance, to raise money for famine relief in Shaanxi in 1484 – inflating the numbers. The certificates were blank; purchasers simply wrote in their names. "Unless we take timely measures," reported a concerned official in 1479, "in the worst situations they might gather together in the mountains and forests to plan criminal acts; and in less serious situations they might manufacture rumours to alarm people's minds. In any event, the harm they do is never small."[13]

The inflation of the Buddhist priesthood continued with another two hundred thousand ordinations in 1486. That very year, however, a new emperor came to the throne. Zhu Yutang, the Hongxi emperor, aspired to be a Confucian perfect prince. He ordered the death or expulsion of the sorcerers who thronged the previous emperor, and expelled over a thousand Buddhist and Taoist monks from court. He restored neglected rites, the reading of Confucian texts, the study of law, and the reform of judicial institutions. He embellished the Temple of Confucius in Qufu with a literary pavilion. When fire destroyed some Taoist institutions in Beijing in 1497, one of the emperor's chief ministers gloated unfeignedly: "If they had possessed numinous power, would they not have been protected by it? Heaven despises such filth."[14] Qixao, the Buddhist monk who occupied the informal position of favourite in the previous reign, was accused of peculation from state funds and dealing in aphrodisiacs. His head was chopped off in 1488.

In practice, however, the spiritual life of the court was woven of many strands, and it was hard to unwind Taoism and Buddhism from it entirely. The emperor still relied on Taoist magic for medicine. He favoured painters who produced celebrations of scholarship, but Confucian heroes never monopolised the artists' subject matter. The emperor's personal favourite was – on the face of it – a surprising choice: an eccentric drunkard from Nanjing, called Wu Wei. Wu became a painter, like so many impoverished mandarins, because his family could not afford to complete his scholarly education and get him a job in the imperial bureaucracy. His father had squandered the family fortune on experiments in alchemy – the sort of practice a Taoist might be prey to but which a good Confucian would eschew. Perhaps in recoil from the shame, Wu cultivated a bohemian reputation, snubbing patrons, whoring, and exhibiting crazy virtuosity – painting masterpieces when apparently so drunk that he could hardly stand, sometimes using his hands to paint

In Wu Wei's painting, a legendary Taoist saint contemplates the sea
with, underfoot, the miraculous crutch that will serve as a raft.

instead of brushes, or smearing the ink on to the paper or silk with bits of tableware. When he did use a brush, he gripped it tightly and wielded it boldly, stabbing and slashing at the surface with angular strokes. The results were stunningly brilliant. Yet despite these offences against propriety – and despite producing many works of Taoist piety for monastic paymasters – Wu knew how to please a Confucian patron.

To understand his appeal, it is worth comparing his work with that of his senior contemporary, Shen Zhou. Shen's mountains soar, his trees tower; the very air in his works seems to vibrate visibly with cosmic power. Human works and lives are reduced to specks in all this immensity. His most famous work, painted in 1487, now in the National Palace Museum in Taipei and known as *Rainy Thoughts*, recalls the tastes and circumstances revealed in the rain-induced mystical experience with which this chapter began. He realised that experience is incomplete until transformed, by some unseen power, into part of oneself. Until then, the bell and drum may as well be mute and the beauties of the landscape invisible. Sounds and vision die on the air. But when they register in the human mind, memory and art perpetuate them. The painter called this transmuting power "will".

"Sounds are cut off, colours obliterated; but my will, absorbing these, endures. What is the so-called will? Is it inside me, after all, or outside? Does it exist in external things or does it come into being because of those things?"[15]

In the calm of his vigil, in mystical interpenetration with the rest of nature, when his being engaged and fused with the stimuli around him, he sensed the answer.

"How great is the power of sitting up at night! One should purify one's heart and sit alone, by the light of a newly trimmed, bright candle. Through this practice one can pursue the principles that underlie events and things, and the subtlest workings of one's own mind. . . . Through this, we shall surely attain understanding."[16]

On another occasion, he recorded "in a chance moment of exhilaration" a night spent in conversation with a friend on a wet night.

Doing a painting in the rain, I borrow its wet richness.
Writing poems by candlelight, we pass the long night.
Next morning, in sun, we open the gate; the spring freshness has spread.
At the lakeshore you leave me among the singing willows.[17]

The real subject is the rain-soaked world. The room where the artists sit draws the eye, because it glows with light, but its scale is insignificant and our view of it indistinct. The rain dominates the composition, seeping into the very paper on Shen Zhou's sopping brush, speckling the air with spongy dabs, dripping from the tall thickets and dense copses that overshadow the painter's flimsy house, blurring the dark mountains that glower in the background.

Wu Wei, by contrast, painted people not as fragments of a landscape or specks in an enveloping cosmos. In his work, humankind is nearly always dominant. Even when he located people in large-scale landscapes, he always made them bigger and more active than Shen Zhou's characteristic figures. When he painted scholars, he made them dominate the composition, as if mastering nature by the power of thought and the resources of knowledge. Typically, his sages are strongly delineated, while the sketchy trees and hills around them seem feeble by comparison.

Although Confucianism never monopolised Chinese values, it did dominate the culture of the late-fifteenth-century court and of the administrative elite throughout the empire. Part of the consensus was that the empire was already big enough for its own purposes. It comprised all that mattered under heaven. It could supply its own wants from its own resources. If the "barbarians" outside its frontiers realised the wisdom of acknowledging Chinese superiority, revering the emperor, paying tribute, and adopting Chinese ways, that was welcome, in the foreigners' own interests. But the best way to attract them was by example, not by war. The state should defend its frontiers but not waste blood and wealth to enlarge them.

Earlier in the century, when factional squabbles displaced the Confucians from power, China had looked briefly as though it might launch

a major effort to found a seaborne empire, reaching out across the Indian Ocean. The Yongle emperor (r. 1402–24) aggressively sought contact with the world beyond the empire. He meddled in the politics of
China's southern neighbours in Vietnam and enticed the Japanese to
trade. The most spectacular manifestation of the new outward-looking
policy was the career of the Muslim eunuch-admiral Zheng He. In
1405, he led the first of a series of naval expeditions, the purpose of
which has been the subject of long and unresolved scholarly debate but
which was intended in part, at least, to exert political power around the
Indian Ocean's shores. He replaced unacceptable rulers in Java, Sumatra, and Sri Lanka, founded a puppet state on the commercially important Strait of Malacca, and gathered tribute from Bengal. He displayed
Chinese power as far away as Jiddah, on the Red Sea coast of Arabia,
and in major ports in East Africa as far south as the island of Zanzibar.
"The countries beyond the horizon," he announced with some exaggeration, "and from the ends of the Earth, have become subjects."[18] He
restocked the imperial zoo with giraffes, ostriches, zebras, and rhinoceroses – all hailed as beasts bringing good luck – and brought Chinese
geographical knowledge up to date.

Can Zheng He's voyages be called an imperial venture? Their official
purpose was to pursue a fugitive pretender to the Chinese throne – but
that would not have required expeditions on so vast a scale to such distant places. The Chinese called the vessels "treasure ships" and emphasised what they called "tribute gathering". (In the more distant spots
Zheng He's ships visited, what happened was more like an exchange.)
Commercial objectives may have been involved. Almost all the places
Zheng He visited had long been important in Chinese trade. In part,
the voyages were scientific missions: Ma Huan, Zheng He's interpreter,
called his own book on the subject *The Overall Survey of the Ocean's
Shores*, and improved maps and data on the plants, animals, and peoples
of the regions visited were among the expeditions' fruits. But flag showing is always, to some extent, about power or, at least, prestige. And the
aggressive intervention Zheng He made in some places, together with

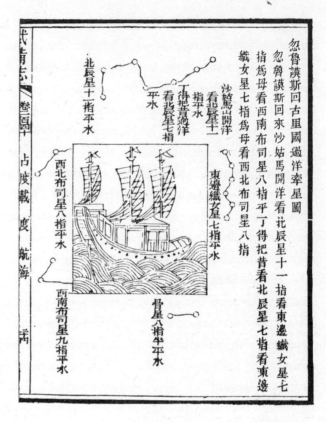

One of the star
charts Ma Huan
composed en route
with Zheng He
between the
Persian Gulf and
Calicut.

the tone of his commemorative inscriptions, demonstrates that the extension or reinforcement of China's image and influence was part of the project.

It is hard to see how else the huge investment the state made in his enterprise could have been justified. Zheng He's expeditions were on a crushing scale. His ships were much bigger than anything European navies could float at the time. The first expedition was said to comprise 62 junks of the largest dimensions ever built, 225 support vessels, and 27,780 men. The vessels – to judge from a recently discovered rudder post – justified the awed terms of contemporary assessments, displacing, perhaps, over three thousand tons; this was ten times the size of the largest ships afloat in Europe at the time. The seventh voyage – probably the longest in reach – sailed 12,618 miles. The voyages lasted on average over two years each. Some silly claims have been made for

Zheng He's voyages. Ships of his fleet did not sail beyond the limits of the Indian Ocean – much less discover America or Antarctica.

His achievements, however, clearly demonstrated China's potential to become the centre of a maritime empire of enormous reach. Strictly speaking, these were not route-finding voyages. As we have seen, the trade routes of the Indian Ocean, across maritime Asia, and into East Africa had been familiar to Chinese merchants for centuries. In the early thirteenth century, Zhao Rugwa provided a practical handbook for commercial travellers in South-east Asia and India. There were certainly opportunities to increase commercial openings by backing initiatives with force. The trades of the region were highly lucrative, including spices, fragrant hardwoods, valuable medicinal drugs, and exotic animal products. The motives for dispatching the "treasure ships", however, transcended commerce. Zheng He was engaged on what would now be called flag-waving missions, impressing the ports he visited with Chinese power and stimulating the awe of the emperor's home constituency with exotica that the Chinese classified as the tribute of remote peoples.[19] The official pretext for his commission – which few believed, then or now – was to search for a fugitive ex-emperor who was supposed to be in hiding abroad. Strategic considerations were clearly involved. Zheng He intervened actively in the politics of some ports in South-east Asia that were important for China's trade and security. A potentially hostile empire had recently arisen in central Asia under the Turkic chief Timur, usually known in the West as Tamerlane or Tamberlaine; apprehension may have sent the Chinese sniffing for allies and intelligence around the edges of the new menace. Whatever the motives of the expeditions, part of the effect was to consolidate Chinese knowledge of the routes Zheng He took, and to compile practical maps and sailing directions for them.

The admiral was a Muslim eunuch of Mongol ancestry. Every feature of his background marked him as an outsider to the Confucian scholar-elites that dominated Chinese political life. When the emperor appointed him to lead the first ocean-going task force in 1403, it was a triumph for four linked factions at court, whose interests clashed with

Confucian values. First, there was the commercial lobby, which wanted to mobilise naval support for Chinese traders in the Indian Ocean. Alongside the merchants, an imperialist lobby wanted to renew the programme of imperial aggression espoused by the previous dynasty but opposed by Confucians, who theorised that the empire should expand, if at all, by peacefully attracting "barbarians" into its orbit. Then there was the always-powerful Buddhist lobby, which wanted to keep state funds out of sceptical or anticlerical Confucian hands by diverting them to other projects, and which perhaps sensed opportunities for spreading the faith under the official aegis of imperial expansion.

The voyages did display China's potential as the launching bay of a seaborne empire: the capacity and productivity of her shipyards; her ability to mount expeditions of crushing strength and dispatch them over vast distances. Zheng He's encounters with opponents unequivocally demonstrated Chinese superiority. On the first expedition, he confronted a Chinese pirate chief who had set up a bandit state of his own in the sometime capital of Srivijaya in Sumatra. The pirates were slaughtered and their king sent to China for execution. On the third voyage, the Sinhalese king of Sri Lanka tried to lure Zheng He into a trap and seize the fleet. The Chinese dispersed his forces, captured his capital, deported him to China, and installed a pretender in his place. On the fourth expedition, a Sumatran chief who refused to co-operate in the exchange of gifts for tribute was overwhelmed, abducted, and, eventually, put to death.

Of all Zheng He's acts of political intervention, perhaps the most significant – in terms of long-term consequences – was his attempt to set up a Chinese puppet kingdom to control the trade of the Strait of Malacca, the vital bottleneck in the normal route between China and India. He chose to elevate Paramesvara, a bandit chief who had been driven from his own kingdom and had established a stronghold in the swamps of what is now known as Melaka, on the Malayan coast. In 1409, Zheng He conferred the seal and robes of kingship upon him. Paramesvara travelled to China to pay tribute in person and established a client relationship with the emperor; Chinese patronage turned his modest stronghold into a great and rich emporium.

Zheng He's own perception of his role seems to have combined an imperial impulse with the peaceful inspiration of commerce and scholarship. A stela he erected in 1432 began in a jingoistic vein: "In the unifying of the seas and continents the Ming Dynasty even goes beyond the Han and the Tang. . . . The countries beyond the horizon and from the ends of the earth have become subjects." That was an exaggeration, but he added, more plausibly, in deference to traders and geographers, "However far they may be, their distances and the routes may be calculated."[20] An "overall survey of the ocean's shores" was one of the fruits of the voyages. Copies of the charts survive thanks to the fact that they were reproduced in a printed work of 1621. Like European charts of the same period, they are diagrams of sailing directions rather than attempts at scale mapping. Tracks annotated with compass bearings show the routes between major ports and represent in visual form the sailing directions Zheng He recorded, all of which have the form "Follow such-and-such a bearing for such-and-such a number of watches". Each port is marked with its latitude according to the elevation of the Pole Star above the horizon, which Zheng He verified by means of "guiding star-boards" – ebony strips of various breadths held at a fixed distance from the observer's face to fill the space exactly between the star and the horizon.

But the Chinese naval effort could not last. Historians have debated why it was abandoned. Part of the answer, at least, is clear. The scholar-elites hated overseas adventures and the factions that favoured them so much that, when they recaptured power, the mandarins destroyed almost all Zheng He's records in an attempt to obliterate his memory. Moreover, China's land frontiers became insecure as Mongol power revived. China needed to turn away from the sea and towards the new threat. The state never resumed overseas expansion. The growth of trade and of Chinese colonisation in South-east Asia was left to merchants and migrants. China, the empire best equipped for maritime imperialism, opted out. Consequently, lesser powers, including those of Europe, were able to exploit opportunities in seas that Chinese power vacated. It became possible for the Ryukyu Islands to be unified as a thriving emporium for the trade of China and Japan with South-east Asia. Sho Shin ruled the islands from 1477. He disarmed the warlords, sent bureaucrats to China for education in Confucian principles, and imposed internal peace.

In many ways, it was to the credit of Chinese decision makers that they pulled back from involvement in costly adventures far from home. Most powers that have undertaken such expeditions and attempted to impose their rule on distant countries have had cause to regret it. Confucian values, as we have seen, included giving priority to good government at home. "Barbarians" would submit to Chinese rule if and when they saw the benefits. Attempting to beat or coax them into submission was a waste of resources. By consolidating their landward empire, and refraining from seaborne imperialism, China's rulers ensured the longevity of their state. All the maritime empires founded in the world in the past five hundred years have crumbled. China is still here.

Ch'oe Pu's diary reflects the successes and limitations of Chinese Confucians' "soft power", as modern political theory would call it. Ch'oe Pu was aware of similar struggles and exchanges of prejudice between Confucians and their Buddhist rivals in Korea. He was such a pious Confucian, so respectful of the rites for the dead, that he refused to doff mourning, even when it might have exempted him from peril of his life, as when his companions were afraid of slaughter – either at the hands of brigands unintimidated by the sight of Ch'oe Pu's official uniform, or by Chinese peasants who mistook the Koreans for Japanese pirates. He declined to pray at a river shrine, which he regarded as superstitious, despite the advisability of deferring to local customs. His contempt for Buddhism was excoriating. He denounced the futility of monks' prayers and rejoiced at the news of secularisations of monasteries because "the abolished temples become people's houses, the destroyed Buddhas become vessels, and the heads that once were bald are now hairy and fill the army's ranks".[21]

He spoke to his Chinese hosts in terms that were calculated to flatter, but which also reflected two long-standing prejudices among Korea's elite: willingness to defer to China, and anxiety to imitate the Chinese. "In heaven," he admitted,

there are not two suns. How under the same heaven can there be two emperors? My king's one purpose is to serve your country devotedly.[22] . . . Though my Korea is beyond the sea, its clothing and culture being the same as China's, it cannot be considered a foreign country. That is especially so now, with Great Ming's unification . . . under one roof. All under Heaven are my brothers; how can we discriminate among people because of distance? That is particularly true of my country, which respectfully serves the celestial court and pays tribute without fail. The Emperor, for his part, treats us punctiliously and tends us benevolently. The feeling of security he imparts is perfect.[23]

Ch'oe Pu learned to make a water wheel he saw in China because "it will be useful to Koreans for all ages to come". But when interrogators asked for military intelligence, he was evasive. When they asked the distance to Korea, he exaggerated. When officials asked him how Korea had managed to repel earlier Chinese attempts at conquest, he sidestepped the question and emphasised his country's strength.[24]

In his day, Korea was experiencing a Confucian revival parallel to China's – only more fragile. After a spell, in the previous reign, of royal dependence on Buddhist advisers and lavish patronage of Buddhist temples, Ch'oe's royal master, Sŏng-jong, who came to the throne in 1470, restored Confucianism, much as the Hongxi emperor did in China. Yet when Chinese dignitaries visited Korea, it struck them as an exotic and barbarous land, more notable for its differences from China than for the continuities Koreans strove to contrive. In 1487 an ambassador arrived in Korea from the court of the new emperor of China. "The ministers," he reported back, "with pins in their hair, stand like ibises in attendance, while old and young gather on the hills to see. . . . The stone lions bask in the sun that rises from the sea. In front of the Kwang-wha Gate they sit east and west, high as the towers, wonderfully hammered out."[25] He watched acrobats masked as lions and elephants in a palace painted red, with green glass windows, in the audience chamber.[26] The level of mealtime hospitality impressed him: five layers of honeyed bread, honey and flour cakes piled a foot high, rice soup, pickled relish, soy, rice wine superior in aroma and flavour to Chinese millet wine, beef, mutton, pork, walnuts, dates, mutton sausages, fish, and lotus roots to sweeten the breath.[27]

He lectured the Koreans on Confucianism, in a way one suspects must have annoyed his hosts: "We proclaim the ceremonies of the Book of Spring and Autumn which says, 'The various states must first see to the rectitude of the individual man.'"[28] In the long run, the lecture was to little avail. Chong-jik, the minister who put the policy of reviving the ceremonies into effect in Korea, died in 1492. After the king's death in 1494, his successor reversed the policy, beheaded Chong-jik's exhumed body, and scourged and exiled other leading Confucians, including Ch'oe Pu.

Japan – the other country Columbus hoped to open trade with – was in no condition to contemplate taking the initiative in reaching out to the rest of the world. Ch'oe Pu, who so admired China, had less respect for Japan. The riches of Japan, he thought, would seem to a Korean like "ice to a summer bug".[29] But the country's problems were not fundamentally economic. Japanese rice could be harvested two or three times a year. Large amounts of copper, swords, sulphur, and sappanwood were exported to China. Japan used Chinese coins, minted, for reasons no one has ever fully been able to explain, from copper produced in Japan. The size and distribution of cities – concentrated, as usual in Japanese history, in the teeming heartland of southern Honshu and northern

Kyushu – suggest that rural production was high and the systems of commerce and communications could dispense large amounts of food efficiently. Kyoto had reputedly two hundred thousand inhabitants before ruinous civil war broke out in the late 1460s. Tennoji in Kawachi province and Hakata in northern Kyushu had over thirty thousand people. More than twenty other towns had more than ten thousand.

Japan's problems were political. Though Japanese statesmen regarded China as their model, in practice the country was very differently managed. The emperor was a sacral, secluded figure, spared the vulgarities of politics by hereditary vicegerents known as shoguns. Control of Kyoto ensured fabulous revenues for the shoguns' government. They could afford to neglect the rest of the country. Provincial power was delegated to or usurped by the warlords as the price of peace. But peace in the hands of a warrior caste is always precarious. Trying to forget "the trials of this world", the poet Shinkei described the effects: "Even within the powerful clans selfish quarrels broke out between lord and retainer and among the rank and file, in which men of various stations fell in great numbers. And though they battled day and night, pitting their might against each other in their various territories, nowhere was the outcome ever decisive."[30]

While squabbles of the aristocracy overspilled into violence, members of the military class known as samurai made common cause with peasants oppressed by the warlords' need of money. Together they formed masterless leagues of self-defence that erupted in rebellion. They were, according to the poet-priest Ikkyu, who was a propagandist for the shogunate, "demons with red faces, their hot blood aroused, . . . turning the whole city into a den of thieves and striking fear in the people as they endlessly looted for treasures. And thus it came about that the people grew weary, the capital fell into ruin, and of the myriad ways of civilized men nothing remained."[31] From the late 1430s, the eastern provinces were steeped in constant warfare: "As the months stretched into years, myriads perished, their bodies torn by the sword as men fell upon each other in their madness, and still the strife showed no signs of letting up." A reforming shogun's attempts to reassert central authority ended in his assassination in 1441. Fifteen years of effective interregnum followed, while his successors were minors. When the shogun Yoshimasa reached maturity, he struggled to recoup power. In 1482, after the failure of all his efforts, he wrote that the daimyo, or warlords, "do as they please and do not follow orders. That means there can be no government."[32]

Meanwhile, in 1461 drought struck

> when not a single tuft of grass grew upon the fields across the land. From the capital and the villages, thousands of starving people, both high and low, wandered out to beg on the wayside, or just sat there till they crumpled over and died. It is impossible to say how many myriads perished in just a single day. The world had turned into a hell of hungry ghosts before my eyes.[33]

In 1467 the two most powerful warlords came to blows, ostensibly over the succession to the shogunate, and were forced to flee when their armies ravaged the capital. "All, high and low, were thrown into utter confusion and scattered in the four directions, their flight swifter than flowers in a windstorm, red leaves beneath the tree-withering blast. Within the capital, it had become a veritable hell." The poet Ichijo Kaneyoshi fled devastation so total that "only layers of cloud cover the remains", while bandits scattered the contents of his library – "the dwellings of hundreds of bookworms . . . that had been passed down for over ten generations".[34] The following ten years were the most destructive in Japan's long history of civil wars.

"How terrible it is," wrote the poet Shinkei, "to have been born in the last days of such an utterly degenerate age". The calamities seemed to him "to presage the world's destruction".[35] Moralists blamed the indifference and self-indulgence of the ruling classes, or the aloof lifestyle of the shogun, or the supposed influence of women at his court, or the corruption of his ministers.

Yet wars, though they warp morals and wreck lives, can stimulate art. A renaissance was under way,[36] with painters and poets who looked back half a millennium for their models and perhaps for escape. In the longueurs of war, fighters competed to write Chinese verses. The shogun Yoshimasa dabbled while Japan burned. His character has puzzled every historian who tried to tackle it fairly. He treated the events of his day as if they were none of his responsibility. In the earliest years of the war, his own poetry expressed optimism amounting to insouciance:

> *Forlorn though the hope,*
> *Still I believe that somehow*
> *Peace will be restored.*
> *Although it is so confused,*
> *I don't despair of the world.*[37]

Pessimism followed, amounting to despair, but deeply dyed with egotism.

> *"What a sad world it is!"*
> *Everyone says the same, but*
> *I'm the only one,*
> *Unable to control it,*
> *Whose grief keeps on growing.*[38]

His life seems a series of evasions. He had an impressive array of virtues: in selecting artists he showed unerring judgement. In organising poetry competitions he displayed unstinting industry. In identifying the problems of government he showed considerable sagacity. But he turned away from every disagreeable task: curbing his wife's avarice,

reprimanding his son's prodigality, punishing the warlords' presump-
tions. He simply ignored the wars that broke out around him, withdrawing first into a circle of artistic mutual admiration in the capital,
then resigning government responsibilities altogether in his country
retreat before taking the final step: ordination as a Zen monk.

His profligacy probably helped cause the dissolution of the state by
ratcheting up taxation, immiserating peasants, and leaving the central
government bereft of an armed force. But at least it can be said to his
credit that much of his spending was on the arts. While in power, he
was a compulsive builder and redecorator of palaces. When he retired
from public life, his hillside villa became like the country retreats of the
Medici – a centre where artists and literati gathered to perform plays,
coin poems, practise the tea ceremony, blend perfumes, paint, and converse. Sometimes, warlords took time out from strife or state building
on their own account in nearby provinces to join the soirées. Yoshimasa
built a supposedly silver-foil-clad pavilion on the grounds, decorated
with "rare plants and curious rocks",[39] begun in 1482 and completed
three years after his death, in 1493. To meet the costs, the government
requisitioned labour from the dwindling number of loyal landowners in
the provinces. In retirement, Yoshimasa boosted his income by engaging in trade in his own right, sending horses, swords, sulphur, screens,
and fans to China and getting cash and books in return.[40] This shows
both that a merchant life was no derogation, even for a former shogun,
and that the troubles did not interrupt the trade.

In some ways, the arts of the time seem strangely indifferent to the
wars. Kano Masanobu painted Chinese rivers and Buddhist worthies on
the walls in styles derived from Chinese models. The critics and painters
Shinkei Geiami and his son Soami coaxed great work from the brushes of
pupils, such as the dynamic Kenko Shokei. But art was ultimately inseparable from the politics of the wars, because warlords paid for so much of it,
and the shogun's patronage was by no means disinterested.

One suspects that Yoshimasa employed artists because, at least in
part, they were cheaper than warriors and more effective as mediators of

propaganda. Patronage of Noh theatre, for instance, was traditional in the shogunal house, exhibiting heroic themes and aligning the shoguns with exemplars from a sometimes mythical past; it was while watching a play that Yoshimasa's father had been assassinated. Because Yoshimasa had to maintain links around the kingdom, he commanded a brisk trade in portraits for distribution to provincial shrines, where they could focus loyalties, like fragments or relics of himself.[41] But Yoshimasa elevated art to a new rank as the Japanese equivalent of the "rites and music" Confucius had prescribed as essential to the health of the Chinese state.[42]

Not everyone succumbed to Yoshimasa's patronage. The painter of landscape in ink Toyo Sesshu visited China in 1467, after years of copying Chinese paintings. He served only provincial houses and declined to paint for Yoshimasa with a characteristically Chinese excuse: it was not right for a mere priest to paint in a "golden palace".[43] Such dissent or fastidiousness was rare. Yoshimasa's taste inspired swaths of the elite and of merchants who sought to spend their way to status. Provincial chieftains imitated his practice, inviting poets, painters, and scholars to elevate their own courts with learning and art. A once-popular theory about the origins of the Italian Renaissance ascribed investment in culture to the mood of hard times: when wars curtail opportunities to make money from trade, capitalists sink their money into works of art. Something of the sort seems to have happened in Japan in the long years of civil war from the late 1460s. The fear – often realised – that frequent burnings in the capital would destroy valuable libraries inspired a feverish enthusiasm for copying manuscripts. The flight of sages and artists from the capital helped spread metropolitan tastes around the country. Warlords competed for the services of poets and painters.[44] Yamaguchi, for instance, became a "little Kyoto", graced by the presence of famous artists.

Shinkei's wanderings are a case in point. In 1468 he left the capital for the east, to use his prestige as a Buddhist sage in the interests of one of the contending parties in the civil wars. He spent most of the next

1492

Tranquillity, sorrow, and reflection in the midst of civil war: Sogi, composing verses with fellow literati by a colleague's grave under the full moon.

four years responding to invitations from nobles to conduct poetical soirées in their castles and camps, endeavouring, he said, "to soften the hearts of warriors and rude folk and teach the way of human sensibility for all the distant ages".[45] Spring afflicted him: "Even the flowers are thickets of upturned blades."[46]

The adventures of another renowned poet exemplify the predicament of artists in a time of civil war. Sogi, an equally famous poet, usually travelled between provincial courts in response to invitations from aspiring patrons. In 1492, however, he stayed in the capital, educating aristocrats on the classics of the Heian era of nearly half a millennium before. He was seventy-three years old, and his taste for travelling was waning. In the summer of that year, however, he made an excursion into the countryside to visit Yukawa Masaharu, a minor warlord with literary ambitions. The sequence of poems he wrote for this patron begins with a prayer for the endurance of the house, likening Masaharu's offspring to a stand of young pines: "[Y]et still more tall may they grow." But "the law", he also wrote, "is not what it was".[47] Piety was past.

> Who will hear it?
> The temple bell from the hills,
> Off in the distance.

Despite Sogi's prayers for him to be spared in the battle he had to face, Masaharu backed the wrong side in the conflict. Within a year of Sogi's visit, his fortunes were in ruins. He disappeared from records after 1493.

Amazingly, this renaissance flourished in conditions of insecurity that might have paralysed the city of Kyoto, where there were never enough loyal soldiers to keep order among the rival gangs who infested the city and the rival armies of warlords who often invested it. After the warlords' armies withdrew from the wreckage in 1477, marauders took over. Full-scale warfare continued in the east of the country.

As war intensified, Japan dissolved into warring states. A self-made, self-appointed leader who came to be known as Hoso Soun demonstrated the opportunities. Having made his reputation in the service of other warlords, he struck out on his own, attracting followers by his prowess. In 1492 he conquered the peninsula of Izu and turned it into a base from which he proposed to extend his rule over the entire country. In 1494 he secured control of the peninsula by capturing the fortress of Odiwara, which commanded the approach to Izu, by posing as the leader of a party of deer hunters. He was never strong enough to get much farther than the neighbouring province of Sagami, but his career was typical of the era, in which scores of new warlords burst on to the scene, established new dynasties, and set up what were in effect small independent states. At the same time, peasant communities organised their own armed forces, sometimes in collaboration with warlords.

One of the earliest editions of Columbus's first report shows the oriental
merchants he expected to find trading with the natives of Hispaniola.

Though China withdrew from imperial ambitions, and Japan, crumbling into political ineffectiveness, had not yet embarked on them, the underlying strength of those countries' economies remained robust, and the vibrancy and dynamism of cultural life were spectacular.

Elsewhere, in widely separated parts of the world, to which we must now turn, expansion unrolled like springs uncoiling. An age of expansion really did begin, but the phenomenon was of an expanding world, not, as some historians say, of European expansion. The world did not simply wait passively for European outreach to transform it as if touched by a magic wand. Other societies were already working magic of their own, turning states into empires and cultures into civilisations. Some of the most dynamic and rapidly expanding societies of the fifteenth century were in the Americas, south-west and northern Asia, and sub-Saharan Africa. Indeed, in terms of territorial expansion and military effectiveness against opponents, some African and American empires outclassed any state in western Europe.

The Indian Ocean, which China forbore to control – "the seas of milk and butter", as ancient Indian legends called the seas that lapped maritime Asia – linked the world's richest economies and carried the world's richest commerce. It constituted a self-contained zone, united by monsoonal winds and isolated from the rest of the world by zones of storms and untraversable distances. For the future of the history of the planet, the big question was who – if anyone – would control the routes of commerce now that the Chinese had withdrawn. In the 1490s, that issue was unresolved. But the Indian Ocean was also an arena of intense, transmutative cultural exchange, with consequences that the world is still experiencing, and to which we must now turn.

Chapter 9

"The Seas of Milk and Butter"

The Indian Ocean Rim

*19 January: Nur ad-Din Abd ar-Rahman Jami dies
at Herat.*

Conventional historiography suffers from too much hot air and not enough wind. For the whole of the age of sail – that is, almost the whole of the recorded past – winds and currents set the limits of what was possible in long-range communications and cultural exchange. Most would-be explorers have preferred to sail into the wind, presumably because, whether or not they made any discoveries, they wanted to get home. Phoenicians and Greeks, for instance – dwellers at the eastern end of the Mediterranean – explored the length of that sea, working against the prevailing wind. In the Pacific, Polynesians colonised the archipelagos of the South Seas, from Fiji to Easter Island, by the same method.

Generally, however, fixed wind systems inhibit exploration. Where winds are constant, there is no incentive to try to exploit them as causeways to new worlds. Either they blow into one's face, in which case

The world map of the Nuremberg Chronicle illustrates the suspicion, derived from Ptolemy, that the Indian Ocean was landlocked.

seafarers will never get far under sail, or they sing at one's back – in which case they will prevent venturers from ever returning home. Monsoon systems, by contrast, where prevailing winds are seasonal, encourage long-range seafaring and speculative voyages, because navigators know that the wind, wherever it bears them, will eventually turn and take them home.

It depresses me to think of my own ancestors, in my family's homeland in north-western Spain, staring out unenterprisingly at the Atlantic for hundreds, perhaps thousands of years, and never troubling to go far out to sea – dabbling, at most, in fishery and coastal cabotage. But the winds pinioned them, like butterflies in a collector's case. They could scarcely have imagined the sensation of the wind, year in, year out, alternately in one's face and at one's back. That is what happens on the shores of maritime Asia, where the monsoon dominates the environment. Above the equator, north-easterlies prevail in winter. When winter ends, the direction of the winds is reversed. For most of the rest of the year they blow steadily from the south and west, sucked in towards the Asian landmass as air warms and rises over the continent.

By timing voyages to take advantage of the predictable changes in the direction of the wind, navigators could set sail, confident of a fair wind out and a fair wind home. In the Indian Ocean, moreover, compared with other navigable seas, the reliability of the monsoon season offered the advantage of a speedy passage in both directions. To judge from such ancient and medieval records as survive, a trans-Mediterranean journey from east to west, against the wind, would take fifty to seventy days. With the monsoon, a ship could cross the entire Indian Ocean, between Palembang in Sumatra and the Persian Gulf, in less time. Three to four weeks in either direction sufficed to get between India and a Persian Gulf port.

In 1417 a Persian ambassador heading for India did it in even less time. Abd er-Razzaq was bound for the southern Indian realm of Vijayanagar. There were too many hostile states in the way for him to go by land. His ship sailed late, in the terrifying, tempestuous spell of weather towards the end of summer, when the caustic heat of the Asian interior drags the ocean air inwards with ferocious urgency. The merchants who were to have accompanied the ambassador abandoned the voyage, crying "with one voice that the time for navigation was past, and that everyone who put to sea at this season was alone responsible for his death". Fright and seasickness incapacitated Abd er-Razzaq for three days. "My heart was crushed like glass," he complained, "and my soul became weary of life." But his sufferings were rewarded. His ship reached Calicut, the famed pepper emporium on the Malabar coast, after only eighteen days' sailing from Ormuz.[1]

The Indian Ocean has many hazards. Storms rend it, especially in the Arabian Sea, the Bay of Bengal, and the deadly belt of habitually bad weather that stretches across the ocean below about ten degrees south. The ancient tales of Sinbad are full of shipwrecks. But the predictability of a homebound wind made this the world's most benign environment for long-range voyaging for centuries – perhaps millennia – before the continuous history of Atlantic or Pacific crossings began. The monsoon liberated navigators in the Indian Ocean and made maritime Asia the home of the world's richest economies and most spectacular states. That is what drew Europeans – Asia's poor neighbours – eastward, and why Columbus and so many of his predecessors, contemporaries, and successors sought a navigable route to what they called the Indies.

In the fifteenth century, the biggest single source of influence for change in the region was the growing global demand for, and therefore supply of, spices and aromatics – especially pepper. No one has ever satisfactorily explained the reasons for this increase. China dominated the market and accounted for well over half the global consumption, but Europe, Persia, and the Ottoman world were all absorbing ever greater amounts. Population growth contributed – but the increase in demand for spices seems greatly to have exceeded it. As we saw in chapter 1, the idea that cooks used spices to mask the flavour of bad meat is nonsense. Produce was far fresher in the medieval world, on average, than in modern urbanised and industrialised societies, and reliable preserving methods were available for what was not consumed fresh. Changing taste has been alleged, but there is no evidence of that: it was the abiding taste for powerful flavours – a taste now being revived as Mexican, Indian, and Szechuan cuisines go global – that made spices desirable. The spice boom was part of an ill-understood upturn in economic conditions across Eurasia. In China, especially, increased prosperity made expensive condiments more widely accessible as the turbulence that brought the Ming to power subsided and the empire settled down to a long period of relative peace and internal stability.

In partial consequence, spice production expanded into new areas. Pepper, traditionally produced on India's Malabar coast, and cinnamon, once largely confined to Sri Lanka, spread around South-east Asia. Pepper became a major product of Malaya and Sumatra in the fifteenth century. Camphor, sappanwood and sandalwood, benzoin and cloves all overspilled their traditional places of supply. Nonetheless, enough local specialisation remained within the region to ensure huge profits for traders and shippers; and the main markets outside South-east Asia continued to grow.

For that brief spell early in the fifteenth century, in the reign of the Yongle emperor, when Chinese navies patrolled the Indian ocean, it looked as if China might try to control trade and even production in spices by force. The emperor exhibited an impressive appetite for conquest. Perhaps because he was a usurper with a lot to prove, he was willing to pay almost any price for glory. From the time he seized the throne in 1402 until his death twenty-two years later, he waged almost incessant war on China's borders, especially on the Mongol and Annamese fronts. He scattered at least seventy-two missions to every accessible land beyond China's borders. He sent silver to the shogun in Japan (who already had plenty of silver), and statues of Buddha and gifts of gems and silks to Tibet and Nepal. He exchanged ill-tempered embassies with Muslim potentates in central Asia. He invested kings in Korea, Melaka, Borneo, Sulu, Sumatra, and Ceylon. These far-flung contacts probably cost more in gifts than they raised in what the Chinese called "tribute": live okapis from Bengal, white elephants from Cambodia, horses and concubines from Korea, turtles and white monkeys from Siam, paintings from Afghanistan, sulphur and spears and samurai armour from Japan. But they were magnificent occasions of display, which gave Yongle prestige in his own court and perhaps some sense of security.[2]

The grandest and most expensive of the missions went by sea. Between 1405 and 1433 seven formidable flag-waving expeditions ranged the Indian Ocean under Admiral Zheng He. As we have seen, the scale of his efforts was massive, but their cultural consequences were, in many ways, more pervasive than their political impact. The voyages lasted, on average, two years each. They visited at least thirty-two countries around the rim of the ocean. The first three voyages, between 1405 and 1411, went only as far as the Malabar coast, the principal source of the world's pepper supply, with excursions along the coasts of

Siam, Malaya, Java, Sumatra, and Sri Lanka. On the fourth voyage, from 1413 to 1415, ships visited the Maldives, Ormuz, and Jiddah, and collected envoys from nineteen countries.

Even more than the arrival of the ambassadors, the inclusion of a giraffe among the tribute Zheng He gathered caused a sensation when the fleet returned home. No one in China had ever seen such a creature. Zheng He acquired his in Bengal, where it had arrived as a curiosity for a princely collection as a result of trading links across the Indian Ocean. Chinese courtiers instantly identified the creature as divine in origin. According to an eyewitness, it had "the body of a deer and the tail of an ox and a fleshy boneless horn, with luminous spots like a red or purple mist. It walks in stately fashion and in its every motion it observes a rhythm." Carried away by confusion with the mythical *qilin* or unicorn, the same observer declared, "Its harmonious voice sounds like a bell or musical tube."

The giraffe brought assurances of divine benevolence. Shen Du, an artist who made a living drawing from life, wrote verses to describe the giraffe's reception at court:

> The ministers and the people all gathered to gaze at it and their joy knows no end. I, your servant, have heard that when a sage possesses the virtue of the utmost benevolence, so that he illuminates the darkest places, then a qilin appears. This shows that your Majesty's virtue equals that of heaven. Its merciful blessings have spread far and wide, so that its harmonious vapours have emanated a ch'i-lin, as an endless blessing to the state for myriad years.[3]

Accompanying the visiting envoys home on a fifth voyage, which lasted from 1416 to 1419, Zheng He collected a prodigious array of exotic beasts for the imperial menagerie: lions, leopards, camels, ostriches, zebras, rhinoceroses, antelopes, and giraffes, as well as a mysterious beast, the *Touou-yu*. Drawings made this last creature resemble a white tiger with black spots, while written accounts describe a "righteous beast" who would not tread on growing grass, was strictly vegetarian, and appeared "only under a prince of perfect benevolence and sincerity". There were also many "strange birds". An inscription recorded: "All of them craned their necks and looked on with pleasure, stamping their feet, scared and startled." That was a description not of the birds but of the enraptured courtiers. Truly, it seemed to Shen Du, "all the creatures that spell good fortune arrive".[4] In 1421, a sixth voyage departed with the reconnaissance of the east coast of Africa as its main objective, visiting, among other destinations, Mogadishu, Mombasa, Malindi, Zanzibar, and Kilwa. After an interval, probably caused by changes in the balance of court factions after the death of the Yongle emperor in 1424, the seventh voyage, from 1431 to 1433, renewed contacts with the Arabian and African states Zheng He had already visited.[5]

Mutual astonishment was the result of contacts on a previously unimagined scale. In the preface to his own book about the voyages, Ma Huan, an interpreter aboard Zheng He's fleet, recalled that as a young man, when he had contemplated the seasons, climates, landscapes, and people of distant lands, he had asked himself in great surprise, "How can such dissimilarities exist in the world?"[6] His own travels with the eunuch-admiral convinced him that the reality was even stranger. The arrival of Chinese junks at Middle Eastern ports with cargoes of precious exotica caused a sensation. A chronicler at the Egyptian court described the excitement provoked by news of the arrival of the junks off Aden and of the Chinese fleet's intention to reach the nearest permitted anchorage to Mecca.

After that, there were no more such voyages. Part, at least, of the context of the decision to abort Zheng He's missions is clear. The examination system and the gradual discontinuation of other forms of recruitment for public service had serious implications. Scholars and gentlemen re-established their monopoly of government, with their indifference towards expansion and their contempt for trade. In the 1420s and 1430s the balance of power at court shifted in the bureaucrats' favour, away from the Buddhists, eunuchs, Muslims, and merchants who had supported Zheng He. When the Hongxi emperor ascended the throne in 1424, one of his first acts was to cancel Zheng He's next voyage. He restored Confucian officeholders, whom his predecessor had dismissed, and curtailed the power of other factions. In 1429 the shipbuilding budget was cut almost to extinction. China's land frontiers were becoming insecure as Mongol power revived. China needed to turn away from the sea and towards the new threat.[7]

The consequences for the history of the world were profound. Chinese overseas expansion was confined to unofficial migration and, in large part, to clandestine trade, with little or no imperial encouragement or protection. This did not stifle Chinese colonisation or commerce. On the contrary, China remained the world's most dynamic trading economy and the world's most prolific source of overseas settlers. Officially, "not a plank floated" overseas from China. In practice, prohibitions had only a modest effect. From the fifteenth century onward, Chinese colonists in South-east Asia made vital contributions to the economies of every place they settled; their remittances home played a big part in the enrichment of China. The tonnage of shipping frequenting Chinese ports in the same period probably equalled or exceeded that of the rest of the world put together. But, except in respect of islands close to China, the state's hostility to maritime expansion never abated for as long as the empire lasted. China never built up the sort of wide-ranging global empire that Atlantic seaboard nations acquired. An observer of the world in the fifteenth century would surely have forecast that the Chinese would precede all other peoples in the discovery of world-girdling, transoceanic routes and the inauguration of far-flung seaborne imperialism. Yet nothing of the sort materialised, and the field remained open for the far less promising explorers of Europe to open up the ways around the world.

Of course, the destiny of the world was not determined by a single decision made in China. China's renunciation of maritime imperialism belongs in a vast context of influences that help to explain the long-term advantages of Atlantic-side European peoples in the global "space race".

These influences can be classified as partly environmental and partly economic. The limits of Zheng He's navigations are a clue to the environmental influences beyond the reach of the monsoons. The Indian Ocean is hard to get out of. Even ships that safely make it through the belt of storms, bound towards the Atlantic around southern Africa, must negotiate lee shores in the region of what is now KwaZulu-Natal, which, in the sixteenth and seventeenth centuries, became a notorious graveyard for ships that ventured there. This was probably the location of the place called Ha-pu-erh on the maps generated by the Zheng He voyages, beyond which, according to the annotations, the ships did not proceed, owing to the ferocity of the storms. On its eastern flank, maritime Asia is hemmed by the typhoon-racked seas of Japan and the vastness of the Pacific.

To undertake voyages into such hostile seas, Indian Ocean navigators would need a big incentive. The Indian Ocean was an arena of such intense commercial activity, and so much wealth, that it would have been pointless for indigenous peoples to look for markets or suppliers elsewhere. When merchants from northern or central Asia or Europe or the African interior reached the ocean, they came as supplicants, generally despised for their poverty, and found it hard to sell the products of their homelands.

Chinese disengagement from the wider world was not the result of any deficiency of technology or curiosity. It would have been perfectly possible for Chinese ships to visit Europe or the Americas, had they so wished. Indeed, Chinese explorers probably did get around the Cape of Good Hope, sailing from east to west, at intervals during the Middle Ages. A Chinese map of the thirteenth century depicts Africa in roughly its true shape. A Venetian mapmaker of the mid-fifteenth century reported a sighting of a Chinese or, perhaps, Javanese junk off the south-west African coast.[8] But there was no point in pursuing such initiatives: they led to regions that produced nothing the Chinese wanted. Although the evidence that Chinese vessels ever crossed the Pacific to America is, at best, equivocal, it is perfectly possible that they

did so. Again, however, it would have been folly to pursue such voyages or attempt systematic contacts across the ocean. No people lived
there with whom the Chinese could possibly wish to do business.

To a lesser – but still sufficient – extent, the same considerations
applied to other maritime peoples of the Indian Ocean and East and
South-east Asia. The Arabs, the Swahili merchant communities, Persians, Indians, Javanese and other island peoples of the region, and the
Japanese all had the technology required to explore the world, but plenty
of commercial opportunities in their home ocean kept them fully occupied. Indeed, their problem was, if anything, shortage of shipping in re-
lation to the scale of demand for inter-regional trade. That was why, in
the long run, they generally welcomed interlopers from Europe in the
sixteenth century, who were truculent, demanding, barbaric, and often
violent, but who added to the shipping stock of the ocean and, therefore,
contributed to the general increase of wealth. Paradoxically, therefore,
poverty favoured Europeans, compelled to look elsewhere because of the
dearth of economic opportunities at home.

The Indian Ocean was by no means unknown to Europeans. The widespread assumption that Vasco da Gama was the first to penetrate deep
inside it when he rounded the Cape of Good Hope in 1498 is a vulgar
error. Italian merchants often plied their trade there during the late
Middle Ages. Typically, they travelled across the Ottoman and Persian
empires, in the rare interstices of war and religious hostility. Or else,
even more commonly, they undertook a long and arduous journey up-
river along the Nile from Alexandria, and overland by camel caravan
from the first or second cataract to the Red Sea coast, where they
awaited the turn of the monsoon before shipping for Aden or Socotra. It
was inadvisable to attempt to join the Red Sea farther north because of
the formidable hazards to navigation.

Most of the Western venturers who worked in the Indian Ocean are
known only from stray references in the archives. Merchants rarely

wrote up their experiences. But two circumstantial accounts survive from the fifteenth century: the first by Niccolò Conti, who had been as far east as Java, and had returned to Italy by 1444; the second by his fellow Florentine Girolamo di Santo Stefano, who made an equally long trading voyage in the 1490s. Conti knew something of the Near East as a result of working as a merchant in Damascus, and therefore chose to travel overland via Persia to the Gulf, where he took ship for Cambay in the Bay of Bengal. Santo Stefano used the other main route. In company with a business partner, Girolamo Adorno, he travelled up the Nile and joined a caravan bound for the Red Sea. He crossed the ocean from Massawah – a port generally under Ethiopian control at the time.

On his return, Conti sought papal absolution for having abjured Christianity in Cairo in order to save the lives of his wife and children, who travelled with him. In Rome, he was able to enhance geographers' knowledge of the East, adding glosses, derived from experience, to the available traditions, which derived in part from the sometimes obscure texts transmitted from classical antiquity, and sometimes from the dubious claims of travellers and pseudo-travellers, like Marco Polo, whom the learned were disinclined to believe. Exchanges of geographical lore had constituted leisure-time conversation for delegates at the Council of Florence in 1439 and had excited much interest in new discoveries: it was an ideal moment to share revelations. Conti told his story to a Florentine humanist, who made a record of it as a morally edifying tale of changing fortunes.

The convention Conti's work established was of "the inconstancy of fortune". When Santo Stefano wrote up his experiences of the Indian Ocean in 1499, he, too, focused on lamentations against ill luck and sententious reflections on the "disastrous journey" he endured "for my sins". Had he eluded his sufferings, he might have retired on the riches that slipped through his hands during his career as a merchant in the Indies and would have avoided the need to throw himself on the mercy of patrons – the obvious subtext of his work. "But who can contend with fortune?" he asked, rhetorically, concluding with "infinite thanks

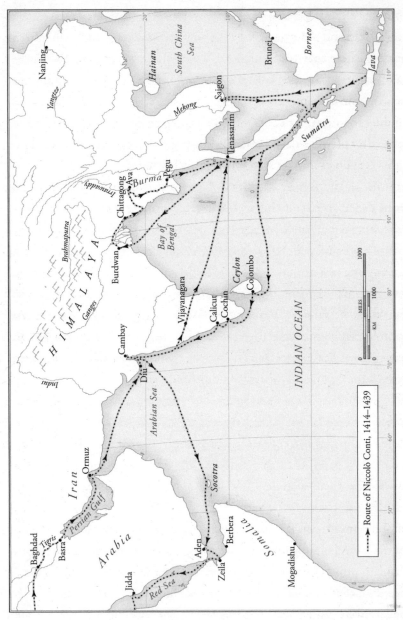

The Indian Ocean with the route of Niccolò Conti.

to our Lord God, for that he has preserved me, and shown me great mercy".[9] He and Adorno got as far east as an emporium in northern Sumatra, where they took ship for Pegu, in Burma, apparently with the idea of engaging in trade in gems. It was painfully slow doing business there. In Sumatra on the way back a local ruler confiscated their cargo, including the valuable rubies they brought from Burma. Adorno died in 1496, "after fifty-five days' suffering" in Pegu, where "his body was buried in a certain ruined church, frequented by none".[10]

In the Maldives, in an attempt to head homeward with what little fortune he had salvaged from his adventures, Santo Stefano waited six months for the monsoon to turn. When it did, it unleashed so much rain that his deckless ship sank with the weight of it, "and those who could swim were saved and the rest drowned".[11] After floating on wreckage from morning to evening, the merchant was rescued by a passing ship. No tale of the ocean would be complete without a shipwreck and a dramatic escape, but if Santo Stefano embellished the truth, he also, like Conti, managed to convey a great deal of representative information about how Westerners perceived the ocean and the lands that lined its rim.

Naturally enough, as they were merchants, both Conti and Santo Stefano inventoried trade goods of all kinds wherever they went, and took special interest in spices and aromatics. Santo Stefano described the drying of green peppercorns at Calicut, the profusion of cinnamon in Sri Lanka, the availability of pepper in Sumatra, the location of sandalwood in Coromandel. Conti's description of aromatic-oil production from cinnamon berries in Sri Lanka reflects personal observation (whereas some of his purported observations seem rather to have been culled from his reading). He reported camphor and durians ("the taste varies, like that of cheese"[12]) in Sumatra. As specialists in gems, both travellers were always interested in where rubies, garnets, jacinths, and crystals "grew". Both showed some interest in military intelligence. Santo Stefano was interested in elephant breeding for war and confirmed Conti's claim that ten thousand war elephants were maintained in the stables of the ruler of Pegu.

These were hard-headed observations. But the writers seemed to go soft in the head when they succumbed to the lure of exotica. They crowded their narratives with descriptions of improbable marvels – the travellers' titbits that readers at the time called "mirabilia". No one was expected to believe them, but readers demanded them. Around the Indian Ocean, Conti and Santo Stefano described a topsy-turvy world in which murder is moral, serpents fly, monsters trap fish by lighting irresistible magnetic fires on shore, and miners use vultures and eagles to gather diamonds.[13] Some of the tales echo stories in the Sinbad corpus, and should be seen as evidence that the authors really did know the East at first hand.

The taste for sensationalism was most apparent in the travellers' obsessions with sex. Santo Stefano devoted much space to polygyny and polyandry. He described how Indian men "never marry a virgin" and hand prospective spouses over to strangers for deflowering "for fifteen or twenty days" before the nuptials. Conti was scrupulous in enumerating the harems of great rulers and commending the sangfroid of wives who committed *suti*, flinging themselves on their dead husbands' funeral pyres. In India he found brothels so numerous, and so alluring with "sweet perfumes, ointments, blandishments, beauty and youth", that Indians "are much addicted to licentiousness", whereas male homosexuality, "being superfluous, is unknown".[14] In Ava, in Burma, the women mocked Conti for having a small penis and recommended a local custom: inserting up to a dozen gold, silver, or brass pellets, of about the size of small hazelnuts, under the skin, "and with these insertions, and the swelling of the member, the women are affected with the most exquisite pleasure". Conti refused the service, because "he did not want his pain to be a source of others' pleasure".[15]

On the whole, the merchants' reports were of a world of abundance and civility. Beyond the Ganges, according to Conti, in a translation made in the reign of Elizabeth I, people "are equal to us in customs, life, and policie; for they have sumptuous and neat houses, and all their vessels and householde stuffe very cleane: they esteeme to live as noble people, avoided of all villainie and crueltie, being courteous people &

riche Merchauntes".[16] But if there was one thing the civilisations of the East lacked, it was shipping adequate to meet the huge demands of their highly productive economies and active trades. Santo Stefano marvelled at the cord-bound ships that carried him along the Red Sea and across the Indian Ocean. He noted the bulkhead construction that divided ships' hulls into watertight compartments. But while ships were well designed, well built, and ingeniously navigated, there were never enough of them to carry all the available freight.

As a result, in the 1490s the Indian Ocean was trembling on the brink of a new future in which European interlopers would cash in on their advantages. For that future to happen, Europeans needed to penetrate the ocean with ships. Because they lacked saleable commodities, they had to find other ways of doing business; shipping and freighting were their best resources. Without ships of their own, visitors such as Conti and Santo Stefano were reduced to little better than peddlers. But the Indian Ocean region was so rich and productive, so taut with demand, and so abundant in supply that it could absorb hugely more shipping than was available at the time. Any European who could get ships into the zone stood to make a fortune.

There was only one way to do it: sail the ships in around the southern tip of Africa. But was such a long and hazardous journey possible? Were the ships of the time equal to its strains? Could they carry enough food and water? In any case, it was not even certain that an approach to the ocean lay along that route. The geographer the age most revered was the second-century Alexandrian Claudius Ptolemy. His *Geography*, which became the favourite book on the subject in the West when the text became widely available in the early fifteenth century, was generally read to mean that the Indian Ocean was landlocked, inaccessible by sea. Maps of the world made to illustrate his ideas – and there were many of them at the time – showed the ocean as a vast lake, cut off to the south by a long tongue of land protruding from south-eastern Africa and curling round to lick at the edges of East Asia. The fabled wealth of India and the spice islands lay enclosed within it, like jewels in a strong room.

Although this was an erroneous view, it was understandable. Indian Ocean merchants kept to the reliable routes, served by predictable monsoons, that guaranteed them two-way passage between most of the trading destinations of maritime Asia and East Africa. There was little reason to venture below about ten degrees south, where the belt of tempests girds the sea, or to risk the coasts south of Mozambique, where the storms tear into lee shores. There were no potential trading partners in the region, no opportunities worth braving those dangers for. From within the monsoon system, the way in and out of it did seem effectively unnavigable.

For anyone who tried to approach from the Atlantic, by contrast, no such inhibitions applied. In 1487 the Portuguese explorer Bartolomeu Dias managed to struggle around the Cape of Storms. The king of Portugal is supposed to have renamed it the Cape of Good Hope in a promotional exercise of brazen chutzpah. But the hope was weak, the storms strong. Beyond the cape, Dias found an adverse current and dangerous lee shores. The way to the Indian Ocean still seemed to be barred. Nor had Dias really gone far enough to prove that the ocean was not landlocked. All he had achieved was to demonstrate how laborious was the journey to the southernmost tip of Africa: to avoid the adverse current along the West African shore, his successors would have to strike far into the South Atlantic – farther from home, longer at sea, than any voyagers had ever been – to find the westerly winds that would carry them around the cape.

So, while Dias explored the way by sea, the Portuguese crown sent agents overland to the Indian Ocean by traditional routes to gather intelligence and, in particular, to settle the question of whether the ocean was open to the south. Pero da Covilhão led the effort. He was one of the many indigent but talented noblemen to cross and recross the permeable border between Portugal and Castile. He spent years in Seville, where he served in the household of the Castilian nobleman the Count (later Duke) of Medina Sidonia. This was probably a useful apprentice-

The Portuguese embassy to Ethiopia in 1520 found Covilhão at the court of the Negus. The official Ethiopian account stresses "Prester John's" magnificence.

ship. The count was an investor in the conquest of the Canary Islands and a major figure in the Atlantic tuna fishery and sugar industry. But when war broke out between the two kingdoms in 1474, Covilhão returned to his native Portugal to serve his king. Missions of an unknown nature – perhaps espionage, perhaps diplomacy – took him to Maghrebi courts, where he learned Arabic.

At about the time Bartolomeu Dias left to explore the approach to the Indian Ocean from the Atlantic, Covilhão, with a companion, Afonso de Paiva, set off up the Nile and across the Ethiopian desert to Zeila on the Red Sea. His inquiries took him east to Calicut and south, perhaps as far as Sofala on the coast of Mozambique – the emporium from which East African gold was traded across the Indian Ocean. By the end of 1490 he was back in Cairo, from where he sent a report of his findings home. It has not survived. But it surely summarised knowledge gleaned on the spot: the Indian Ocean was indeed open to the south. Covilhão then turned to a further aspect of mission: establishing diplomatic contact with the court of the ruler of Ethiopia, who retained the Portuguese visitor in his service. Covilhão was still there when the next Portuguese mission got through in 1520.

Policy makers in Portugal thought the Ethiopian ruler was important to their plans to send ships to the Indian Ocean, because they knew that his realm was Christian, and they identified him as "Prester John" – a legendary potentate of supposedly fabulous wealth whom Westerners had sought at intervals for three and a half centuries in the hope of securing an ally against Islam. For between the withdrawal of the Chinese in the 1430s and the arrival of the Europeans in the 1490s, the Indian Ocean was a Muslim lake. Most of the states that lined it were under Muslim rule or dominance and had substantial, usually majoritarian, Muslim populations. Muslim merchants – Arabs, Gujaratis, Persians – carried much of the commerce that crossed the ocean, though Hindu, Jain, and Buddhist merchants were also of great importance. The latest sailing directions, on which pilots relied, were the work of the great Muslim oceanographer Ahmad ibn Majid, who compiled his account of the East African coast from personal surveying expeditions. His reputation grew to the point where sailors from Aden regarded him as a saint and offered him prayers for their safety when they launched their boats.

There were, of course, regions intractable to Islam. In some circles, Islam met a sceptical reception. Kabir of Benares was a poet of secularist inclinations.

> Feeling your power, you circumcise –
> I can't go along with that, brother. If your God favoured circumcision
> why didn't you come out cut?

Hindus fared little better in the face of Kabir's scepticism:

If putting on the thread makes you a brahmin,
What does the wife put on? . . . Hindu, Muslim, where did they
come from?[17]

Fanaticism was more effective than scepticism in setting limits to the spread of Islam. Hindus generally resisted Muslim proselytisation with tenacity. In southern India, the warlike state of Vijayanagar proclaimed its defiance in its name, which means "city of victories". In 1443 it impressed a Muslim visitor as "such that the eye has seen nothing like it", inside its sixty-mile ring of sevenfold walls. Vijayanagar's rajahs called themselves "Lords of the Eastern and Western Oceans". According to the maxims of an early-sixteenth-century ruler,

[a] king should improve the harbours of his country and so encourage its commerce that horses, elephants, precious gems, sandalwood, pearls and other articles are freely imported. . . . Make the merchants of distant foreign countries who import elephants and good horses attached to yourself by providing them with villages and decent dwellings in the city, by affording them daily audience, presents, and allowing decent profits. Then those articles will never go to your enemies.[18]

In practice, however, the capital was as far from the sea as you could get, and outlying provinces were hard to control. By 1485, the power of Vijayanagar's neighbours seemed not only to have arrested the expansion of the state but to threaten its very existence. Taxation from coastal emporia dried up as the frontiers withdrew inland. Muslim warlords usurped frontier areas. So a frustrated general, Saluva Narasimha, mounted a putsch and organised the state for war. The relief was temporary. After his death in 1491 renewed struggle for the throne almost extinguished the kingdom, until in 1492 another ambitious general, Narasa Nayaka, took effective power without proclaiming himself king. Thanks to these strong men, the state survived precariously to resume expansion a generation later.

Jihad was one means of spreading and consolidating Islamic appeal, or, at least, Muslim power. Aggressive sultanates justified their wars by invoking religion. In 1470, the Russian merchant Afanasyi Nikitin reported on them, describing their military might in awe-struck terms and recounting some of their raids against Hindu lands. His account of what he called his "sinful wanderings" is skewed by his renunciation of his merchant's vocation – he insists that the pepper and textiles of India are valueless – and by terrible guilt that overcame him at the compromises and evasions of faith he was forced to make in order to trade and even to survive in the realms of rulers who prided themselves on Muslim fanaticism. He frequently protests – too much – that he remained faithful to Christianity, but his own evidence makes it plain that he had to renounce his religion, at least outwardly. The main purpose of his book seems to be solemnly to warn fellow Christians not to trade in India, in peril of their souls. After many months in the Bahmanid kingdom in the Deccan, India, he was unable to compute the date of Easter.

> I have nothing with me; no books whatever; those that I had taken from Russia were lost when I was robbed. And I forgot the Christian faith and the Christian festivals and knew not Easter nor Christmas . . . for I am between the two faiths.[19]

Nikitin reported that the Bahmanids commanded an army a million strong, armed with firearms, including heavy cannon. The sultan's armour was of gold inlaid with sapphires and diamonds. His counsellors were borne through the streets on couches of gold. Hundreds of armour-clad elephants accompanied him, each bearing an armoured howdah bristling with gunmen. The state was indeed near the height of its power. Under the enterprising favourite Mahmud Gawan, in the 1460s and 1470s the sultan's authority grew at the expense of the nobles, and the frontiers at the expense of neighbours. But the campaigns both inside and outside the kingdom provoked resentment and overtaxed the strength of the state. In 1482 the sultan had the minister murdered, allegedly because he "dared to come in our way and he tried to join forces with our enemies".[20] His master soon followed him to the grave, leaving the throne to a twelve-year-old, Shihabu'd-din Mahmud. The power struggles that followed among the ministers and generals unleashed massacres, provoked a popular rebellion, and made it easy for provincial power brokers to usurp authority and, in effect, secede from the realm. By 1492 the Bahmanid kingdom was in a state of fission. Over the next couple of years, Shihabu'd-din reasserted his authority in a series of victories against recalcitrant subordinates – but only temporarily arrested the dissolution.

The strength of the Muslim sultanate of Gujarat peaked at roughly the same time. Mahmud Shah Begarha (1469–1511) conquered Champaner from its Hindu masters in 1484 and began rebuilding the city on the grand scale still visible in the sumptuous ruins of palaces, bazaars, squares, gardens, mosques, irrigation tanks, and ornamental ponds. There were workshops producing fine silk, textiles, and arms, and Hindu temples were allowed outside the walls. The sultan's mightiest subject, Malik Ayaz, came to Gujarat in the 1480s as a Russian slave famous for valour and archery in the entourage of a master who presented him to the sultan. Freed for gallantry in battle – or, in another account, for killing a hawk that had besmirched the sultan's head with its droppings – he received the captaincy of an area that included the ancient site of a harbourside settlement, just re-emerging, thanks to Malik's immediate predecessors, from centuries of accumulated jungle. He turned Diu into an impressively fortified emporium and induced shippers from the Red Sea, the Persian Gulf, Melaka, China, and Arabia to use it as their gateway to northern India. His style of life reflected the value of the trade. When he visited the sultan, he had nine hundred horses in his train. He employed a thousand water carriers and served Indian, Persian, and Turkish cuisine to his guests off china plates.

No state in India at the time could compare with the sultanate of Delhi, which began in the tradition of the many hegemonies that invading dynasts had founded in India; it was more of a racket than a state, a supremacy shared among predatory clan members and ethnic cronies. When Bahlul, the founding father, arrived from Afghanistan, he wrote home advertising the wealth of India and enticing his kinsmen to abjure their native poverty and follow him. They swarmed in – it seemed to locals – "like ants or locusts". But the size and diversity of his domains and opportunities soon had Bahlul recruiting help more widely. He had twenty thousand Mongols in his service. As the frontiers widened, it became increasingly prudent and increasingly necessary to employ natives – as long as they were or would be Muslims.

Bahlul's successor, Sikandar Lodi, who was on the throne in 1492, adopted indigenous court rituals and "favoured nobles and shaikhs from Arabia, Persia, and various parts of Hind".[21] Sikandar Lodi's maternal grandfather was a commoner – a goldsmith – a taint that almost cost him the throne. In matters of manners and morals he had high standards and tough practices. Like all Muslim rulers of the time, he commissioned annalists who celebrated him so lavishly as to undermine all credibility – excusing, for instance, as "for the sake of his health" the toping of this supposedly uncompromising enforcer of the sharia. He certainly exempted himself from his own rules, including the prohibition of shaving. He performed miracles, commanded jinns, and had a magic lamp that illuminated for him news of far-off events.[22] He flogged nobles who besmirched a polo match by brawling. He deflected the erotic attentions of an over-admiring sheikh by singeing his beard.

His fanaticism disgusted even his own chroniclers. He destroyed Hindu temples, smashed images, proscribed rites. When a sheikh disputed the justice of prohibiting Hindus' sacred baths, the sultan raised his sword against the man in anger. His vocation was as a conqueror:

that is why he called himself Sikandar – the local form of the name of Alexander the Great. He got as far as annexing Bihar and Dholpur. But he left the state overextended and impoverished. He chopped up Hindu idols and gave the pieces to Muslim butchers to use for weighing meat. He turned temples into mosques and madrassas. He burned a Hindu holy man alive for saying, "Islam and Hindu Dharma are both equally acceptable to God if followed with a sincere heart." He frequently razed temples and erected mosques in their place, as evidenced by his behaviour at Mandrail, Utgir, and Narwar. He issued orders, backed by threats of punishment by death, against the Hindu custom of bathing and shaving to mark the midsummer festival.[23]

Aggression, however, probably contributed less to the spread of Islam than peaceful proselytisation: acculturation by trade, and the slow, sometimes unrewarding work of missionaries. In what would become Malaysia and Indonesia, as in Africa, the other great arena of Islamic expansion at the time, the means of propagation was the "jihad of words".[24]

Trade shunted living examples of Muslim devotion between cities and installed Muslims as port supervisors, customs officials, and agents to despotic monopolists. Trading states speckled the Swahili coast, but the conventional notion that they housed ocean-going peoples is false. For generations, the Swahili responded to the racism of Western masters by cultivating a non-African image, emphasising their links of culture and commerce with Arabia and India. After independence, some of their hinterland neighbours took revenge, treating them as colonists, rather as the inland communities of Liberia and Sierra Leone treated the descendants of resettled slaves in Monrovia and Freetown as an alien and justly resented elite. In Kenya, political demagogues threatened to expel the Swahili, as if they were foreign intruders. Yet the Swahili language, though peppered with Arabic loanwords, is closely akin to other Bantu languages. The Swahili came to the coast from the interior, perhaps thousands of years ago, and retained links with the hinterland that their trade with visitors from the Indian Ocean never displaced.

The coastal location of Swahili cities conveys a misleading impression of why the sea was important to them: they were sited for proximity to fresh water, landward routes, and sources of widely traded coral as much as for ocean access. The elite usually married their daughters to business partners inland rather than to foreign sojourners. Few cities had good anchorages. More than half had poor harbours, or none at all. The town of Gedi, which covered eighteen acres inside ten-foot-high walls and had a palace over a hundred feet wide, was four miles from the sea. Swahili traders plied their own coasts and frequented their own hinterlands, acquiring gold, timber, honey, civet, rhinoceros horn, and ivory to sell to the Arabs, Indians, and Gujaratis who carried them over the ocean. They were classic middlemen who seem to have calculated that the risks of transoceanic trading were not worthwhile as long as customers came to their coasts.

Visiting Portuguese in the early sixteenth century noticed the love-hate relationship that bound the Swahili to the hinterland. On the one hand, the two zones needed each other for trade; on the other, religious enmity between the Muslims and their pagan neighbours committed them to war. This, thought Duarte Barbosa, was why the coastal dwellers had "cities well walled with stone and mortar, inasmuch as they are often at war with the Heathen of the mainland".[25] There were material causes of conflict, too. The Swahili needed plantations, acquired at hinterland communities' expense, to grow food, and slaves to serve them. Coastal and interior peoples exchanged raids and demands for tribute as well as regular trade. When Portuguese observers arrived in the early sixteenth century, they got the impression that Mombasa, the greatest of the Swahili port cities, lived in awe of its neighbours, the "savage", poison-arrow-toting Mozungullos, who had "neither law nor king nor any other interest in life except theft, robbery, and murder".[26] But Islam provided the standard excuse for hostilities, if not their real cause. The religion was well established among the urban Swahili, after nearly half a millennium of proselytisation by visiting merchants and the Sufis and sheikhs they sometimes carried in their ships. By the early fourteenth century, visiting Muslims commonly praised their orthodoxy. It was probably not until the sixteenth century, when Portuguese piracy disrupted the Indian Ocean trade of the Swahili coast, that local Islam began to diverge from the mainstream.

For some cities, the ocean was all-important. Kilwa was one of the greatest of Swahili emporia because the monsoon made it accessible to transoceanic traders in a single season. Ports farther south, like Sofala, though rich in gold, were accessible only after a laborious wait, usually in Kilwa, for the wind to turn. Merchants from Gujarat seem rarely to have bothered to go farther south than Mombasa or Malindi, where merchants congregated with products from all along the coast as far as Sofala. The Gujaratis paid for their purchases with fine Indian textiles of silk and cotton.

On the opposite shore of the ocean, in South-east Asia, it was harder for Islam to penetrate agrarian states with only limited interest in long-range trade. In what came to be called Indochina, the Khmer kingdom was a self-contained unit, which produced enough rice to feed its people. The rulers never showed any interest in going into business in their own right, though around the turn of the century they shifted their capital to what is now Phnom Penh in an apparent effort to increase their control over the revenue from maritime trade. Vietnam – which was culturally and physically close to China – adopted policies actively hostile to overseas commerce. Le Thanh Ton, who ruled from 1460 to 1497, forbade the waste of land, broke up great estates, colonised frontier zones with prisoners and demobilised soldiers, and gave fiscal exemptions to diggers of ditches and planters of mulberries. He almost doubled the size of his kingdom by southward conquests that took the frontier beyond Qui Nonh. He issued regulations that seem too perfect ever to have been put into practice, in which all his subjects were arrayed in order of rank under the rule of royally appointed bureaucrats. He scattered temples of literature around the country, where aspiring mandarins could study the works of Confucius and prepare for civil-service examinations on the Chinese pattern. While empowering

1492

Confucian bureaucrats and imposing a strict law code inspired by Confucius, Le held on to popular sensibilities by representing himself as the reincarnation of a heroic ancestor.

Native kings in the region had a lot to lose if they committed to Islam: the awe inspired by reincarnation, the role of preceding the Buddhist millennium or incarnating a Hindu deity, the custodianship of relics sacred to Hindus and Buddhists. Ramathibodi II, for instance, who came to the throne of Ayutthaya – the kingdom that became Siam – in 1491, engaged in trials of magic power with neighbouring kings. Khmer kingship relied on the notion that kings were Buddhas or incarnations of Shiva. In a region of divine kingship and agrarian states, it was hard for Islam to get a toehold: neither merchants nor missionaries could exert much influence.

The Malay world that flanked Indochina and lay offshore was more permeable, full of trading states and seafaring traditions. As the sultan of Melaka observed in 1468, "to master the blue oceans people must engage in trade, even if their countries are barren".[27] Camõens, who ranged the East and celebrated it in verse in the late sixteenth century, described the Malay world:

> *Malacca see before, where ye shall pitch*
> *Your great Emporium, and your Magazins:*
> *The Rendezvous of all that Ocean round*
> *For Merchandizes rich that there abound.*
> *From this ('tis said) the Waves impetuous course,*
> *Breaking a passage through from Main to main,*
> *Samatra's noble Isle of old did force,*
> *Which then a Neck of Land therewith did chain:*
> *That this was Chersonese till that divorce,*
> *And from the wealthy mines, that there remain,*
> *The Epithite of "Golden" had annext:*
> *Some think, it was the Ophyr in the Text.*[28]

◆   ◆   ◆

Muslim merchants frequented the region for centuries before any natives accepted Islam. Some of them formed communities in port cities.
Missionaries followed: scholars in search of patronage, discharging the
Muslim's obligation to proselytise on the way; spiritual athletes in
search of exercise, anxious to challenge native shamans in contests of
ascetic ostentation and supernatural power. In some areas Sufis made
crucial contributions. They could empathise with the sort of popular
animism and pantheism that "finds Him closer than the veins of one's
neck".[29] As missionaries, Sufis were the most effective agents. As always
with conversion stories, it is hard to distinguish miracle tales, invented
in retrospect to hallow events, from real evidence. The legends of conversions engineered by Sufis are untrustworthy, partly because they are
often warped by the writers' wider agendas, and partly because they
tend to be shaped by traditional topoi.

Sacred autobiography is predictably full of stories of childish orchard
raiding and youthful peccadilloes, suddenly visited darkness, suddenly
glimpsed light. The crucial questions relate to the self-reprofiling of
whole societies. This is a process, still little understood, by which the
term "Islam" becomes part of the collective self-designation of whole
communities, embracing numbers of people who have never had a conversion experience or anything like it. Underlying collective realign-
ments of this sort are further, remoter processes, by which Islam
captures elites or becomes part of the landscape of life in a particular
society or – if I may be permitted another metaphor – a thread in the
fabric of social identity. For most people in the society that plays host to
the new religion, it commonly involves passive reception of new doc-
trines and devotions, without any active commitment.

According to tradition, the first ruler to embrace Islam in South-east
Asia, in Pasai, on Sumatra, in the late thirteenth century, received the
message of the faith in a dream. He then invited a holy man over to

complete his conversion. In the following century, other Sumatran states followed suit, and there were Muslim-led states on the Malayan mainland. Early in the fifteenth century, Melaka's ruler adopted Islam. From the end of the century conversions multiplied, spread by dynastic marriages or by a radiation-like process in which Sufis fanned outwards from each successive centre to which they came. Melaka seems to have provided manpower for the conversion of states in Java, which in turn, around the beginning of the new century, did the same job for Ternate in the Moluccas, from where missionaries continued to neighbouring islands. Provincial rulers guaranteed the flow of revenue to the sultans' courts in exchange for the unmolested exercise of power. "As for us who administer territory," said a nobleman in a Malay chronicle, "what concern is that of yours? . . . What we think should be done we do, for the ruler is not concerned with the difficulties we administrators encounter. He only takes account of the good results we achieve."[30]

Shortly before his death in 1478, the Sufi proselytiser Abu-al-Mewahib al-Shadili summarised what he called the "maxims of illumination" – *Qawanin Hikam al-Ishraq*. Sufis, he thought, were an elite: others were "people of deviation and innovation".[31] Every one of his maxims began with a text from the Quran. Mystical experience was like memory. To be "immersed in the sea of unity" with God, the mystic had to efface all thoughts of his attributes, concentrate on his essence, and "then the distance that is between him and you is effaced".[32] Abandon intelligence, reason, experiment, and authority, al-Shadili urged.[33] Lose consciousness of the universe. Practise permanent penance, for "the repentance of ordinary men is a passing mood". Sufis could approach enlightenment because they had come to acknowledge the power of evil over them and the need to repent of it. The author quoted the Gospels as well as the Quran.[34]

Al-Shadili recommended watchfulness as a means to identification with God. "The thought of Truth's sentinel came to the heart of a servant who was lonely among men." "There passed through the heart and thought of a longing person a glimpse of the splendour and beauty of the loved one which turned him like unto a person bewitched by the sorcery of the Babylonians: all this took place when his longings and nightingales of joy were loosed." The author was glib with images from the mystical repertoire common to many cultures and dangerous in Islam – likening experience of God to physical love, pagan magic, even drunkenness. A mystical experience overcame him in a garden, when the trees rustled:

> The winds of union with them blew at daybreak,
> With gusts of yearning in the heart.
> The branch of love merrily shook in me,
> When fruits of love fell here and there.
> Suns of union with penetrating rays
> Pierced the awnings of the veils.
> Clear joy shone over us and thus sparkled
> The face of compassion which dispelled all blame.[35]

While Columbus was beginning preparations for his first transoceanic voyage, one of the greatest mystics of the age died in what is now Afghanistan. Nur ad-Din Abd ar-Rahman Jami was a consummate poet – the last great Persian poet, some say, and the biographer of a long line of Sufis. He was one of the most celebrated intellectuals of the age, whose fame in Asia was wider and deeper than any mere hero of the Renaissance could have achieved, at the time, within the narrow limits of Christendom. The rulers of the Ottoman Empire and the heirs of the Mongol khans competed unsuccessfully for his services as a political adviser: he preferred a life of art and meditation. Some of his works were translated into Chinese and sustained considerable influence over the next two hundred years in Buddhist as well as Muslim mysticism. Besides accounts of his mystical experiences, he wrote an explanation of mystical principles, called *Gleams* (*Lawa'ih*). Sense veiled reality. The self was a distraction: "[T]ry to conceal yourself," he recommended, "from your own gaze."[36] Learning was a snare – a judgement many

Franciscan mystics in Europe would have endorsed. "How can love," he demanded, "appear from the folds of your books?"[37] He would have agreed with most Western mystics on another point: mystics had to beware of self-indulgence and make love practical. Jami advised, "Don't count the Real as apart from the world, for the world is in the Real, and in the world the Real is none but the world."[38] For himself, however, his goals were otherworldly. The world was hardly worth contemplation. He dismissed it with a shrug – almost a smirk – of ennui: "I've had my fill of every loveliness not eternal."[39] Jami was aware that annihilation meant the eclipse of consciousness: "Annihilation of annihilation is in-cluded in annihilation. . . . If you are conscious of the tip of a hair and speak of annihilation's road, you've left the road."[40] Even religion was irrelevant to the mystic, whose "custom is annihilation and whose rule poverty". When you achieve union with God, why consort with mul-lahs? The same sort of thought occurred to Christian mystics.

His acknowledged masterpiece was his immensely long last poem, *Yusuf and Zulaikha*, a searing love story that encodes a religion of Jami's devising, which, without any overt tampering with Islam, is utterly per-sonal, and takes stunning liberties with the Quran. He takes the Quranic story of Yusuf – the biblical Joseph – and the seductress he encountered in his flight from his abusive brethren, and turns it into a treatise on love as a sort of ladder of Bethel – a means of ascent to personal union with God. The author begins by addressing readers who seek mystical experi-ence. "Go away and fall in love," he counsels. "Then come back and ask me." Loving union is a way of connecting with God, "who quickens the heart and fills the soul with rapture". Zulaikha first sees her future lover in a vision so powerful that lust impedes her from loving him truly. While the world goggles at his splendour and beauty, his wife tortures herself with reproaches and longs for death. If she had grasped the inward form instead of embracing the body that conceals it, she would have found that conjugal love can be a means of ascent to God.

She begins to glimpse the truths of mysticism – the possibilities of self-realisation through self-immersion in love, but carnality obstructs her. Jami says, "As long as love has not attained perfection, lovers' sole preoccupation is to satisfy desire. . . . They willingly prick the beloved with a hundred thorns." Zulaikha has to go through a series of terrible purgations, which are like the classic stages of mystical ascent: despair, renunciation, blindness, oblivion. She endures repeated rejection by Yusuf and loses everything that once mattered to her – her wealth, her beauty, and her sight – before the lovers can be united. Zulaikha perceives the mystic truth:

> In solitude, where Being signless dwelt,
> And all the universe still dormant lay
> Concealed in selflessness, One Being was
> Exempt from "I" or "Thou"-ness, and apart
> From all duality; Beauty Supreme,
> Unmanifest, except unto Itself
> By Its own light, yet fraught with power to charm
> The souls of all; concealed in the Unseen,
> An Essence pure, unstained by aught of ill.[41]

Carnal love shatters like a graven idol. Yusuf's real beauty strikes his inamorata afresh, like a light so dazzling that he seems lost in it.

> From Everlasting Beauty, which emerged
> From realms of purity to shine upon
> The worlds, and all the souls which dwell therein.
> One gleam fell from It on the universe
> And on the angels, and this single ray
> Dazzled the angels, till their senses whirled
> Like the revolving sky. In diverse forms
> Each mirror showed it forth, and everywhere
> Its praise was chanted in new harmonies.
> The cherubim, enraptured, sought for songs
> Of praise. The spirits who explore the depths

1492

Of boundless seas, wherein the heavens swim
Like some small boat, cried with one mighty voice,
"Praise to the Lord of all the universe!"[42]

Nowadays, most people, I suspect, will find it hard to think of mysticism as modern. It was, at least, a gateway to one of the great mansions of modernity: the enhanced sense of self – the individualism, sometimes edging narcissism or egotism, that elbows community to the edge of our priorities. Without the rise of individualism, it would be hard to imagine a world organised economically for "enlightened self-interest" or politically along lines of "one person, one vote". Modern novels of self-discovery, modern psychology, feel-good values, existential angst, and the self-obsessions of the "me generation" would all be unthinkable. Liberation from self-abnegation had to begin – or at least have one of its starting points – in religious minds, because godly institutions, in the Middle Ages, were the major obstacles to self-realisation. The watchfulness of fellow congregants disciplined desire. The collective pursuit of salvation diminished individuals' power. The authority of godly establishments overrode individual judgement. Mysticism was a way out of these constraints. For worshippers with a hotline to God, institutional religion is unnecessary. Sufis, Catholic and Orthodox mystics, and Protestant reformers were all, therefore, engaged, in one sense, in the same project: firing the synapses that linked them to divine energy; freeing themselves to make up their own minds; putting clerisy in its place. Whatever modernity is, the high valuation of the individual is part of it. The mystics' role in making modernity has been overlooked, but by teaching us to be aware of our individual selves, they helped to make us modern.

Chapter 10

"The Fourth World"

Indigenous Societies in the Atlantic and the Americas

6 March: A young Montezuma celebrates
tlacaxipehualiztli, the spring fertility festival, and
witnesses the sacrifice of human captives – their hearts
ripped out, their bodies rolled down the high temple steps.

In 1493, when Columbus got back from his first voyage, no one – least of all the explorer himself – knew where he had been. In the received picture of the planet, the earth was an island, divided between three continents: Europe, Asia, and Africa. For most European scholars, it was hard to believe that what they called "a fourth part of the world" existed. (Some Native American peoples, by coincidence, called the earth they trod "the fourth world" – to distinguish it from the heavens, the waters, and the underground darkness.) Humanist geographers, who knew ancient writers' speculations that an "antipodean" continent awaited discovery, groped towards the right conclusion about what Columbus had found. Others assumed – more consistently with the evidence – that he had simply stumbled on "another Canary

Guamán Poma's early-
seventeenth-century
drawing of work on a
rope bridge under the
supervision of the Inca
inspector of bridges,
whose ear-spools
denote his elite status.

Island": another bit of an archipelago that Spanish conquistadores were already struggling to incorporate into the dominions of the crown of Castile. This was a pardonable error: Columbus's newfound lands were on the latitude of the Canaries. Their inhabitants, by Columbus's own account, were "like the Canary Islanders" in colour and culture. Despite Columbus's urgent search for valuable trade goods, the new lands seemed, even to the discoverer, more likely to be viable as sources of slaves and locations for sugar-planting – just as the Canaries had been.

The conquest of the Canary Islands was a vital part of the context of Columbus. The archipelago was a laboratory for conquests in the Americas: an Atlantic frontier, inhabited by culturally baffling strangers, who seemed "savage" to European beholders; a new environment, uneasily adaptable to European ways of life; a land that could be planted with new crops, exploited with a new, plantation-style economy, settled with colonists, and wrenched into new, widening patterns of trade.

In the Canaries, the conquest of the Atlantic world was already under way when Columbus set sail. The core of the financial circle that paid for his first transatlantic voyage formed when a consortium of Sevillan bankers and royal treasury officials combined to meet the costs of conquering Grand Canary in 1478–83. Columbus's point of departure was the westernmost port of the archipelago, San Sebastián de la Gomera, which became fully secure only when a Spanish army uprooted the last native resistance on that island in 1489. The Spaniards did not reckon the conquest of the most intractable islands as complete until 1496.

The natives – all of whom disappeared in the colonial era owing to conquest, enslavement, disease, and assimilation – were among the last descendants of the pre-Berber inhabitants of North Africa. For a sense of what they were like, the nearest surviving parallels are the Imraguen and Znaga – the poor, marginal fishing folk who cling to the coastal rim of the Sahara today, surviving only by occupying places no one else wants. Along with the advantages of isolation, the islanders enjoyed – before Europeans arrived – a mixed economy, based on pastoralism supplemented by farming cereals in small plots, from which they made *gofio* – slops of powdered, toasted grain mixed with milk or soup or water that are still eaten everywhere in the islands but appreciated, as far as I know, nowhere else. They made a virtue of isolation, abandoning navigation and barely communicating from island to island, even though some islands lie within sight of one another – rather like the ancient Tasmanians or Chatham Islanders or Easter Islanders, who imposed isolation on themselves. They forswore the technology that took them to their homes, as if they were consciously withdrawing from the world, like dropouts of a bygone era. Insulation from the rest of the world, however, has disadvantages. Contact with other cultures stimulates what we call development, whereas isolation leads to stagnation. The material culture of the Canarians was rudimentary. They lived in caves or crudely extemporised huts. They were armed, when they had to face European invaders, only with sticks and stones.

The ferocity and long-sustained success of their resistance gives the lie to the notion that superior European technology guaranteed rapid success against "primitives" and "savages". Adventurous European individuals and ambitious European states launched expeditions at intervals from the 1330s. They depleted some islands by enslaving captives, but they could not establish any enduring presence until a systematic effort in the early fifteenth century, launched by adventurers from Normandy, secured control of the poorest and least-populated islands of Lanzarote, Fuerteventura, and Hierro. The conquerors installed precarious but lasting colonies, which, after some hesitation and oscillation between the crowns of France, Portugal, and Aragon, ended owing allegiance to Castile.

After that, the conquest stalled again. The remaining islands repelled many expeditions from Portugal and Castile. In the mid-fifteenth century, the Peraza family – minor noblemen of Seville who had acquired the lordship of some islands, and claimed the right of conquest over the rest – gained a footing in Gomera, where they built a fort and exacted tribute from the natives, without introducing European colonists. Repeated rebellions culminated in 1488, when the natives put the incumbent lord, Hernán Peraza, to death, and the Spanish crown had to send an army to restore order. In revenge, the insurgents were executed or enslaved in droves, with dubious legality, as "rebels against their natural lord". The Spaniards put a permanent garrison on the island. The treatment of the natives, meanwhile, touched tender consciences in Castile. The monarchs commissioned jurists and theologians to inquire into the case. The inquiry recommended the release of the slaves, and many of them eventually returned to the archipelago to help colonise other islands. Their native land, however, was now ripe for transformation. In the next decade, European investors turned it over to sugar production.

Ferdinand and Isabella, who were not yet committed to the exhausting effort of conquering Granada, thought intervention worthwhile be-

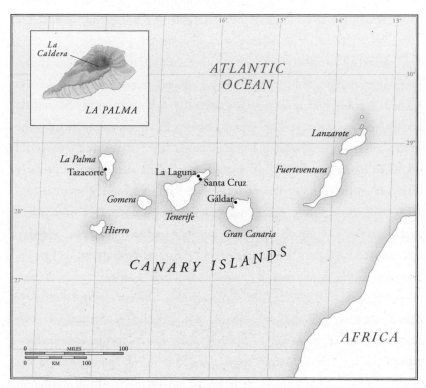

The Canary Islands.

cause of Castile's rivalry with Portugal, which made the Canaries seem important. Castilian interlopers in the African Atlantic had long attracted Portuguese complaints, but the war of 1474–79, in which Afonso V of Portugal challenged Ferdinand and Isabella for the Castilian throne, intensified Castilian activity. The monarchs were open-handed with licences for voyages of piracy or carriage of contraband. Genoese merchant houses with branches in Seville and Cadiz and an eye on the potential sugar business were keen to invest in these enterprises. The main action of the war took place on land, in northern Castile, but a "small war" at sea in the latitude of the Canaries accompanied it. Castilian privateers broke into Portugal's monopoly of trade and slaving on the Guinea coast. Portuguese attacks menaced Castilian outposts in the Canary Islands. The value of the unconquered islands of the archipelago – Grand Canary, Tenerife, and La Palma, which were the largest and most promising economically – became obvious. When Ferdinand and Isabella sent a force to resume the conquest in 1478, a Portuguese expedition in seven caravels was already on its way. The Castilian intervention was a pre-emptive strike.

Other, longer-maturing reasons also influenced the royal decision. First, the monarchs had other rivals than the Portuguese to keep in mind. The Perazas' lordship had descended by marriage to Diego de Herrera, a minor nobleman of Seville, who fancied himself as a conquistador. His claim to have made vassals of nine native "kings" or chiefs of Tenerife and two on Grand Canary was, to say the least, exaggerated. He raided the islands in the hope of extracting tribute by terror, and attempted, in the manner of previous would-be conquistadores, to dominate them by erecting intimidating turrets. Such large, populous, and indomitable islands, however, would not succumb to the private enterprise of a provincial hidalgo. Effective conquest and systematic exploitation demanded concentrated resources and heavy investment. These were more readily available at the royal court.

Even had Herrera been able to complete the conquest, it would have been unwise for the monarchs to let him do so. He was not above intrigue with the Portuguese, and he was typical of the truculent paladins whose power in peripheral regions was an affront to the crown. Almost since the first conquerors seized power in the Canaries, lords and kings had been in dispute over the limits of royal authority in the islands. Profiting from a local rebellion against seigneurial authority in 1475–76 – one of a series of such rebellions – Ferdinand and Isabella decided to enforce their suzerainty and, in particular, the most important element in it: the right to be the ultimate court of appeal throughout the colonies of the archipelago. In November 1476 they launched an inquiry into the legal basis of lordship in the Canaries. The results were enshrined in an agreement between seigneur and suzerain in October 1477: Herrera's rights were unimpeachable, saving the superior lordship of the crown; but "for certain just and reasonable causes", which were never specified, the right of conquest should revert to Ferdinand and Isabella.

Beyond the political reasons for intervening in the islands, there were economic motives. As always in the history of European meddling in the African Atlantic, gold was the spur. According to a privileged chronicler, King Ferdinand was interested in the Canaries because he wanted to open communications with "the mines of Ethiopia"[1] – a general name, at the time, for Africa. The Portuguese denied him access to the new gold sources on the underside of the African bulge, where the trading post of São Jorge da Mina opened in 1482. Their refusal must have stimulated the search for alternative sources and helps explain the emphasis Columbus's journals placed on the need for gold. Meanwhile, the growth of demand for sugar and dyes in Europe made the Canaries worth conquering for their own sake: dyes were among the natural products of the archipelago; sugar was the boom industry European colonists introduced.

The conquest was almost as hard under royal auspices as under those of Diego de Herrera. Native resistance was partly responsible. Finance and manpower proved elusive. One of Ferdinand's and Isabella's chroniclers could hardly bring himself to mention the campaigns in the Canaries without complaining about the expense. Gradually, although the monarchs' aims in arrogating the right of conquest included the desire to exclude private power from the islands and keep it in the "public" domain, they had to allow what would now be called "public-private partnerships" to play a role. Formerly the monarchs had financed the war by selling indulgences – documents bishops issued to penitents remitting the penalties their sins incurred in this world. Ferdinand and Isabella claimed and exercised the right to sell these to pay for wars against non-Christian enemies. But as the war dragged on and revenues fell, they made would-be conquerors find their own funds. Increasingly, instead of wages, conquistadores received pledges of conquered land. Instead of reinvesting the crown's share of booty in further campaigns,

1492

the monarchs granted away uncollected booty to conquerors who could raise finance elsewhere. By the end of the process, ad hoc companies financed the conquests of La Palma and Tenerife, with conquerors and their backers sharing the proceeds.

The islands – as a royal secretary remarked of Grand Canary – might have proved insuperable, but for internal divisions the Spaniards were able to exploit. For the first three years of the conquest of Grand Canary, the Castilians, undermanned and irregularly provisioned, contented themselves with making raids on native villages. Working for wages, and therefore with little incentive to acquire territory, the recruits from urban militia units did not touch the mountain fastnesses on which the Canarians used to fall back for defence. Rather, they concentrated on places in the low plains and hills, where food, not fighting, could be found – the plains where the natives grew their cereals, the hillsides up and down which they shunted their goats. It was a strategy of mere survival, not of victory. Between raids, the invaders remained in their stockade at Las Palmas, where inactivity bred insurrection.

The arrival of Pedro de Vera as military governor in 1480 inaugurated more purposeful strategies. He planned amphibious excursions to the otherwise barely accessible west coast. He erected a new stockade – a second front – in a strategic spot at Agaete in the north-west. His first major victory was the result of a miscalculation by the native leaders, who marched their forces to the plain of Tamaraseite near Las Palmas to offer conventional battle, with disastrous results. If the chronicler who described the battle can be believed, Pedro de Vera slew one of his principal opponents with his own hand, in what sounds suspiciously like a chivalric or Homeric encounter. Towards the end of 1480 or 1481, when the natives broke off the fighting in order to sow their crops, the truce was celebrated with a mass baptism, to which, presumably, many natives submitted cheerfully without necessarily understanding the significance of the sacrament.

Still, some natives clearly saw the ceremony as marking a new phase in their relations with the Spaniards. A group of chiefs or notables arrived at the court of Ferdinand and Isabella in May 1481. The monarchs contrived a timely display of Christian charity. They bestowed a letter of privilege on the visitors, declaring that they had taken the people of Grand Canary "beneath our protection and royal defence, like the Christians they are", promising them freedom from enslavement and guaranteeing their right to move and trade among Castilian dominions on an equal footing with Castilian-born subjects. From that moment on, "loyalism" and adherence to Christianity increased among the natives.

In coming campaigns, Pedro de Vera was able to play off rival factions. In 1482, the capture and conversion of one of the most important chiefs, known to tradition as Tenesor Semidan but better identified by his baptismal name of Don Fernando Guanarteme, immeasurably strengthened de Vera's hand, as Don Fernando was able to induce many of his compatriots to submit, especially around his power base in the north of the island.

Yet victory still proved elusive. Frustrated by the inaccessibility of the insurgents who held out in the central mountains, beyond perilous goat walks and precipitous defiles, Pedro de Vera turned to a policy of terror and scorched earth. Innocent natives burned to death in reprisal for the loss of Spanish soldiers. Spaniards seized supplies and livestock to deny them to the enemy. Gradually, coerced by these tactics or persuaded by Don Fernando, the natives surrendered. Some abandoned hope and ended their struggle in ritual suicide, flinging themselves from terrible heights.

A remnant continued resistance in justified confidence, for they could still win battles. In the winter of 1483, stalked in a remote ravine, they destroyed a corps of Basque freelances by their usual tactic: precipitating an avalanche to bury the enemy column. De Vera implicitly acknowledged that force could not prevail against them on their chosen terrain. He withdrew to Las Palmas and invited his adversaries to make

1492

honourable terms. While a few recalcitrants continued to roam the mountaintops, almost the entire island was at peace by the summer of 1483. La Palma, meanwhile, had an unconquerable reputation, despite the fact that mutually hostile groups of natives divided the island uneasily among themselves. The Spaniards usually called them "bands" and identified twelve of them. The varied topography of the island, sprinkled with microclimates, ensured that there were enough resources to go around, and plenty of terrain that was almost invulnerable to invaders. The natives, whatever their material differences, all practised the same way of life, mixing goat herding with farming what the Spaniards identified as wheat to make *gofio*. Cairns marked their sacred places, where they left offerings of meat and gathered for athletic contests, especially wrestling in the formal, almost balletic style still popular in the Canary Islands. They disposed of the irremediably sick, or those moribund with age, by what we would now call assisted suicide, laying the victims on a goatskin to await death in a cave mouth, with a flask of milk alongside them, more for comfort than sustenance.

In 1402 the adventurers from Normandy tried to subdue the island and failed. Henry the Navigator launched repeated expeditions. All came to grief. In the mid-fifteenth century the Peraza family launched the most unremitting effort of all. The natives defeated their armies and killed Guillén Peraza, the young heir on whom were centred the family's hopes for the next generation. The incident inspired a ballad, replete with chivalric imagery that masks the squalid reality of the Perazas' wars:

> *Weep, ladies, weep, if God give you grace,*
> *For Guillén Peraza, who left in that place*
> *The flower, now withered, that bloomed in his face.*
> *Guillén Peraza, child of chance,*
> *Where is your shield and where is your lance?*
> *All is destroyed by Fortune's glance.*[2]

La Palma remained intractable until a woman intervened. There are so many stories of women who are instrumental in conquests that it is tempting to see them all as examples of tradition distorting truth. But Francisca Gazmira's role in the conquest of La Palma has left a trail in the archives as well as a trace in romance. In 1491, when Ferdinand and Isabella were laying siege to Granada, they received news of how the governor and clergy of Grand Canary had selected a pious native slave woman, who had been born in La Palma, to return to the island on an evangelising mission "to talk to the leaders and chiefs of the communities of the said island, because they had sent a message to say that they wished to become Christians and entrust themselves to Your Highnesses' lordship".[3]

That an episcopal licence should have been conferred on a lay, native, female missionary suggests that Francisca had remarkable charismatic powers, which she seems to have put to good use among her people. She won plenty of her compatriots to the Spaniards' side. She returned from the island with four or five chiefs, who were baptised and clothed in the cathedral of Grand Canary. "And after they became Christians," the local authorities reported, "she returned them to the said island of La Palma so that they could arrange for the members of their communities to become Christians under Your Highnesses' lordship."[4] The governor ordered that no one should dare enslave any members of the affected communities, and the ecclesiastical authorities invoked a bull of Pope Eugenius IV, of 1434, to forbid enslavement of natives who wished to become Christians and who kept the terms of the peace treaties Francisca's converts had made.

Francisca's success created an opportunity for invaders to harness the help of native allies and at last exploit native divisions to their own advantage. A would-be conquistador was already struggling to get financial backing for a renewed assault on the island. Alonso de Lugo had the perfect profile for the job. He had the right experience. He had fought against the Moors before joining the conquest of Grand Canary, where he was instrumental in capturing Don Fernando Guanarteme. He had the right character: unremittingly ruthless, unrestrainedly ambitious, unhesitatingly reckless, indefeasibly tough. He was a calculating entrepreneur who undertook risks for money as well as glory. He had started the first productive sugar mill on Grand Canary and realised that even if slaving opportunities in La Palma were in decline, the climate and soil suited sugar and promised profit. But the Granada war was now at a critical phase. It was a bad time to raise money and men for more-distant adventures.

According to legend, Lugo was idling disconsolately in Seville Cathedral when he got the money for the conquest of La Palma: St Peter himself appeared in the guise of a mysterious old man and thrust a bagful of doubloons into his grasp. The story represents a feeble attempt to sanctify a morally shabby conquest. Lugo's real backers came from that same group of private financiers in Seville some of whom had already invested in Columbus's enterprise.

Lugo's small, scratch force arrived in the late summer of 1491 on the west coast of the island, to a welcome from the bands Francisca Gazmira had evangelised. If later traditions are reliable, Mayantigo, who was or aspired to be "chief of chiefs" of the island, led the collaborators. The terms of the treaty Lugo made with him suggest a more active alliance than formerly. There was to be "peace and union" between the parties. Mayantigo would acknowledge and obey the Castilian monarchs. He would continue to rule his own band, and would govern on the monarchs' behalf. His people would enjoy all the rights and privileges of the Castilian subjects of the crown. Like so many later Spanish campaigns in the Americas, the war that followed was an internecine struggle, in which natives slaughtered each other, leaving the Spaniards as the beneficiaries of the conflict and the heirs of dead or displaced elites.

Reinforced by the Christian bands, Lugo marched clockwise around the coast, attacking communities who made no effort to unite in resistance. He defeated them piecemeal before withdrawing to winter quarters. The interior of the island was the scene of fiercer defence, for there volcanic activity and erosion have combined to create a vast natural fortress, La Caldera, a cauldron-like crater at the foot of two miles of precipitous, savagely forested slopes. A single people, under a fiercely independent leader whom tradition calls Tanausú, occupied it. Native allies had to carry Lugo on their shoulders to get him over the broken terrain. When the first attack was repulsed, he planned his next assault by an even more tortuous route – reputedly impossible and therefore unguarded. But Tanausú's skill in skirmish and ambush seemed insuperable.

If our sole surviving source can be trusted, Tanausú might have resisted indefinitely had Lugo not tricked him into attending a sham parley at which the Spaniards overcame him and decimated his followers. The story goes that Lugo sent a native emissary, Juan de La Palma, to offer the same terms of submission that the Christian bands had accepted. Tanausú insisted that he would consider proposals only if Lugo's forces withdrew from his lands. He would then take part in a parley on the frontier. Lugo complied, but his sincerity – if he had any – was riven with suspicion. Tanausú was late for the meeting; so Lugo regarded the agreement as null and void. He set out in arms. When the attackers and defenders met, Tanausú's counsellors advised against resumed negotiations, but the leader – in what looks like a literary commonplace rather than an account of real events – rejected their advice. Trusting in Lugo's good faith, he headed into what he thought would be talks but turned out to be a battle. In custody, he could not commit suicide in the spectacular manner of earlier Canarian leaders in defeat. He starved himself to death.[5]

Here for once the chronicle tradition seems to depart from a heroic version of events. The surviving text dates from the last years of the sixteenth century, when boldly revisionist friars were rewriting the history of the conquest of the Canaries. They wanted to make it match the idealised image of New World peoples crafted in the work of the Dominican moralist Bartolomé de Las Casas. Until his death in 1567, this impassioned critic of empire bombarded the royal court with endless examples of the lobbyists' art, praising the natural virtues of the natives and defending their rights. No doubt the received version of the death of Tanausú is as warped as that of the contemporary chronicles, which reflect a perception saturated in chivalric literature. But cruelty and ruthless daring are thoroughly characteristic of everything that is known for certain about Alonso de Lugo.

Partly, perhaps, because of his early reputation for rapacity, Lugo's operations suffered from shortage of finance and from legal entanglements with his backers. In 1494, he narrowly escaped destruction during his attempted invasion of Tenerife after being lured into a trap near the mouth of the spectacular Orotava Valley. He returned with larger forces in 1495 and recruited to his side many natives who felt alienated by the arrogance of the leader of resistance, the chief of Taoro – Tenerife's richest chieftaincy. A battle on a flat plain near La Laguna favoured the Spaniards' cavalry and crossbows, but even after his victory Lugo felt insecure and hunkered down in winter quarters. He sallied forth gingerly in the spring of 1496 to find that a mysterious disease had depleted and debilitated the natives. It was the first of a series of plagues that caused a demographic disaster, comparable, on the island's smaller scale, with those that later devastated the New World. Lugo's triumphal march through what was becoming a wasteland drove the chief of Taoro to ritual suicide in the manner now familiar to Spanish campaigners. Surprisingly, no chronicler recorded the event, but the spot where the chief met his end became a celebrated landmark and appeared over the next few years in many records of land grants. The communities that remained in arms submitted over the next few weeks, and by June 1496, Lugo was able to parade their leaders before the monarchs at court.

It is probably no exaggeration to say that but for the accidents that made the Canaries Castilian, the New World could not have become predominantly Spanish. The wind pattern of the ocean makes the archipelago the ideal staging post on the outward journey, almost directly in the path of the trade winds that carried imperialists on to America. Philip IV, early in the seventeenth century, called the islands "the most important possession I have" because of their strategic location, dominating the Atlantic winds.

The conquest of the Canaries was Spain's education for empire. Here the crucial problems were anticipated: vast distances, unfamiliar environments, spectacularly broken terrain, intellectually and morally challenging cultures, hostile peoples whom the Spaniards had to divide to conquer. In the light of these similarities, the apparent contrast with the course of the conflicts that followed in the New World seems incomprehensible. The Canaries were small and sparsely populated with defenders whose war technology was rudimentary. Yet it took nearly a century to subdue the archipelago, and each island resisted successive expeditions with surprising tenacity and effectiveness. Yet the tally of American conquests accumulated with dizzying rapidity. In most of the Caribbean, wherever Spaniards wanted to seize islands, they did so with relative ease and speed, applying more or less directly the lessons of the Canaries. Columbus scythed through native opponents of Spanish colonisation of Hispaniola in a few months of campaigning in 1496. Thereafter, resistance was confined to what were in effect guerrilla operations in the bush and the high mountains. The conquest of nearby islands – Puerto Rico, Cuba, Jamaica – followed a similar pattern.

On the mainlands of the Americas, conquistadores faced some densely populated, dazzlingly rich societies, which could put scores of thousands of well-armed men into the field, in environments hostile to the Spaniards, who were far less favourably placed than their counterparts in the Canaries – much farther from home and from hope of reinforcement. Yet almost at a gulp, Spain seemed to gobble up the empires of the Aztecs and the Incas, both of whom looked, at first sight, like insuperable foes. The conventional explanations – that the Spaniards were inherently superior, that they were mistaken for gods and preceded by omens, that their technology was decisive, that disease undermined defence, and that their enemies were subverted by corroded morale – are all false. But a glance at the Aztec and Inca realms in about 1492 helps explain how so dramatic a debacle was possible.

They were part of a rich world that lay just beyond Columbus's reach. The Caribbean is a hard sea to cross. On average, in the sixteenth century, it took Spanish convoys almost twice as long to get from Santo Domingo to Veracruz, on the coast of Mexico, as it did to cross the entire breadth of the Atlantic. For more than a generation after Columbus's first crossing of the Gulf of Mexico, in 1502, Spanish pilots struggled to learn the pattern of the currents. In 1527, the navigators of the expedition of Pánfilo de Narvaez still had not done so: bound for Mexico from Cuba, they actually sailed backwards – imperceptibly driven back, night after night, by the Gulf Stream. When they reached what they thought was their destination, they were on the west coast of Florida.

Nonetheless, Columbus did get an inkling of what was in store on the mainland. In 1502, vainly scouring the American isthmus for a way through to the Pacific, he caught a glimpse of a huge, laden trading canoe that proved the existence in the vicinity of societies wealthy enough to exchange their surpluses. It was a sign that the kind of rich, recognisably "civilised" peoples he had sought since his arrival in the New World really existed and lived not far off.

Indeed, great civilisations stretched, almost continuously, interrupted only by sea, across Eurasia, North Africa, and Meso-American and Andean America like a girdle around the world. But the girdle was still unbuckled. The Americas remained isolated. Because of the lie of the land and the drift of the currents, it was hard for the inhabitants to explore their own hemisphere and get to know each other's civilisations. The Aztecs and Incas knew almost nothing of each other. Nowadays scholars deprecate comparisons between these two great hegemons, because their differences were more interesting and – to most people – more surprising than their similarities. But it is worth beginning with an appreciation of the similarities.

Both occupied high altitudes with corresponding advantages and disadvantages: the defensibility of mountain fastnesses, the moderation of high-altitude climates in tropical zones, the richness – which only precipitate mountains can confer – of many different ecosystems concentrated in a small space at different altitudes and on slopes and in valleys of contrasting relationships to sun and wind. In both regions, animal proteins were relatively scarce by Old World standards: there were no big quadrupeds; domesticable meat-producing species were few and small. Albeit for different reasons, both the Aztecs and the Incas relied heavily on maize and treated it as a sacred substance.

Similar paradoxes dappled the technologies of both peoples. Both built monumentally in stone without developing the arch. Both traded and travelled across vast distances without making use of the wheel. Both favoured cityscapes apparently symbolic of cosmic order, rigidly geometric and symmetrical. Both worked only soft metals and despised iron. Both were upstart empires, erected with astonishing rapidity, from small regional states, in a few generations. Both encompassed astonishing environmental diversity – far exceeding anything Europeans could achieve, or even imagine – and both relied for their cohesion, and perhaps their survival, on their ability to shift products between eco-zones to meet local shortages, ensure a variety of supply, and cheat drought and famine. Both faced resentful and rebellious subject or victim populations. Both practised religious rites that demanded human sacrifices, and therefore needed methods of war and government calculated to provide specimens. Both were committed to warfare of increasing range and therefore escalating costs, without knowing how to cope with the consequences. Both, in about 1492, were at or near their peak: their time of fastest expansion and greatest security.

"Aztecs" is a vague term for a group of communities who collaborated in dominating central Mexico. Scholars have never agreed on whom to include in it. The term rarely occurs in sources earlier than the eighteenth century, and it is doubtful whether anyone thought of himself as an Aztec before then: Aztecs called themselves "Mexica" – a

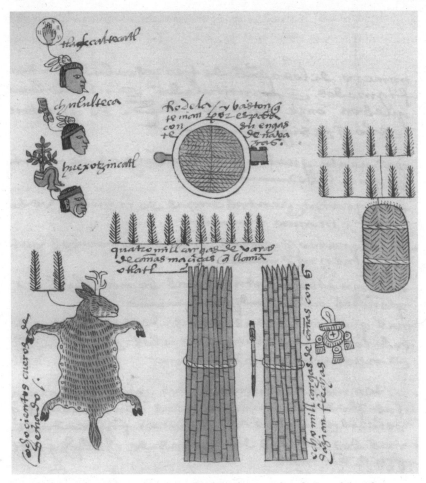

Detail of the tribute claimed by Tenochtitlan, showing deerskins and "smoking tubes", dues from the implacably hostile mountain communities of Tlaxcala and Huexotzinco.

plural noun in Nahuatl, the language they shared with many other peoples of central Mexico – or spoke of themselves as members of their own particular communities, the city-statelets that filled the densely crammed world of their high valley. The best perspective from which to see their world is that of an unmistakably Aztec place, which in today's language we think of as the Aztec "capital": the hegemonic city-state of

Tenochtitlan, which stood on the present site of Mexico City, in the middle of what was then a huge lake.

Tenochtitlan was at the centre of the complex web of tribute exchange that crisscrossed Meso-America, receiving food, textiles, luxury goods, and victims for human sacrifice from hundreds of other states, and garnering vastly more than it disbursed. It is hard to retrieve a sense of what the city was like, because the Spaniards who conquered it in the 1520s razed it and smothered it with a new city, adjusted to a European aesthetic. Today, even the lake has disappeared under the sprawl of Mexico's capital. For Tenochtitlan, however, the lake determined the way of life. It provided security, but – in combination with the dizzying altitude, which froze many important crops – it made agriculture hard. In 1519, Spanish adventurers first saw Tenochtitlan's marketplace, which they described with awestruck admiration. But almost all the fabulous array of goods on show had to come from elsewhere, paddled in canoes or borne on human porters' backs – for no beasts of burden existed – across the causeways that linked the city to others on neighbouring islands and on the lakeshore.

The huge population – now incalculable except by guesswork, but usually reckoned at between fifty and a hundred thousand people – made the Spaniards liken Tenochtitlan to Europe's biggest cities: such a vast concentration of manpower could not be self-supporting; the Tenochca, the people of Tenochtitlan, were committed to war and commerce. Their success was measurable in the height and spread of the huge temples and palaces of stone that enclosed the central plazas. The temples, elevated on tall stepped pyramids, dominated the skyline. When the Spaniards first saw them from afar, they seemed fantastic and fearful, like the castle turrets of a fairy-tale ogre, at once gloomy and gaudy, daubed with images of monstrous gods and human sacrifices in which telluric reds and aquatic blues predominated. When the beholders got close up, the impression they got was even more perplexing: the cruelly steep temple steps were stained with the blood of human sacrifices.

The obliteration of the indigenous cities means that the impressions we have of them are not really our own: we see them through the frightened eyes of early observers. But many smaller-scale works of Aztec art survive, demonstrating sensibilities modern Westerners can understand sympathetically – even identify with. The contrast between Aztec and Inca art in this respect could hardly be greater. The world vision reflected in Inca art is painfully, uncompromisingly abstract. Weavers and goldsmiths splayed and straightened human and animal forms. Textiles and reliefs embody an unbending imagination, in which tense lines and sharp angles contain every image like the bars and walls of prisons. There is less naturalism in Inca art than in that of orthodox Islam, in which an abstract aesthetic traditionally prevails. The Incas recorded data and perhaps literature in knotted strings, which are probably as efficient a medium of symbolic notation as what we call writing – but it is a method that excludes pictures of the rich, vivid kind that flowed from Aztec minds on to the pages even of their most prosaic records.

The Aztecs' most characteristic art – in which they excelled and introduced new refinements to Meso-American tradition – was sculpture in the round. The pieces most engaging to a modern eye are small-scale, wrought into lifelike shapes by a respect for nature, meticulously observed. A couple – human in some sense but simian featured – sit, each with an arm around the other, exchanging looks with tilted heads that suggest suddenly questioned affection. A serpent with yawning jaws and a malevolent eye stretches a long, forked tongue lazily over his own coils. A dancing monkey personifies the wind, with a belly distended by trapped flatulence and an erupting fart suggested by the way his tail is raised. A rabbit strains nervously to sniff food or danger, with a nose just raised or wrinkled to evoke a twitch.[6]

The imperial self-image of the Tenochca leaps fully armed from the vividly illustrated pages of documents from their archives, or from copies or abstracts made soon after the Spanish conquest. The most spectacular records are gathered in a book probably made in the early 1540s

for a Spanish viceroy who wanted to report to Spain on the tribute levels, conquest rights, and structures of provincial government practised
by the Aztecs before the Spaniards arrived. The compilation never
reached Spain. French pirates captured the ship in which it travelled.
The French king's geographer snaffled it, then sold it in 1580 to an English intelligence gatherer, who hoped to glean from it something about
the vulnerabilities of the Spanish monarchy. An English scholar of language first coveted and then appropriated it, in the hope of learning
about the Aztecs' writing system. The document, known as *Codex
Mendoza*, ended up in the library of the University of Oxford, where the
pictures that enliven it still gleam with the brash colours of native dyes.

The first illustrated page discloses one of the Tenochcas' favourite
myths of themselves. It depicts the foundation of Tenochtitlan, reputedly in the year 1324 or 1325, recalling the waterlogged site, strewn
with aquatic plants, and the squat, flimsy, reed-thatched huts that preceded the vast temples, palaces, and plazas, all of stone, that glorified
imperial Tenochtitlan. The legendary founder, Tenuch, whose name
was as obviously derived from the city's as that of Romulus was from
Rome, appears with his face blackened by sacred dye, surrounded by his
nine companions, each identified with a name glyph. Ozmitl, for instance, means "pierced foot" in the language of the Aztecs, and a foot
with an arrow through the ankle appears on the document in explanation, with a tie line to Ozmitl's portrait.

A rampant eagle dominates the scene. Though we can be sure, from
external evidence, that a native painter created it, the way he drew the
eagle, with wings outspread and claw extended, owes something to the
conventions of European heraldry, as if the draughtsman wanted to
equate the power of his people's ancestors with that of European hegemons, who also affected eagle symbols: the Romans, obviously, or the
Habsburg dynasty, who at the time ruled so much of Europe, including
Spain, and claimed overlordship over the rest. For the Tenochca, the eagle image recalled the story of how an eagle led Tenuch to her island

Codex Mendoza's depiction of the legendary culture hero, Tenuch, guided by an eagle to found Tenochtitlan in its defiantly mountainous lake-bound island.

eyrie, where a prickly pear grew out of a rock as a sign from the gods that he should found his city there. In the image, the eagle perches on the name glyph for Tenochtitlan: a fruiting cactus (called *nochtli* in Nahuatl) and a stone (*tetl* in the same language). A skull rack, like those on which the Aztecs exhibited the rotting heads of the captives they sacrificed, stands by the eagle's nest, just as the bloody bones of her own victims piled up around her home. The Tenochca saw themselves as eagle-like. They adorned their shields with clumps of eagle down and enriched their war gear with costly eagle feathers. Some of the elite wore eagle disguises for important rituals, including war, and they levied tribute in the form of live eagles from some of their subject peoples. Their city was their eyrie, and they stained it with blood and adorned it with bones.

In North America, most native origin myths depict the people as having sprung from the land, with a right of occupancy that dates from the beginning of time. The Aztecs saw themselves differently. They were self-proclaimed migrants who came from elsewhere and whose rights were rights of conquest. They told two rival stories about their past. In one, they were Chichimeca, dog people, former nomads and savages who ascended to the valley of Mexico from the deserts to the north and who survived as victims of longer-established denizens, through sufferings that demanded vengeance. In the second version of the myth, they were descendants of former hegemons, the Toltecs, whose homeland lay to the south, where the ruins of their great city of Tula had lain abandoned for centuries. Strictly speaking, the two stories are mutually contradictory, but they convey a consistent message: of warlike provenance, lost birthright, and imperial destiny.

Tenochtitlan could not even have survived, let alone launched an empire, without an ideology of violence. Its site is over seven thousand feet above sea level, at an altitude where some of the key crops that nourished Meso-American ways of life will not grow. There is no cotton, of which, by the late fifteenth century, Tenochtitlan consumed hundreds of thousands of bales every year for everyday clothing and for the manufacture of the quilted cotton armour that trapped the enemy's

1492

blades and arrowheads. Cacao, which Meso-Americans ground into the theobromine-rich infusion that intoxicated the elite at parties and in rituals, is a lowland crop that grows only in hot climates. The Tenochca speckled their lake with "floating gardens" laboriously dredged from the lake bed, for producing squashes, corn, and beans. But even these every-day staples were impossible to grow in sufficient amounts for the burgeoning lake-bound community. Only plunder on a grand scale could solve the logistical problems of keeping the city fed and clothed.

As the reach of Aztec hegemony lengthened, demand for exotic luxuries increased. Hundreds of thousands of bearers arrived laden with exotic tribute from the hot plains and forests, coasts, and distant highlands: quetzal feathers and jaguar pelts; rare conches from the gulf; jade and amber; rubber for the ball game that, like European jousting, was an essential aristocratic rite; copal for incense; gold and copper; cacao; deerskins; and what the Spaniards called "smoking-tubes with which the natives perfume their mouths". Elite life, and the rituals on which the city depended to stay in favour with the gods, would have collapsed without regular renewals of these supplies. The flow of tribute was both the strength and the weakness of Tenochtitlan: strength, because it showed the vast reach of the city's power; weakness, because if the tribute flow stopped, as it would do soon after the Spaniards arrived and helped rouse the subject peoples against the empire, the city would shrivel and starve.

In and around 1492, no such prospect loomed: it was probably unthinkable. Ahuitzotl became Aztec paramount in 1486. In 1487, at the dedication of a new temple in his courtly centre at Tenochtitlan, the captives sacrificed were reliably estimated at more than twenty thousand. By the time of his death in 1502, tribute records credited him with the conquest of forty-five communities – two hundred thousand square kilometres. In the reign of his successor, Montezuma II, who was still ruling in Tenochtitlan when the conquistadores arrived, forty-four communities are listed, but the momentum never relaxed. Montezuma's armies shuttled back and forth from the River Pánuco in the north, on the gulf coast, across the isthmus and as far south as Xonocozco, on what is now the frontier of Mexico and Guatemala. The Spaniards did not find a spent empire, or a state corroded by diffidence or undermined morale. On the contrary, it is hard to imagine a more dynamic, aggressive, or confident band of conquerors than the Aztecs.

For the Aztecs' victims, the experience of conquest was probably more of a short, sharp shock than an enduring trauma. The fact that many communities appear repeatedly as conquests in the rolls the Aztecs preserved, as records of who owed them tribute, suggests that many so-called conquests were punitive raids on recalcitrant tributaries. The glyph for conquest is an image of a burning temple, suggesting that defeat was a source of disgrace for local gods. One of the astonishing features of Meso-American culture before the conquest is that people revered the same pantheon throughout and beyond the culture area the Aztecs dominated. So maybe the worship of common deities spread with war. But nothing else changed in the culture of the vanquished.

Typically, existing elites remained in power, if they paid tribute. Wherever records survive in the Aztec world, ruling dynasties at the time the Spaniards took over traced their genealogies back to their own heroes and divine founders, in unbroken sequences of many hundreds of years. It was rare for Tenochtitlan to intrude officials or install garrisons. In early colonial times the Spaniards, who were looking hard for indigenous precedents for their own style of government in an attempt to represent themselves as continuators, rather than destroyers, of indigenous tradition, could find only twenty-two cases of communities ruled directly from Tenochtitlan, and most of those were recent conquests or frontier garrison towns, suggesting that direct rule, where it occurred, was a transitional, temporary device.

So the hegemony of Tenochtitlan was not an empire in the modern sense of the word. For years, when I was teaching Meso-American history to undergraduates, I sought a neutral word to describe the space the Aztecs dominated. I felt immensely pleased with myself when I thought of calling it by the vague German term *Grossraum*, which literally means "big space". But my pleasure fled when I realised, first, that the under-graduates could not understand what I meant and, second, that it was an absurd evasion to pluck a term from a culture that had nothing to do with the case. We may as well call it what it was: a tribute system of unparalleled complexity.

The complexity is obvious from the lists of goods that fill documents from the pre-conquest archives of the Tenochca state. For Tenochtitlan, no tributary was more important than the city's nearest neighbour, Tlatelolco, which was on an adjoining island in a shared lake. Its strategic proximity was dangerous, and its loyalty was essential. Indeed, Tlatelolco was the only ally that never deserted Tenochtitlan but fought on, during the siege of 1521, until the end, while the Spaniards detached all the other formerly allied and subject communities, one by one, from Tenochtitlan's side, by intimidation or negotiation. In keeping with the city's supreme importance, Tlatelolco got special treatment from the illustrators of *Codex Mendoza*. Instead of using a simple name glyph to signify the city, they devoted much space to a lively depiction of the city's famous twin towers – the double pyramid, reputedly the highest in the Aztec world, that adorned the central plaza. They also showed the conquered chief of Tlatelolco, whom the Tenochca called Moquihuixtl, hurling himself drunkenly down the temple steps in despair. More remarkable than the way they depicted the city is the tribute they listed – including large quantities of cotton and cacao, which could no more grow in Tlatelolco than they could elsewhere in the region. So Tlatelolco was evidently receiving tribute from farther afield and passing it on to Tenochtitlan.

Other cities privileged in the imperial pecking order levied and exchanged tribute in similar ways. Tenochtitlan topped the system, but it was not entirely exempt from the exchange. Annually, in mock battles, the city engaged in a ritualised exchange of warriors for sacrifice with Tlaxcala, a community on the far side of the mountain range to the south-east of Tenochtitlan. The terms of exchange favoured the hegemonic city, and Tlaxcala was also listed as paying tribute in other

The fall (1473) to Tenochca conquerors of the neighbouring
city of Tlatelolco with the spectacular death of the defeated ruler,
Moquihuixtl.

forms, including deerskins, pipes for tobacco, and cane frames for
loading goods on porters' backs. But the system marked Tlaxcala out as
special. When the Spaniards arrived, the Tlaxcalteca tested them, welcomed them, allied with them, used them against their own regional
enemies, and supplied more men and material for the siege of Tenochtitlan than any other group.

Power in the Aztec world was many-centred, elusive, and exercised
through intermediaries. Traditionally, historians represented the Inca
hegemony as a complete contrast: highly centralised, systematic, and
uniform. Inca imperialism was indeed different from that of the Aztecs,
but not in the ways commonly supposed. Peter Shaffer's play of 1964,
The Royal Hunt of the Sun, the best-ever dramatisation of the conquest of
Peru, captures received wisdom in a brilliant passage of dialogue. Under

the supreme Inca's all-seeing gaze, symbolising the reach of his intelligence service, the Spaniards interrogate natives about the nature of the empire and hear that its organisation is comprehensive, inflexible, and irresistible. The population is divided not among disparate natural communities but into bureaucratically contrived units of a hundred thousand families. The state controls all food and clothing. Every month, the people unite in the apportioned tasks of the season: ploughing, sewing, roof mending. Obligations to the state dominate every phase of life. The ruler interrupts the dialogue to explain: "Nine to twelve years, protect harvests. Twelve to eighteen, care for herds. Eighteen to twenty-five, warriors for me – Atahuallpa Inca!"

The image is appealing, but misleading. The Inca system was not centralised. It did not resemble the "state socialism" that Shaffer's Cold War-era play portrays. On the contrary, the empire had distinctive relationships, crafted to meet each individual case, with almost every one of its subject communities.

The vision of Inca power crushing diversity out of the empire was a construction of early colonial historians. Some of them were clerics or conquistadores. They exaggerated Inca power to flatter the Spaniards who overthrew it and the saints who supposedly helped. Other makers of the myth were the descendants of the Inca themselves, who aggrandized their ancestors by making them seem equal or superior to European empire builders. Garcilaso de la Vega, for example, the most accomplished writer on the subject in the sixteenth century, whose book on his ancestors appeared eighty years after the Spaniards arrived in Peru, was the son of an Inca princess. He lived as what Spaniards called a *señorito*, embodying gentlemanly affectations, in the Andalusian town of Montilla, which was small enough and remote enough for him to be the most important local personage. His status is measurable in his scores of godchildren. For him the Incas were the Romans of America, whose perfectly articulated empire exhibited all the qualities of order, organisation, military prowess, and engineering genius his European contemporaries admired in their own accounts of ancient Rome.

Roman models, however, are almost useless for understanding what the Incas were like. The best route is via the ruins of the states and civilisations that occupied the Andes before them. From the seventh century to the tenth, the metropolis of Huari, nine thousand feet up in the Ayacucho Valley, preceded and in some ways prefigured the Inca empire. The town had barracks, dormitories, and communal kitchens at its centre for a warrior elite, while a working population of some twenty thousand gathered around it. Satellite towns around the valley imitated it, probably because they were colonies or subject communities. To judge from similar evidence farther afield, the influence or power of Huari reached hundreds of miles over mountains and deserts to Nazca. The Huari zone overlapped with the Incas' home valley of Cuzco, and the memory of their achievements remained potent.

Deeper inland, higher into the mountains, in an area that became a target for Inca imperialism, lay the ruins of the city of Tiahuanaco, near Lake Titicaca, with an impressive array of raised temples, sunken courtyards, triumphal gateways, fearsome reliefs, crushing monoliths, and daunting fortifications. Spread over forty acres at an altitude higher than that of Lhasa in Tibet, it was a real-life Cloud Cuckoo Land, twelve thousand feet above sea level. Potatoes fed it. No other staple would grow so close to the snow line. To cultivate the tubers, the people built platforms of cobbles, bedding the potatoes into topsoil of clay and silt. To supply irrigation, and for protection from violent changes of temperature, they dug surrounding channels from Lake Titicaca. The potato fields stretched nine miles from the lakeside and could yield thirty thousand tons a year. The state warehoused huge amounts and converted crops into chuñu, a gastronomically unappealing but vital substance made by freeze-drying potatoes in the conducive climate of the high Andes. Tiahuanaco was obviously an imperial enterprise. To supplement potatoes, and to ensure against blight, the inhabitants had to conquer fields at lower altitudes, where they could grow quinoa and what modern Americans call corn – that is, maize.

The Incas did much the same as their predecessors in Huari and Tiahuanaco, only on a vastly larger scale, all over the culture area they called Tawantinsuyú, "land of four quarters", which comprised the Andes and the mountains' flanks as far as the coasts and the forests. They practised ecological imperialism, switching products between climates and sometimes shifting whole communities hundreds of miles in order to adjust the supply of labour to the needs of empire.

Much of the Inca world was settled at altitudes too high for maize, but the Incas' partiality for the crop was close to an obsession. They systematically shifted populations towards valleys suitable for growing maize. They stockpiled it in warehouses higher than its zone of cultivation, where it could feed armies, pilgrims, and royal progresses while supplying maize beer for ritual purposes. They engaged in what we now think of as state-sponsored science, developing new strains, adapted for high yields.[7] Maize was not necessarily the best crop, from either an environmental or a nutritional point of view. The Incas favoured it for more than utilitarian reasons: it was sacred to them, rather as the wheat of the Eucharist is sacred to Christians, perhaps in a way that the routine staples of the Andes, such as potatoes and sweet potatoes, could not attain, because they were too familiar.

The Incas also needed lowland products. Coca sustained a life of a higher order than corn. For the elites for whom it was reserved, it unlocked realms of imagination and stimulated ritual. Whereas maize beer, the commoners' tipple, could intoxicate, coca could inspire. The Urubamba Valley specialised in producing it, in an arc along the rivers Torontoy, Yanatil, and Paucartambo,[8] where the Incas imported labour from the lowlands on either side of the mountains to supply the manpower. Even more than coca, cotton and chillies were vital: the one for clothing, the other to flavour food and animate life. Chillies grew well alongside the River Vilcanota north of Cuzco and were among the products for which the supreme Inca, Huayna Capac, located his estate at Yucay in the early sixteenth century. Honey, and exotic feathers for elite costumes, were among the products the forests produced. Though the

Incas always disparaged the forest as a wild and fretful place, they adapted to it. Indeed, when the Spaniards drove the Inca rulers from the highlands, they took refuge in the forest and sustained a luxurious life in a new, lavish capital at Vilcabamba until the Spaniards descended and burned it, extinguishing the last independent Inca state, in 1572.

The meaning of the Inca name is in some ways easier to grasp than that of the Aztecs. It was, at least, a name they used of themselves. It denoted at first – perhaps until the mid-fifteenth century – a member of a group defined by kinship in the Cuzco Valley. But it came to apply to selected members of a widespread elite, scattered, by the end of the century, along and around the Andes from northern Ecuador to central Chile. In part – and here a parallel with the Romans is inescapable – the extension of the name's embrace was a strategy of the state, rather like the progressive broadening of the label "Roman citizen". Inca rulers conferred the status of Inca on subjects of the imperial heartland, sent them into remote provinces, and admitted some collaborative elites in conquered territories to Inca ranks.

In some ways, the Incas did make stunningly despotic interventions in the lives of the peoples of the empire, chiefly in the form of massacres and mass deportations. Terror was an organ of government. When, at an uncertain date, the Incas conquered the rival kingdom of Chimú, they razed the principal city of Chanchan almost to the ground and carried off the entire population. A few years before the coming of the Spaniards, Inca Huayna Capac drowned – it was said – twenty thousand Cañari warriors in Lake Yahuar Cocha. The same ruler levied one hundred thousand workers – if colonial-period estimates can be believed – to build his summer palace, and relocated fourteen thousand in the Cochabamba Valley, from as far away as Chile, to provide labour for new agricultural enterprises. When the Spaniards captured Atahuallpa, the supreme Inca they ransomed and put to death, he had fifteen thousand people in his camp, whom he had forced from their homes in northern Ecuador and was transferring to new settlements. A census the Spaniards called for in 1571 showed that the population of Cuzco included the children and grandchildren of at least fifteen ethnic groups whom the Incas shipped in to supervise newly established economic activities, especially the manufacture of textiles that were formerly regional specialities. At least forty groups featured among workers in Yucay, where Huayna Capac had an estate.[9] Colonial historians thought that the Incas routinely selected six or seven thousand families for resettlement every time they added a new place to their empire. In Moho, when the Spaniards announced the fall of the Inca empire, the entire population rose and left, returning to the homes from which the Incas had uprooted them. The resettlement policies the Incas enforced had nothing to do with homogenising culture; on the contrary, migrants were required to preserve their own languages and customs and forbidden to mix with neighbouring communities.

Power over the environment matched this power over human lives. The Incas maintained a road network over 30,000 kilometres – getting on for 18,000 miles – long, with teams of runners capable, on favoured routes, of covering 240 kilometres (or 150 miles) a day. Between Huarochirí and Jauja they climbed passes 16,700 feet high. Way stations studded the system at altitudes of up to 13,000 feet. Here workers were rewarded with feasts and pain-numbing doses of maize beer. Armies found refreshment. Prodigious bridges linked the roads. The famous Huaca-cacha ("Holy Bridge") stretched 250 feet on cables thick as a man's body, high above the gorge of the River Apurimac at Curahasi. The roads streaked the empire with a uniform look that impressed Spanish travellers of the early colonial era and helped to create the impression that the Incas were homogenisers and centralisers whose roads were like grapples, holding the empire in a single grip. And the Incas did have what one might call a signature style – a kind of architecture that shaped the way stations, warehouses, barracks, and shrines that they built along the roads and at the edges of their empire: the habit of stamping the land with buildings that proclaimed their presence or passing was a tradition they learned from Huari and Tiahuanaco. Similarly, they helped spread the use of their language, Quechua, from its heartlands in the northern and central Andes – though it was probably already a lingua franca of trade.

The roads were there not only to speed Inca commands and to carry Inca armies. They also linked sacred sites. The management of the sacred landscape of the Andes – the maintenance of shrines, the promotion of pilgrimages – was all part of the value the empire added to lives lived in its shadow. Rituals encoded political relationships in ways hard for modern Westerners to understand – scores of different ways, each appropriate to the traditions of the peoples involved. The Incas kept the images of local and regional deities from around the empire hostage in Cuzco, and literally scourged them when the guardian peoples of their shrine defaulted on payments of tribute or obligations of service. Lines, on to which roads were often mapped, radiated like sun rays from Cuzco, linking mountaintop shrines and pilgrimage places. A thousand scribes in Cuzco knotted memorials of sacred places, their calendars, and their rites into the woven braids that the Incas used to record data.

One of the most startling pieces of evidence was recorded among the Checas, a people of the Huarochirí Valley, between Cuzco and the coast. As they recalled their history, late in the sixteenth century, a supreme Inca, beset by enemies, had once, in a mythical past, called upon the guardians of shrines all over the Inca world to march to his aid. The manuscript represents the negotiations as dialogues between gods, who travelled to conferences on litters. Perhaps this is really how diplomacy unfolded. The Incas regularly assembled their mummified former rulers, who shared a meal together – the viands consumed by attendants – and conversed through professional shamans. The presence of divine images at parleys hallowed the events; and the convention that the words spoken proceeded from the minds of gods, rather than from their human spokesmen, would add diplomatic distance to the exchanges and freedom to the debate. But in this case none of the provincial gods would support the Incas, except Paria Caca, the eponymous lord of the mountain where the Checas went to worship, who offered to turn stones into warriors – for that was the image the Incas regularly used to evoke successful recruitment. All the god demanded in return was that the Incas offer sacrifice at his shrine by dancing there annually.

What did the Checas get by imposing this ritual on their ally? At one level, the dance was symbolic, showing that the god of the Checas could command the Incas and that the Checas' relationship to the dynasts of Cuzco was not one of simple submission. At another level, it was a matter of some practical utility. It ensured that the supreme Inca was available for regular consultations and that the obligations of hospitality were indefinitely renewed. The arrangement mattered deeply to the Checas. That was why they remembered it and wrote it down. Their reason for siding with the Spaniards in the war to overthrow the Incas was that the rulers in Cuzco dishonoured the sacred promise to perform the annual dance.

Marriages also helped the empire cohere. Inca monarchs took brides from all over Tawantinsuyú, to attract the services of their kin – a practice the Spaniards would imitate to advantage – and to be hostages for their communities' good behaviour. Huayna Capac had six thousand wives to help ensure the loyalties of subject communities. His mother had originally come to the Inca court from a frontier region in what is now Ecuador. When nobles who were her kin threatened to leave Huayna Capac's service, he brought out her mummified carcass or, perhaps, a statue, and bid her dissuade them by speaking to them – which she did through the medium of a native shaman.[10] More evidence comes from the Huayllacan people who lived in towns near Cuzco. They recalled a time when one of their princesses married a supreme Inca. But they forfeited Inca friendship by allowing her and her son to be taken hostage by neighbouring enemies, with whom the Incas then established a new marriage-based alliance. When the Huayllacans tried to retrieve the situation by a successful conspiracy to kill the offspring, the Incas took revenge, crushing them in battle, killing and banishing their leaders, and seizing much of their land.[11]

The results of the marriage habit were equivocal. Supreme Incas begat huge broods of emulous sons who soaked up expenditure, conspired for power, and usually ended up being slaughtered when one of them succeeded in the contest for the throne. Seraglio politics disfigured court life, where pillow talk was often of politics. As in the Ottoman Empire on the other side of the world in the same period, favoured concubines used their privileged access to the supreme ruler to manipulate patronage and even to interfere with the succession. Partly to arrest this form of corruption, late in the fifteenth century supreme Incas took to marrying their full sisters and limiting the right of succession to the offspring of these impeccably royal unions.

Tribute was the cement of empire. At the installation of a new supreme Inca, hundreds of children from all the subject communities were strangled in sacrifice and buried, together with great numbers of other offerings from the provinces: llamas, rare shells from the coast, artworks in gold and silver, and rich apparel, including cloaks made from bats' skins in Puerto Viejo and Tumbes. Parties of sacrificers set out from Cuzco, with children in their train, to repeat the offerings at important shrines around the empire, at distances of up to about 1,250 miles from Cuzco.[12] Pots, woven goods, footwear, slaves, and coca arrived, as well as foodstuffs, people, and objects for sacrifice. From Huancayo in the Chillún Valley, the Incas levied a proportion of everything produced locally: coca, chillies, maté for making tea, dried birds, fruit, and crayfish. Fabulous amounts of gold served to "plant" the Incas' gardens with corncobs of gold and to plate the temples of Cuzco with gold and silver. In the garden of the Temple of the Sun at Cuzco, according to a wide-eyed Spanish report, "the earth was lumps of gold and it was cunningly planted with stalks of corn that were of gold". No wonder the Incas were not surprised when the Spanish conquistadores demanded a roomful of gold as Atahuallpa's ransom.

Rather as the Aztec hegemony relied on continual expansion to feed the growth of Tenochtitlan and the demands of its high-roller elite, so Cuzco, with its huge and growing establishment, needed the momentum of conquest to continue indefinitely. "Most of the inhabitants," according to Pedro Pizarro, "served the dead."[13] The dead, it was said, "ate from the best lands". Expansion was necessary to provide domains for each successive supreme Inca's mummy. The system created potentially fatal instability at the heart of the empire: huge rival constituencies at court controlled their own resources and could back rival candidates for power. The results included instability at the core and friction on the frontiers. The rate of expansion had slowed by the time the Spaniards arrived, and the violence and trauma of succession conflicts jarred and weakened the state.

Nothing in pre-Hispanic Andean chronology is certain. The Jesuit missionary Bernabé Cobo, who struggled to understand Peru's past in the early seventeenth century, thought it was because the Incas were indifferent to chronology. He complained of how, if you asked natives for dates, they would speak vaguely of "a long time ago". But the Incas did have a sense of chronology, which they expressed in ways unintelligible to Europeans, associating events together, counting generations, and reckoning in eras of unequal lengths, identified by the names of real or legendary rulers. No records are reliable enough, therefore, to justify the assigning of events to particular years, but the Inca realm was expanding fast in the generation or two preceding the arrival of the Spaniards. Inca conquests of that period brought most sedentary peoples of the Andes into a single system, reaching nearly to the River Bío-bío in the south. According to the traditional chronology, Inca Tupac Yupanqui was on the throne in 1492. According to memories Spanish and native chroniclers recorded in the early colonial era, he was the widest-ranging of Inca conquerors. His father, Pachacuti, had launched the empire-building project, taking the Inca state from a regional power in the valley of Cuzco and its environs into what are now Ecuador, Bolivia, and coastal Peru. Tupac Yupanqui extended the conquests to comprise almost all the sedentary peoples of the Andean culture era and, it was said, scoured the sea for "isles of gold" to add to the empire.

Meanwhile, the world Columbus sought – which, as he said, "Alexander laboured to conquer" – eluded him. But another world awaited, of wealth more easily exploited than that of Asia and the Indian Ocean, on the far side of the Atlantic and the Caribbean, just beyond his reach. As it turned out, the densely populated zone that stretched from East Asia across Europe and North Africa did not stop at the ocean's edge. There were uncontacted outposts of intense settlement and city life in Meso-America and the Andean region, in and around the lands of the peoples we know as the Aztecs and Incas. The route Columbus reported led Europe towards them and their gold and silver and millions of productive people. Beyond them, and in the Caribbean islands along the route, was a vast, underexploited terrain that could be adapted for ranchland and farmland and for a potential plantation economy that would enrich the West.

The incorporation of the Americas – the resources, the opportunities – would turn Europe from a poor and marginal region into a nursery of potential global hegemonies. It might not have happened that way. If Chinese conquerors had bothered with the Americas, we would now think of those areas as part of "the East", and the international dateline would probably sever the Atlantic.

The World We're In

History has no course. It thrashes and staggers, swivels and twists, but never heads one way for long. Humans who get caught up in it try to give it destinations. But we all pull in different directions, heading for different targets, and tend to cancel each other's influence out. When trends last for a short spell, we sometimes ascribe them to "men of destiny" or "history makers", or to great movements – collectively heroic or myopic – or to immense, impersonal forces or laws of social development or economic change: class struggle, for instance, or "progress" or "development" or some other form of History with a capital H. But usually some undetectably random event is responsible for initiating big change. History is a system reminiscent of the weather: the flap of a butterfly's wings can stir up a storm.

Because history has no course, it has no turning points. Or rather, it has so many that you might as well try to straighten a tornado as attempt to sort them out.

1492

Random mutations, however, sometimes have enduring effects in history, rather as in evolution. Evolution generally makes a bad model for understanding history, but in some ways it offers useful analogies. In evolution, a sudden, uncaused, unpredictable biological mutation intersects with the grindingly slow changes that transform environments. Something works for a while – a big, reptilian body, a prehensile tail, an expanded cranium – and a new species flourishes for a span before it becomes a fossil. Similar changes happen in human communities. Some group or society acquires a distinctive feature, the origins of which we struggle – usually unsuccessfully – to explain. It therefore enjoys a period of conspicuous success, usually ending in disaster, or "decline and fall", when the society mutates unsustainably or when the environment – cultural or climatic – changes, or when people in some other place benefit from an even more exploitable innovation. We scour the past to spot those moments of mutation, to try to identify those random convulsions that seem briefly to pattern chaos. It's like looking at a seismograph and seeing the first lurch.

The lines in the current pattern are conspicuous enough. We live in a world of demographic explosion. Western hegemony (which the United States exercises now virtually single-handedly and without much chance of keeping going, at present costs, for much longer) crafts the world, along with global intercommunication and, increasingly, global economic interdependence. Other features we can probably all perceive include cultural pluralism and the tensions it generates; competing religious and secular values – with consequent intellectual uncertainty; culture wars, which threaten to become "clashes of civilisations"; rapid technological turnover; information overkill; hectic urbanisation; pell-mell consumption; growing wealth gaps; expensive but effective medical priorities; and environmental angst. The nearest things we have to universal values – apart, perhaps, from obsessions with health – are varieties of individualism, which favour some widespread trends towards, for instance, representative forms of government, codified human rights, and liberal economics. At the same time, ours is a ditherers' world, tacking without much sense of consistent direction, oscillating between addictions and antidotes. Wars alternate with revulsion from war. Generations alienated from their parents bring their children up to be their friends. Spells of social and economic overplanning are interspersed with madcap deregulation. People satiated with permissiveness go "back to basics".

This world already looks doomed to extinction. Western power is going the way of previous dinosaurs. The United States – the last sentinel of Western supremacy – is in relative decline, challenged from East and South Asia. Pluralism looks increasingly like a path to showdown instead of a panacea for peace. Population trends on a global level are probably going into reverse. Capitalism seems to have failed and is now stigmatised as greed. A reaction against individual excess is driving the world back to collective values. Fear of terror overrides rights; fear of slumps subverts free markets. Consumption levels and urbanisation are simply unsustainable at recent rates in the face of environmental change. The throwaway society is headed for the trash heap. People who sense that "modernity" is ending proclaim a "postmodern age".

Yet this doomed world is still young: 1492 seems, on the face of it, too far back to look for the origins of the world we are in. Population really started to grow worldwide with explosive force only in the eighteenth century. The United States did not even exist until 1776, and only became the unique superpower in the 1990s. The tool kit of ideas we associate with individualism, secularism, and constitutional guarantees of liberty really came together only in the movement we call the Enlightenment in eighteenth-century western Europe and parts of the Americas, and even then they struggled for survival – bloodied by the French Revolution, betrayed by romanticism.

Most of the other features of our world were barely discernible before the nineteenth century, when industrialisation empowered Western empires and made a genuinely global economy possible. Much of the intellectual framework familiar in today's world was new in the early twentieth century – the first era of relativity, quantum mechanics, psychoanalysis, and cultural relativism. Individualism had to fight wars against collectivism. Democracy, pitted against totalitarianisms, won a solid-looking victory only when the twentieth century was nearly over. Environmentalism has emerged as a powerful worldwide ideology only in the past forty years or so. Some of the science and technology that make the way we think and live and fear distinctive are of more recent origin – nuclear weapons, micro-IT, the genetics of DNA, the currently fashionable techniques of disease control, the food-production methods that now feed the world. These sudden and rapid new departures are reminders that "modernity" – which, allowing for the variety of more or less equivalent terms, is every generation's self-description – never starts, but is perpetually renewed.

In any case, it is a fallacy to assume that origins are always remote, or that historical events are like big species – with long ancestries – or big plants with long roots. One of the lessons of our time, for those as old as I am or older, is that changes happen suddenly and unpredictably. Long-running pasts crunch into reverse gear. We who are middle-aged – who have not even seen out a normal lifetime – have watched the British Empire collapse, the Cold War melt, the divisions of Europe heal in "ever-closer" union, the Soviet bloc dissolve. Supposedly autochthonous national characters have self-transformed. The English, for instance – my mother's people – whom my father described after the Second World War, with their stiff upper lips and umbrellas as tightly rolled as their minds, have turned into people he would no longer recognise: as mawkish and exhibitionist as everybody else. The stiff upper lips have gone wobbly. The Spanish – my father's people – have changed just as much, in an even shorter time. The values of austerity, sobriety, quixotism, and lividly, vividly dogmatic Catholicism I knew as a child have vanished, conquered by consumerism and embourgeoisement. Spain is no longer – as the tourist slogans used to say – different. Almost every community has undergone similarly radical changes of character.

Structures based on class and sex today are unrecognisable from those of my childhood. Moralities – usually the most stable ingredients of the societies that adopt them – have metamorphosed. Gays can adopt children – an innovation my parents' generation could never have imagined. The pope has prayed in a mosque. Almost every morning brings an awakening like Rip van Winkle's into a transmuted world. I struggle to understand my students' language: we no longer share the same cultural referents, know the same stories, recognise the same icons. When I search in class for art we all have in common, it seems that we have hardly ever even seen the same movies or learned the same advertising jingles. The most bewilderingly abrupt changes have been environmental: a melting icecap, desiccated seas, diminished rain forests, engorged cities, perforated "ozone", species extinguished at unprecedented rates. The world we live in seems to have been made in a single lifetime. It is so mutable, so volatile, that to reckon its gestation at half a millennium or so, and date it from 1492, seems almost quaint.

The big change, I think, that has overtaken my own discipline in my lifetime is that we historians have more or less abandoned the search for long-term origins. What we used to call the *longue durée* has collapsed like a tidied-away telescope. When we want to explain the decline and fall of the Roman Empire, we no longer do as Edward Gibbon did in his classic on the subject and go back to the age of the Antonine emperors (who were doing very well in their day), but say that migrations in the late fourth and early fifth centuries provoked a sudden and unmanageable crisis. When we try to explain the English Civil War of the 1640s, we no longer look back as Macaulay did to traditions supposedly traceable to the "Germanic woods", or even to the supposed "rise of Parliament" or of "the bourgeoisie" in the late Middle Ages and Tudor period, but see English government strained to the breaking point by a war with Scotland that started four years before the breakdown. To explain the French Revolution we no longer do as Tocqueville did in his unsurpassed history and look at the reign of Louis XIV, but see the financial conditions of the 1780s as crucial. To understand the outbreak of the First World War we no longer do as Albertini did and blame the deficiencies of the nineteenth-century diplomatic system – which was actually rather good at preserving peace – but at the relatively sudden collapse of that system in the years preceding the war, or even at the intractabilities of the railway timetables of 1914, which, according to A. J. P. Taylor's notoriously seductive theory, made the mobilisation of armies irreversible once it was under way.

Still, it has long been the vocation of historians to thumb back through time, looking for the previously unglimpsed origins of what is conspicuous in every age. With surprising unanimity, the quest for the origins of most of what is distinctive in the modern world has led back to the fifteenth or sixteenth century and to Europe. Most textbooks still make a break – the start of a new volume or part – around 1500. Some of them still call this the beginning of the modern world. Historians – even those who disapprove of traditional periodisation – loosely call the few centuries prior to about 1800 the "early modern period".

The intellectual movements we call the Renaissance and Reformation, for instance, have become associated with claims or assumptions that they made modern social, political, cultural, philosophical, and scientific developments possible. The work of European explorers and conquerors around the globe makes a convincing starting point for the modern history of imperialism and globalisation. The date textbooks used to treat as "the beginning of modernity" was 1494, when a French invasion of Italy supposedly unlocked influences from the Renaissance and began to spread them around Europe. A few writers have claimed to trace such supposed constituent features of modern thought as scepticism, secularism, atheism, capitalism, and even ironic humour to medieval Jewish tradition, and have argued that the absorption of these ideas into the European mainstream began with the effectively enforced conversion of Spanish Jews to Christianity.[1] These claims are untrue but are suggestive in the present context, because the biggest bonanza of conversions almost certainly occurred in the year 1492, when all Jews who refused conversion were expelled from the Spanish kingdoms.

So dating the beginnings of the modern world to a time close to 1500 or thereabouts has a long tradition behind it. I reject the thinking

that underpins the tradition. In the breakers' yard of history, supposedly cosmic events get pounded into fragments, reduced to a series of
local or individual significance. What once seemed world-shattering
revolutions are reclassified as transitions. Almost all the claims made
for the Renaissance and the Reformation, for instance, have turned out
to be wrong. The supposed consequences in our own world – deism,
secularism and atheism, individualism and rationalism; the rise of capitalism and the decline of magic; the scientific revolution and the American dream; the origins of civil liberties and shifts in the global balance
of power – all appear less convincingly consequential as time goes on.
In recent years, revisionist scholarship and critical thinking have loos-
ened the links in these chains of consequence, one by one.

In any case, the Renaissance and Reformation were, in global terms,
small-scale phenomena. The Renaissance was, in part, a product of cultural cross-fertilisation between Islam and the West. It was not a unique
"classical revival" but an accentuation of uninterrupted Western self-
modelling on ancient Greece and Rome. It edged the West only a little
way towards secularism: most art and learning was sacred in inspiration and clerical in control. It was not "scientific": for every scientist
there was a sorcerer. The Reformation was not a revolution: most reformers were social and political conservatives, whose movements were
part of a general trend among the godly of Christendom towards the
communication of a more acutely felt, actively engaged form of Christianity to previously under-evangelised or unevangelised reaches of society and regions of the world. The reformers' work did not inaugurate
capitalism or subvert magic or promote science. Western imperialism,
though it started in a conspicuous way in 1492, was not a world-
transforming phenomenon until the eighteenth or nineteenth century.

Nevertheless, the world did change in 1492. Events of that year
started to change the balance and distribution of power and wealth
across the globe, launching communities in western Europe across
oceans, empowering a mighty Russian state for the first time, and pre-
figuring (though not of course producing) the decline of maritime Asia

and of traditional powers around the Indian Ocean and its adjacent seas. Until the 1490s, any well-informed and objective observer would surely have acknowledged these regions as homes to the planet's most dynamic and best-equipped exploring cultures, with the most impressive records of long-term, long-range achievement. In that fateful decade, rivals from western Europe leapfrogged ahead, while the powers that might have stopped them or outstripped them remained inert.

At the western end of the Indian Ocean, for instance, the Ottomans were confined or limited by their geographical position. The Egypt of the Mamluks, similarly, exchanged embassies with Gujarat, exercised something like a protectorate over the port of Jiddah, and fomented trade with India via the Red Sea; but, because of that sea's hostility to navigation, Egypt was ill placed to guard the ocean against infidel intruders. Abyssinia ceased to expand after the death of the negus Zara-Ya'cob in 1468; after defeat at the hands of Muslim neighbours in Adel in 1494, hopes of revival dispersed; survival became the aim. Persia was in protracted crisis, from which the region would emerge only in the new century, when the boy-prophet Ismail reunited it. Arab commerce ranged the Indian Ocean from southern Africa to the China Seas, without relying on force of arms for protection or promotion. In southern Arabia, yearning for a maritime empire would arise later, perhaps in imitation of the Portuguese, but there were no signs of it yet.

In the central Indian Ocean, meanwhile, no Indian state had interest or energy to spare for long-range expansion. Vijayanagar maintained trading relations all over maritime Asia but did not maintain fleets. The city that housed the court underwent lavish urban remodelling under Narasimba in the 1490s, but the state had ceased to expand, and Narasimba's dynasty was doomed. The Delhi of Sikandar Lodi, meanwhile, sustaining traditionally landward priorities, acquired a new province in Bihar, but the sultan bequeathed to his heirs an overstretched state that tumbled easily to invaders from Afghanistan a generation later. Gujarat had a huge merchant marine, but no long-range political ambitions. Its naval power was designed to protect its trade, not force it on others. There were of course plenty of pirates. Early in the 1490s, for instance, from a nest on the western coast of the Deccan, Bahadur Khan Gilani terrorised shipping and, for a time, seized control of important ports, including Dabhol, Goa, and Mahimn, near present Bombay.[2] But no state in the region felt the temptation either to explore new routes or to initiate maritime imperialism.

Farther east, China, as we have seen, had withdrawn from active naval policy and never resumed it. In Japan in 1493, the shogun was under siege in Kyoto as warlords divided the empire between them. South-east Asia was between empires: the aggressive phase of the history of Majapahit was in the past; Thai and Burmese imperialism were still underdeveloped and, in any case, never took on maritime ambitions. There had been maritime empires in the region's past: Srivijaya in the seventh century, the Java of the Sailendra dynasty in the eighth, the Chola in the eleventh, and King Hayan Wuruk's Majapahit in the fourteenth all tried to enforce monopolies on chosen routes. But at the time Europeans burst into the Indian Ocean around the Cape of Good Hope, no indigenous community felt the need or urge to explore further, and nothing like the kind of maritime imperialism practised by Portugal, and later by the Dutch, existed in the region.

Europe's conquest of the Atlantic, in short, coincided with the arrest of exploring and imperial initiatives elsewhere. This did not mean that the world was instantly transformed, or that the balance of wealth and power would shift quickly to what we now call the West. On the contrary, the process ahead was long, painful, and interrupted by many reversals. Yet that process had begun. And the Atlantic-rim communities that had launched it – especially those of Spain and Portugal – retained their momentum and continued their dominance in exploration for most of the next three centuries. The opening of a viable route to and fro between Europe and productive regions of the Americas ensured that the global balance of resources would tilt, in the long run, in favour of the West. The balance of the global distribution of power and wealth would change. In preparing that change, or making it possible, 1492 was a decisive year.

In 1492, with extraordinary suddenness after scores – perhaps hundreds – of millions of years of divergent evolution, global ecological exchange became possible: the way life-forms could now overleap oceans, for the first time since the break-up of Pangaea, did more to mould the modern environment than any other event before industrialisation. Events of 1492 assured the future of Christianity and Islam as uniquely widespread world religions, and helped to fix their approximate limits.

Though the Indian Ocean is no longer an Islamic lake, Islam has clung tenaciously to most of the rim. Islam cannot, by nature, be as flexible as Christianity. It is consciously and explicitly a way of life rather than of faith; except in marriage discipline, its code is stricter, more exclusive, more demanding on converts than Christianity. It requires adherents to know enough Arabic to recite the Quran. Its dietary regime is unfamiliar to most cultures. Aspects of today's emerging global culture are particularly inhospitable: liberal capitalism, consumerism, individualism, permissiveness, and feminism have all made more or less easy accommodations in Christendom; Islam seems full of antibodies that struggle to reject them. It may have reached the limits of its adaptability. Buddhism, the third great global religion, has so far achieved only a modest degree of diffusion, but it has established thoroughly flexible credentials, subsisting alongside Shinto in Japan and contributing to the eclecticism of most Chinese religion. It has never captured whole societies outside East, central, and South-east Asia, but it now demonstrates the power to do so, making converts in the West and even reclaiming parts of India from Hinduism. Hinduism, meanwhile, despite a thousand years of quiescence with no proselytising vocation, also appears to be able now to make significant numbers of converts in the West and perhaps has the potential to become a fourth world religion.

As well as events that refashioned the world, we have glimpsed others that represent vivid snapshots of changes under way: the ascent of mysticism and personal religion; the transformation of magic into science; the spread and increasing complexity of webs of commerce and cultural exchange; the increase of productivity and – still very patchily

until the eighteenth century – of population in most of the world; the
retreat of nomads, pastoralists, and foragers; the growing authority and
might of states at the expense of other traditional wielders of power,
such as aristocracies and clerical establishments; the realism with which
artists and mapmakers beheld the world; the sense of a "small world"
every bit of which is accessible to all the rest.

So in a way, the prophets in Christendom who predicted that the
world would end in 1492 were right. The apocalypse was postponed,
but the events of the year ended the world with which people of the time
were familiar and launched a new look for the planet, more "modern", if
you like – more familiar, that is, to us than it would have been to people
in the Middle Ages or antiquity. The world the prophets knew vanished, and a new world, the world we are in, began to take shape.

Notes

Chapter 1: "This World Is Small"

1. L. Pastor, *History of the Popes*, vol. 5 (St Louis, B. Herder, 1898), 371.
2. F. Fernández-Armesto, *So You Think You're Human?* (Oxford: Oxford Univ. Press, 2004), 111.
3. Mark 13:12–26; Matt. 24; Luke 21.
4. Rev. 15:17.
5. Bachiller Palma, *Divina retribución sobre la caída de España*, ed. J. M. Escudero de la Peña (Madrid: n.p., 1879), 91.
6. C. Varela, ed., *Cristobal Colón: textos y documentos completos* (Madrid: Alianza, 1984), 36.
7. G. Ledyard, in *The History of Cartography*, vol. 2, bk. 2, *Cartography in the Traditional East and Southeast Asian Societies*, ed. J. B. Harley and D. Woodward (Chicago: Univ. of Chicago Press, 1994), 44–49.
8. Quoted in C. G. Gillespie, *Dictionary of Scientific Biography*, 16 vols. (New York: Scribner, 1970–80), 11:351.
9. P. Freedman, *Out of the East: Spices and the Medieval Imagination* (New Haven: Yale Univ. Press, 2008), 3–4.
10. G. J. Samuel, *Studies in Tamil Poetry* (Madras: Mani Pathippakam, 1978), 62–72.
11. F. B. Pegolotti, *La pratica della mercatura*, ed. A. Evans (Cambridge, Mass.: Medieval Academy of America, 1936).

12. E. G. Ravenstein, *Martin Behaim, His Life and His Globe* (London: G. Philip & Son, 1908), 39.

13. Ravenstein, *Martin Behaim, His Life and His Globe*, 39.

14. D. L. Molinari, "La empresa colombina y el descubrimiento", in R. Levee, ed., *Historia de la nación argentina*, vol. 2 (Buenos Aires: Academia Nacional de la Historia, 1939), 320–27.

15. Quran 2:189.

16. G. L. Burr, *The Witch Persecutions* (Philadelpia: Univ. of Pennsylvania Press, 1902), 7–10; M. Summers, *The Geography of Witchcraft* (Whitefish, Mont.: Kessinger Publishing, 2003), 533–36.

Chapter 2: "To Constitute Spain to the Service of God"

1. A. de Santa Cruz, *Crónica de los Reyes Católicos*, ed. J. de M. Carriazo (1951), vol. 1, 41–43.

2. J. Goñi Gaztambide, "La Santa Sede y la reconquista de Granada", in *Hispania Sacra*, vol. 4 (1951), 28–34.

3. L. Suárez Fernández and J. de Mata Carriazo Arroquia, *Historia de España*, vol. 17, pt. 1 (Madrid: Editorial Espasa Calpe, 1969), 409–52.

4. "Historia de los hechos de Don Rodrigo Ponce de León, marqués de Cádiz", in *Colección de documentos inéditos para la historia de España*, vol. 116 (Madrid: Real Academia de la Historia, 1893), 143–317, at p. 198.

5. *El tumbo de los Reyes Católicos del Concejo de Sevilla*, ed. R. Carande and J. de Mata Carriazo Arroquia, 5 vols., (Seville: Universidad Hispalense, 1968), vol. 3, 193; L. Suárez Fernández and J. de Mata Carriazo Arroquia, *Historia de España*, vol. 17, 433.

6. D. de Valera, Epistle XXXIV, in M. Penna, ed., *Prosistas castellanos del siglo XV*, vol. 1 (Madrid: Atlas, 1959), 31.

7. M. A. Ladero Quesada, *Las guerra de Granada en el siglo XV* (Madrid: Ariel, 2002), 49.

8. Suárez and Mata, *Historia de España*, vol. 17, 888.

9. F. Fernández-Armesto, *Ferdinand and Isabella* (London: Weidenfeld, 1974), 89.

10. *The Diary of John Burchard*, ed. A. H. Mathew, 2 vols. (London: Francis Griffiths, 1910), 1:317–19.

11. Fernández-Armesto, *Ferdinand and Isabella*, 95.

12. L. P. Harvey, *The Muslims in Spain, 1500–1614* (Chicago: Chicago Univ. Press, 2005), 33.

13. Harvey, *Muslims in Spain*, 47.

14. D. de Valera, "Doctrinal de Príncipes", in M. Penna, ed., *Prosistas*, 173.

15. See B. F. Weissberger, *Isabel Rules: Constructing Queenship, Wielding Power* (Minneapolis: Univ. of Minnesota Press, 2004), 135.

16. H. de Pulgar, "Crónica de los Reyes de Castilla Don Fernando e Doña Isabel," in C. Rosell, ed., *Crónicas de los Reyes de Castilla*, vol. 3 (Madrid: Biblioteca de Autores Españoles, 1878), 255–57.

17. E. Pardo Canalís, *Iconografía del rey católico* (Zaragoza: Institución Fernando el Católico, 1951).

18. Translation of the Latin version in A. Alvar Ezquerra, *Isabel la católica, una reina vencedora, una mujer derrotada* (Madrid: Temas de Hoy, 2002), 316.

19. D. Clemencía, *Elogio de la Reina Católica Doña Isabel* (Madrid: Real Academia de la Historia, 1820), 355–57.

20. P. K. Liss, *Isabel the Queen* (New York: Oxford Univ. Press, 1992), 24.

21. F. de Pulgar, *Letras*, ed. J. Domínguez Bordona (Madrid: Editorial Espasa Calpe, 1949), 151.

Chapter 3: "I Can See the Horsemen"

1. N. Davis, *Trickster Travels: In Search of Leo Africanus* (London: Faber and Faber, 2007), 145–47.

2. H. A. R. Gibb and C. Beckingham, eds., *The Travels of Ibn Battuta*, vol. 4 (Cambridge: The Hakluyt Society, 2001), 317–23.

3. Gibb and Beckingham, *The Travels of Ibn Battuta*, 323.

4. J. Matas i Tort and E. Pognon, eds., *L'atlas català* (Barcelona: Diàfora, 1975), 4.

5. Gibb and Beckingham, *The Travels of Ibn Battuta*, 335.

6. Leo Africanus, *The History and Description of Africa*, ed. R. Brown, 3 vols. (London: The Hakluyt Society, 1896), 3:827.

7. N. Levtzion and J. F. P. Hopkins, eds., *Corpus of Early Arabic Sources for West African History* (Princeton, NJ: Markus Wiener Publishers, 2000), 82.

8. Levtzion and Hopkins, *Early Arabic Sources*, 76–85, 107–12.

9. Levtzion and Hopkins, *Early Arabic Sources*, 119.

10. T. Insoll, *The Archaeology of Islam in Sub-Saharan Africa* (Cambridge: Cambridge Univ. Press, 2003).

11. Leo Africanus, *History*, 3:824.

12. Leo Africanus, *History*, 3:825.

13. Leo Africanus, *History*, 1:156.

14. L. Kaba, *Sonni Ali-Ber* (Paris: ABC, 1977), 77.

15. Kaba, *Sonni Ali-Ber*, 79.

16. E. N. Saad, *Social History of Timbuktu* (New York: Cambridge Univ. Press, 1983), 42.

17. S. M. Cissoko, *Tomboctou et l'empire songhay* (Dakar: Les Nouvelles Éditions Africaines,1975), 55.

18. Cissoko, *Tomboctou*, 57.

19. Saad, *Social History of Timbuktu*, 45.

20. I. B. Kake, and G. Comte, *Askia Mohamed* (Paris: ABC, 1976), 58.

21. Kake and Comte, *Askia Mohamed*, 60.

22. Kake and Comte, *Askia Mohamed*, 68.

23. Leo Africanus, *History*, 3:833–34.

24. F. Fernández-Armesto, *Before Columbus* (London: Folio Society, 1986), 194.

25. Fernández-Armesto, *Before Columbus*, 195.

26. J. Thornton, "The Development of an African Catholic Church in the Kingdom of Kongo, 1491–1750", *Journal of African History* 25:2 (1984), 147–67.

27. S. Axelson, *Culture and Confrontation in Lower Congo* (Stockholm: Gummesson, 1970), 66.

28. A. Brásio, *Monumenta missionaria africana*, vol. 1 (Lisbon: Agença Geral do Ultramar, 1952), 266–73.

29. Brásio, *Monumenta*, 294–323, 470–87.

30. F. Alvares, *The Prester John of the Indies*, ed. C. Beckingham and G. Huntingford (Cambridge: The Hakluyt Society, 1961), 303–4, 320–21.

Chapter 4: "No Sight More Pitiable"

1. A. Bernáldez, *Historia de los Reyes Católicos* (Madrid: Atlas, 1953), 617–53.

2. A. Bernáldez, *Memorias del reinado de los Reyes Católicos*, ed. M. Gómez Moreno and J. de Mata Carriazo (Madrid: Consejo Superior de Investigaciones Científicas, 1962), 96–101.

3. F. Fita, "El martirio del santo niño", *Boletín de la Real Academia de la Historia* 11 (1887): 12–13.

4. Libro de Alborayque, quoted in J. Pérez, *History of a Tragedy: The Expulsion of the Jews from Spain* (Urbana: Univ. of Illinois Press, 2007), 69.

5. Y. Baer, *History of the Jews in Christian Spain*, 2 vols. (Philadelphia: The Jewish Publication Society, 1966), 2:527.

6. Perez, *History of a Tragedy*, 79.

7. Perez, *History of a Tragedy*, 90.

8. R. Conde y Delgado de Molina, *La expulsión de los judíos de la Corona de Aragón: Documentos para su estudio* (Zaragoza: Institución Fernando el Católico, 1991), 95–96.

9. P. León Tello, *Los judíos de Ávila* (Ávila: Institución Gran Duque de Alba, 1963), 91–92; L. Suárez Fernández, *Documentos acerca de la expulsión de los judíos* (Valladolid: Consejo Superior de Investigaciones Científicas, 1964), 391–95.

10. Perez, *History of a Tragedy*, 86.

11. Fernández-Armesto, *Before Columbus*, 201.

12. Bernáldez, *Memorias*, 113.

13. Leo Africanus, *History*, 2:419.

14. Leo Africanus, *History*, 2:424, 443, 447–48.

15. Abraham ben Solomon, quoted in D. Raphael, ed., *The Expulsion 1492 Chronicles* (North Hollywood: Carmi House Press, 1992), 175.

16. Leo Africanus, *History*, 2:453, 461.

17. Leo Africanus, *History*, 2:477.

18. Raphael, *Expulsion 1492 Chronicles*, 87.

19. Davis, *Trickster Tales*, 137.

20. V. J. Cornell, "Socioeconomic Dimensions of Reconquista and Jihad in Morocco: Portuguese Dukkala and the Sadid Sus, 1450–1557", *International Journal of Middle East Studies* 22, no. 4 (November 1990): 379–418.

21. Quoted in Davis, *Trickster Tales*, 32.

22. Raphael, *Expulsion 1492 Chronicles*, 23, 115.

23. H. Beinart, *The Expulsion of the Jews from Spain* (Oxford: Littman Library of Jewish Civilization, 2002), 279.

24. Bernáldez, *Memorias*, 113.

25. Konstantin Mihailovc, *Memoirs of a Janissary*, quoted in H. W. Lowry, *The Nature of the Early Ottoman State* (Albany: SUNY Press, 2003), 47.

26. G. Necipoğlu, *Architecture, Ceremonial, and Power: The Topkapi Palace in the Fifteenth and Sixteenth Centuries* (New York: Architectural History Foundation; Cambridge, Mass.: MIT Press, 1991), 8.

27. S. Shaw, *The Jews of the Ottoman Empire and the Turkish Republic* (London: Macmillan, 1991), 30, 32.

28. Lowry, *Early Ottoman State*, 48.

29. Shaw, *Jews of the Ottoman Empire*, 33.

Chapter 5: "Is God Angry with Us?"

1. E. Armstrong, *Lorenzo de' Medici* (London and New York: Putnam, 1897), 308–9.

2. Armstrong, *Lorenzo de' Medici*, 314.

3. J. Burchard, *At the Court of the Borgia*, ed. G. Parker (London: Folio Society, 1963), 412.

4. Lorenzo de' Medici, *Lettere*, vol. 6, ed. M. Mallett (Florence: Barbèra, 1990), 100.

5. L. Martines, *April Blood* (Oxford; New York: Oxford Univ. Press, 2006), 214–20.

6. Martines, *April Blood*, 221–23.

7. E. B. Fryde, "Lorenzo de' Medici's Finances and Their Influence on His Patronage of Art", in *Humanism and Renaissance Historiography* (London: Hambledon Press, 1983), 145–57.

8. *Lorenzo de Medici: Selected Poems and Prose*, ed. J. Thiem et al. (University Park: Pennsylvania State Univ. Press, 1991), 67 (translation modified).

9. L. Polizzotto, "Lorenzo il Magnifico, Savonarola and Medicean Dynasticism", in B. Toscani, ed., *Lorenzo de' Medici: New Perspectives* (New York: Peter Lang Publishing Group, 1993), 331–55.

10. F. W. Kent, *Lorenzo de' Medici and the Art of Magnificence* (Baltimore: Johns Hopkins Univ. Press, 2004), esp. 91; J. Beck, "Lorenzo il Magnif-

ico and His Cultural Possessions", in Toscani, ed., *Lorenzo*, 138.

11. L. Martines, *Scourge and Fire: Savonarola and Renaissance Italy* (London: Jonathan Cape Ltd, 2006), 12–14 (translation modified).

12. D. Beebe et al., eds., *Selected Writings of Girolamo Savonarola: Religion and Politics, 1490–1498* (New Haven, Conn.: Yale Univ. Press, 2006), 27.

13. Beebe et al., *Writings of Girolamo Savonarola*, 72.

14. Beebe et al., *Writings of Girolamo Savonarola*, 68–69.

15. Beebe et al., *Writings of Girolamo Savonarola*, 73.

16. G. Savonarola, "Prediche ai Fiorentini", in. C. Varese, ed. *La letteratura italiana*, vol. 14 (Milan: Garzanti, 1955): 90.

17. S. Meltzoff, *Botticelli, Signorelli and Savonarola: Theology and Painting from Boccaccio to Poliziano* (Florence: L. S. Olschki, 1987), 53.

18. Beebe et al., *Writings of Girolamo Savonarola*, 72.

19. Burchard, *Court of the Borgia*, 1:372–73.

20. Y. Labande-Mailfert, *Charles VIII: Le vouloir et la destinée* (Paris: Fayard, 1986), 27–28.

21. J. d'Arras, *Mélusine*, ed. C. Brunet (Paris: Brunet, 1854), 121.

22. *Historia de la linda Melosina*, ed. I. A. Corfis (Madison: Hispanic Seminary of Medieval Studies, 1986), chap. 23, p. 54.

23. Labande-Mailfert, *Charles VIII*, 17.

24. Labande-Mailfert, *Charles VIII*, 101; A. Denis, *Charles VIII et les italiens: histoire et mythe* (Geneva: Librairie Droz, 1979), 23.

25. Labande-Mailfert, *Charles VIII*, 110–16.

26. P. Martyr Anglerius, *Opus Epistolarum* (1670), 67–68.

27. Pastor, *History of the Popes*, 366.

28. Pastor, *History of the Popes*, 469–70.

29. Meltzoff, *Botticelli, Signorelli and Savonarola*, 80.

30. P. Schaff, *History of the Christian Church* (New York: Scribner, 1910), 6:68.

31. Beebe et al., *Writings of Girolamo Savonarola*, 137.

32. S. dell'Aglio, *Il tempo di Savonarola* (Tavarnuzze: Galluzzo, 2006), 204.

Chapter 6: Towards "the Land of Darkness"

1. G. Bezzola, *Die Mongolen in abendländisches Sicht* (Bern and Munich: Francke, 1972).

2. J. J. Saunders, "Matthew Paris and the Mongols", in T. A. Sandquist and M. R. Powicke, eds., *Essays in Medieval History Presented to Bertie Wilkinson* (Toronto: Univ. of Toronto Press, 1969), 116–32.

3. F. Fernández-Armesto, "Medieval Ethnography", in *Journal of the Anthropological Society of Oxford* (1982), xiii.

4. J. Fennell, *The Crisis of Medieval Russia* (London; New York: Longman, 1983), 88.

5. R. C. Howes, *The Testaments of the Grand Princes of Moscow* (Ithaca, N.Y.: Cornell Univ. Press, 1967), 295.

6. D. Ostrowski, *Muscovy and the Mongols* (Cambridge; New York: Cambridge Univ. Press, 1998), 144–55.

7. R. Mitchell and N. Forbes, eds., *The Chronicle of Novgorod, 1016–1471* (Hattiesburg, Miss.: Academic International, 1970), 9–15.

8. R. Cormack and D. Glaser, eds., *The Art of Holy Russia* (London: Royal Academy of Arts, 1998), 180.

9. Y. Slezkine, *Arctic Mirrors* (Ithaca: Cornell Univ. Press, 1991), 33–34.

10. J. L. B. Martin, *Medieval Russia* (Cambridge; New York: Cambridge Univ. Press, 1995), 288.

11. M. Isoaho, *The Image of Aleksandr Nevskiy in Medieval Russia* (Leiden; Boston: Brill, 2006), 173.

12. J. Fennell, *Ivan the Great of Moscow* (London: Macmillan, 1963), 41.

13. Fennell, *Ivan the Great*, 43.

14. Fennell, *Ivan the Great*, 46, 55.

15. Fennell, *Ivan the Great*, 59.

16. G. Alef, *Rulers and Nobles in Fifteenth-Century Muscovy* (London: Variorum Reprints, 1983), item 5, p. 54.

17. F. Fernández-Armesto, *Millennium* (London: Bantam, 1995), 124.

18. D. Obolensky, *Byzantium and the Slavs* (Crestwood, NY: St Vladimir's Seminary Press, 1994), 185.

19. Alef, *Rulers and Nobles*, item 9, p. 8.

20. Fennell, *Ivan the Great*, 121.

21. Alef, *Rulers and Nobles*, item 9, p. 7.

22. Alef, *Rulers and Nobles*, item 5, p. 25; Ostrowski, *Muscovy and the Mongols*, 226.

23. Isoaho, *Aleksandr Nevskiy*, 292.

24. R. Feuer-Toth, *Art and Humanism in Hungary in the Age of Mathias Corvinus* (Budapest: Akadémiai Kiadó, 1990), 97.

25. Howes, *Grand Princes of Moscow*, 267–98.

Chapter 7: "That Sea of Blood"

1. F. Fernández-Armesto, *Columbus* (London: Duckworth Publishers, 1996), 2.

2. *Don Quixote*, 2:16.

3. C. Varela, *Cristóbal Colón: Textos y documentos completos* (Madrid: Alianza, 1984), 15–16.

4. F. Fernández-Armesto, *Columbus on Himself* (London: Folio Society, 1992), 43.

5. Fernández-Armesto, *Columbus on Himself*, 16.

6. B. de Las Casas, *Historia de las Indias*, 2 vols. (Mexico City: Fondo de Cultura Económica, 1951), 1:189.

7. Varela, *Cristobal Colón*, 23–24.

8. Fernández-Armesto, *Columbus on Himself*, 56; Varela, *Cristobal Colón*, 22–24.

9. Varela, *Cristobal Colón*, 27–30.

10. F. Fernández-Armesto, "Colón y los libros de caballería", in *Colón*, ed. C. Martínez Shaw (Valladolid: Junta de Castilla y León, 2006).

11. Varela, *Cristobal Colón*, 83–84.

12. Varela, *Cristobal Colón*, 97–101.

13. S. E. Morison, *Journals and Other Documents on the Life and Voyages of Christopher Columbus* (New York: Heritage Press, 1963), 216–19.

14. Las Casas, *Historia*, vol. 1, 313.

15. Fernández-Armesto, *Columbus*, 95.

Chapter 8: "Among the Singing Willows"

1. J. Cahill, *Parting at the Shore: Chinese Painting of the Early and Middle Ming Dynasty* (New York: Weatherhill, 1978).

2. G. Uzielli, *La vita e i tempi di Paolo dal Pozzo Toscanelli*, Raccolta Colombiana 5 (Rome: Reale Commissione Colombiana, 1894), 571–72.

3. J. Meskill, ed., *Ch'oe Pu's Diary: A Record of Drifting Across the Sea* (Tucson: Univ. of Arizona Press, 1965), 22.

4. Meskill, *Ch'oe Pu's Diary*, 50.

5. Meskill, *Ch'oe Pu's Diary*, 52.

6. Meskill, *Ch'oe Pu's Diary*, 53.

7. Meskill, *Ch'oe Pu's Diary*, 65.

8. Meskill, *Ch'oe Pu's Diary*, 63, 93–94.

9. Meskill, *Ch'oe Pu's Diary*, 65.

10. D. Twitchet and F. W. Mote, eds., *The Cambridge History of China*, vol. 8, pt. 2 (Cambridge: Cambridge Univ. Press), 699.

11. I. A. Sim, "The Merchant Wang Zhen, 1424–1495", in *The Human Tradition in Premodern China*, ed. K. J. Hammond (Wilmington, Del.: Scholarly Resources, 2002), 157–64.

12. Meskill, *Ch'oe Pu's Diary*, 107.

13. Twitchet and Mote, *Cambridge History of China*, 920.

14. Twitchet and Mote, *Cambridge History of China*, 878.

15. Cahill, *Parting at the Shore*, 90.

16. Cahill, *Parting at the Shore*, 90.

17. Cahill, *Parting at the Shore*, 89.

18. J. Duyvendak, "The True Dates of the Chinese Maritime Expeditions in the Early Fifteenth Century", *T'oung Pao* 34 (1938): 399–412.

19. R. Finlay, "The Treasure Ships of Zheng He", *Terrae Incognitae* 23 (1991): 1–12.

20. Duyvendak, "Chinese Maritime Expeditions", 410.

21. Meskill, *Ch'oe Pu's Diary*, 8, 146.

22. Meskill, *Ch'oe Pu's Diary*, 57.

23. Meskill, *Ch'oe Pu's Diary*, 65.

24. Meskill, *Ch'oe Pu's Diary*, 93.

25. *Transactions of the Royal Asiatic Society, Korean Branch*, 2 (1902), 36 (translation modified).

26. *Transactions*, 37.

27. *Transactions*, 36, 39–40.

28. *Transactions*, 38.

29. Meskill, *Ch'oe Pu's Diary*, 65.

30. E. Ramirez-Christensen, *Heart's Flower: The Life and Poetry of Shinkei* (Stanford, Calif.: Stanford Univ. Press, 1994), 20.

31. D. Keene, *Yoshimasa and the Silver Pavilion: The Creation of the Soul of Japan* (New York: Columbia Univ. Press, 2003), 70.

32. Keene, *Yoshimasa*, 5.

33. Ramirez-Christensen, *Heart's Flower*, 20–24.

34. D. Keene, ed., *Travellers of a Hundred Ages* (New York: Holt, 1989), 211.

35. Ramirez-Christensen, *Heart's Flower*, 20.

36. K. A. Grossberg, *Japan's Renaissance: The Politics of the Muromachi Bakufu* (Ithaca: Cornell Univ. Press, 2001).

37. Keene, *Yoshimasa*, 69.

38. Keene, *Yoshimasa*, 117.

39. Keene, *Yoshimasa*, 88.

40. Grossberg, *Japan's Renaissance*, 62.

41. Q. E. Phillips, *The Practices of Painting in Japan, 1475–1500* (Stanford, Calif.: Stanford Univ. Press, 2000), 148.

42. Keene, *Yoshimasa*, 164.

43. Keene, *Yoshimasa*, 107.

44. Phillips, *Practices of Painting*, 3.

45. Ramirez-Christensen, *Heart's Flower*, 155.

46. Ramirez-Christensen, *Heart's Flower*, 152.

47. D. Carter, *The Road to Komatsubara: A Classical Reading of the Renga Hyakuin* (Cambridge, Mass.: Council on East Asian Studies, Harvard Univ., 1987), 117, 143.

Chapter 9: "The Seas of Milk and Butter"

1. R. H. Major, ed., *India in the Fifteenth Century* (London: The Hakluyt Society, 1857), 7–13.

2. S.-S. H. Tsai, *Perpetual Happiness: The Ming Emperor Yongle* (Seattle: Univ. of Washington Press, 2001), 178–208.

3. J. Duyvendak, "Chinese Maritime Expeditions", 399–412; T. Filesi and D. Morison, eds., *China and Africa in the Middle Ages* (London: Frank Cass, 1972), 57–61.

4. Duyvendak, "Chinese Maritime Expeditions", 399–406.

5. L. Levathes, *When China Ruled the Seas* (New York: Scribner, 1994).

6. Ma Huan, *The Overall Survey of the Ocean's Shores*, ed. J. R. V. Mills (Cambridge: The Hakluyt Society, 1970), 69, 70, 179.

7. E. L. Dreyer, *Early Ming China* (Stanford, Calif.: Stanford Univ. Press, 1982), 120.

8. Kuei-Sheng Chang, "The Ming Maritime Enterprise and China's Knowledge of Africa Prior to the Age of Great Discoveries", *Terra Incognita* 3 (1971): 33–44.

9. Major, *India*, 10.

10. Major, *India*, 6.

11. Major, *India*, 8.

12. Major, *India*, 9.

13. Major, *India*, 30.

14. Major, *India*, 23.

15. Major, *India*, 11.

16. N. M. Penzer, ed., *The Most Noble and Famous Travels* (London: The Argonaut Press, 1929), 169.

17. C. E. B. Asher and C. Talbot, *India Before Europe* (New York: Cambridge Univ. Press, 2006), 107.

18. Asher and Talbot, *India Before Europe*, 77.

19. Major, *India*, 18.

20. H. Khan Sherwani, *The Bahmanis of the Deccan* (New Delhi: Munshiram Manoharlal, 1985), 238.

21. A. Wink, *Al-Hind: The Making of the Indo-Islamic Worlds*, vol. 3 (Leiden: Brill Academic Publishers, 2004), 136.

22. A. Halim, *History of the Lodi Sultans of Delhi and Agra* (Delhi: Idarah-I-Adabiyat-I-Delli, 1974), 108–13.

23. See, however, K. S. Lal, *Twilight of the Sultanate* (Delhi: Munshiram Manoharlal Publishers, 1963), 191–94.

24. M. N. Pearson, "The East African Coast in 1498: A Synchronic Study", in *Vasco da Gama and the Linking of Europe and Asia*, ed. A. Disney and E. Booth (Delhi: Oxford Univ. Press, 2000), 116–30.

25. M. L. Dames, ed., *The Book of Duarte Barbosa*, 2 vols. (London: The Hakluyt Society, 1918, 1921), vol. 1, 29.

26. Pearson, "East African Coast", 119.

27. N. Tarling, ed., *The Cambridge History of Southeast Asia*, vol. 1 (Cambridge; New York: Cambridge Univ. Press, 1992), 483.

28. *The Lusiads in Sri Richard Fanshawe's Translation*, ed. G. Bullough (London: Centaur, 1963), 329.

29. R. Winstedt, *The Malays: A Cultural History* (London: Routledge, 1958), 33–44.

30. Tarling, *Cambridge History of Southeast Asia*, 409.

31. E. J. Jurji, *Illumination in Islamic Mysticism* (Princeton: Princeton Univ. Press, 1938), 37.

32. Jurji, *Illumination*, 30.

33. Jurji, *Illumination*, 33.

34. Jurji, *Illumination*, 110.

35. Jurji, *Illumination*, 63.

36. W. C. Chittick, trans., "Gleams", in *Chinese Gleams of Sufi Light*, by S. Murata (Albany: SUNY Press, 2000), 144.

37. Chittick, "Gleams", 192.

38. Chittick, "Gleams", 180.

39. Chittick, "Gleams", 140.

40. Chittick, "Gleams", 148.

41. *Joseph and Zuleika by Jami*, ed. C. F. Horne (Ames, Iowa: Lipscombe, 1917), 17.

42. *Joseph and Zuleika*, 18–19.

Chapter 10: "The Fourth World"

1. J. López de Toru, "La conquista de Gran Canaria en la cuarta década del cronista Alonso de Palencia", *Anuario de estudios atlánticos* 16 (1970): 325–94.

2. M. R. Alonso Rodríguez, "Las endechas a la muerte de Guillén Peraza", *Anuario de estudios atlánticos* 2 (1956): 457–71.

3. M. Ruíz Benítez de Lugo-Mármot, *Documentos para la historia de Canarias* (Las Palmas: Gobierno de Canarias, 2000), 35.

4. J. Alvarez Delgado, "Primera conquista y colonización de la Gomera", *Anuario de estudios atlánticos* 6 (1960): 445–92.

5. J. Viera y Clavijo, *Historia de Canarias*, 3 vols. (Madrid: n.p., 1771–75; vol. 2, 1773), 2:151–55.

6. F. Solis, *Gloria y fama mexica* (Mexico City: Smurfit, 1991), 98–112.

7. R. A. Covey, *How the Incas Built Their Heartland* (Ann Arbor: Univ. of Michigan Press, 2006), 52.

8. Covey, *Heartland*, 227.

9. Covey, *Heartland*, 219.

10. T. N. D'Altroy, *The Incas* (Oxford: Blackwell Publishing, 2002), 104.

11. Covey, *Heartland*, 151.

12. D'Altroy, *Incas*, 95, 173.

13. D'Altroy, *Incas*, 97.

Epilogue: The World We're In

1. Summary in D. Nirenberg, "Figures of Thought and Figures of Flesh: 'Jews' and 'Judaism' in Late-Medieval Spanish Poetry and Politics", *Speculum* 81 (2006): 425.

2. S. Subrahmanyam, *The Career and the Legend of Vasco da Gama* (Cambridge: Cambridge Univ. Press, 1997), 111.

Provenance of Illustrations

Page 2: Hartmann Schedel, *Weltchronik* [*The "Nuremberg Chronicle"*] (Nuremberg, 1493), engraving by Michael Wohlgemut and Wilhelm Pleydonwurff.

Page 7: Albrecht Dürer, *Apocalipsis cum figuris* (Nuremberg, A. Dürer, 1498).

Page 8: Nuremberg Chronicle.

Page 28: Woodcut from D. de San Pedro, *Cárcel de amor* (Barcelona: Rosembach, 1493).

Page 82: Fra Mauro's Ethiopia map from O. G. S. Crawford, *Ethiopian Itineraries*, circa 1400–1524 (Cambridge, 1958). Courtesy of The Hakluyt Society. The Hakluyt Society was established in 1846 for the purpose of printing rare or unpublished Voyages and Travels. For further information please see their website at: www.hakluyt.com.

Page 84: Diogo Homem's map of West Africa from J. W. Blake, *Europeans in West Africa*, I (London, 1942). Courtesy of The Hakluyt Society.

Page 90: Nuremberg Chronicle.

Page 107: Nuremberg Chronicle.

Page 109: Nuremberg Chronicle.

Page 117: Nuremberg Chronicle.

Page 129: Girolamo Savonarola, *Tractato contra li astrologi* (Florence: Bartolommeo di Libri, ca. 1497). Courtesy of the Trustees of the British Library.

Page 131: Girolamo Savonarola, *Dialogo della verità prophetica* (Florence: Tubini, Veneziano and Ghirlandi, 1500).

Page 148: S. von Herberstein, *Notes Upon Russia* (London, 1852). Courtesy of The Hakluyt Society.

Page 196: Giuliano Dati, *Lettera delle isole che ha trovato il re di Spagna* (Florence: Morigiani and Petri, 1493).

Page 207: Detail from Shen Zhou, *Night Vigil*. Hanging scroll, National Museum, Taipei.

Page 220: Detail from Wu Wei, *Two Daoist Immortals*. Hanging Scroll, Shanghai Museum.

Page 224: Ma Huan, *Ying-yai Sheng-lan: "The Overall Survey of the Ocean's Shores"*, ed. J. V. G. Mills (Cambridge: The Hakluyt Society, 1970). Courtesy of The Hakluyt Society.

Page 236: Nishikawa Sukenobu, *Ehon Yamato Hiji* (10 vols.; Osaka, 1742).

Page 238: *De Insulis Nuper in Mari Indico Repertis* (Basle, 1494).

Page 242: Nuremberg Chronicle.

Page 257: C. F. Beckingham and G. W. Huntingford, *The Prester John of the Indies* (Cambridge: The Hakluyt Society, 1961). Courtesy of The Hakluyt Society.

Page 274: F. Guamán Poma de Ayala, *Nueva corónica y buen gobierno (codex péruvien illustré)* (Paris: Institut d'Ethnologie, 1936).

Page 290: J. Cooper Clark, ed., *Codex Mendoza*, 3 vols. (London, 1938), iii. Original in the Bodleian Library, Oxford.

Page 294: J. Cooper Clark, ed., *Codex Mendoza*, 3 vols. (London, 1938), iii. Original in the Bodleian Library, Oxford.

Page 299: J. Cooper Clark, ed., *Codex Mendoza*, 3 vols. (London, 1938), iii. Original in the Bodleian Library, Oxford.

Index

Page numbers in italics refer to maps and illustrations.